Adobe
Audition CC
Second Edition

CLASSROOM IN A BOOK®
The official training workbook from Adobe

axim Jago

Adobe Audition CC Classroom in a Book®, Second Edition

Adobe Press is an imprint of Pearson Education, Inc. For the latest on Adobe Press books, go to www.adobepress. com. To report errors, please send a note to errata@peachpit.com. For information regarding permissions, request forms and the appropriate contacts within the Pearson Education Global Rights & Permissions department, please visit www.pearsoned.com/permissions.

Writer: Maxim Jago
Executive Editor: Laura Norman
Development Editor: Victor Gavenda
Technical Reviewer: Alberto Moreno
Senior Production Editor: Tracey Croom
Copyeditor: Linda Laflamme
Composition: Danielle Foster
Proofreader: Becky Winter
Indexer: Jack Lewis
Cover Illustration: bchance.net/petergaillard
Cover Designer: Eddie Yuen
Interior Designer: Mimi Heft

ISBN-13: 978-0-135-22832-6
ISBN-10: 0-135-22832-8

WHERE ARE THE LESSON FILES?

Purchase of this Classroom in a Book in any format gives you access to the lesson files you'll need to complete the exercises in the book.

You'll find the files you need on your **Account** page at peachpit.com on the **Registered Products** tab.

1 Go to www.peachpit.com/register.

2 Sign in or create a new account.

3 Enter the ISBN: 9780135228326.

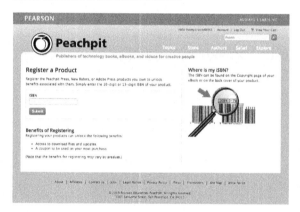

4 Answer the questions as proof of purchase.

5 The lesson files can be accessed through the Registered Products tab on your Account page.

6 Click the Access Bonus Content link below the title of your product to proceed to the download page. Click the lesson file links to download them to your computer.

CONTENTS

ACKNOWLEDGMENTS

Producing effective learning materials for such an advanced technology is a team effort. Friends, colleagues, fellow filmmakers, and technology experts have all contributed to this book.

Everything on these pages was inspected by a team of experienced editors who checked and corrected typos, spelling errors, naming errors, false attributions, suspect grammar, unhelpful phrasing, and inevitably inconsistent descriptions. This wonderful team didn't just highlight text that needed correcting. They offered perfect replacements that I could simply agree to, so in a literal sense, this book is the product of many people's contributions. I'd like to thank the teams at Peachpit and Adobe Press, who made it possible to produce such a beautifully finessed work.

As each draft chapter was completed, the most amazing and highly experienced Victor Gavenda checked over the text to make sure it was ideally accessible for learners, and all references to the technology were run by the remarkable audio expert Alberto Moreno, a multi-award-winning sound engineer with an incredible understanding of audio workflows. The extraordinary copy editor Linda Laflamme helped make sense of complex technical descriptions for new readers, and Tracey Croom made sure the layout was clear and accessible.

A considerable amount of the content of this book is derived from material written by Craig Anderton in the previous edition. Craig worked out the original table of contents. Although I have updated his chapters, rephrased and reworded them, a substantial amount is significantly informed by his original work, especially the step-by-step exercises and most of the media assets. I tip my hat to Craig for such an incredible understanding of audio technology.

And let's not forget Adobe! The passion and enthusiasm demonstrated by those wonderful individuals, who are so committed to creatives like you and me is quite extraordinary. Many thanks to the whole team.

Maxim Jago
Filmmaker, Futurist, Keynote Speaker—maximjago.com

Important!

The video clips, audio clips, and other media files provided with this book are practice files, provided for your personal use in these lessons. You are not authorized to use these files commercially or to publish, share, or distribute them in any form without written permission from Adobe Systems, Inc., and the individual copyright holders of the various items. Do not share videos or audios created with these lesson files publicly. This includes, but is not limited to, distribution via social media or online video services including YouTube and Vimeo. You will find a complete copyright statement on the copyright page at the very start of this book.

GETTING STARTED

Adobe Audition CC is a professional audio editing application that provides multichannel audio acquisition, advanced audio waveform editing, professional multitrack recording editing, and multi-format audio delivery in one fully integrated system.

There are two main modes when working in Audition: the Waveform Editor for working on single pieces of audio and the Multitrack Editor for building layered sound compositions by combining multiple pieces of audio.

Although these two modes have a consistent design and similar tools, they offer fundamentally different approaches to audio editing, mixing, effects, and project organization.

Each view is ideally suited to a particular approach to audio editing, and understanding the differences between the two is key to unlocking the potential of this amazing application.

The two modes are so well integrated that audio included in a multitrack session can be quickly edited, with great precision, in the Waveform Editor and any changes made will automatically update in the multitrack session.

Multitrack sessions can be mastered in mono, stereo, or 5.1 surround. The final mix can be burned to a recordable CD, which is created according to the standard Red Book specification, exported as a high-quality, uncompressed master file or converted into compressed formats, such as MP3 and FLAC.

Audition includes dedicated tools for video soundtrack production. You can send a sequence from Adobe Premiere Pro to Audition, or you can open a Premiere Pro project directly in Audition. Existing audio level adjustments and effects will appear in Audition where you can continue to edit them.

The Multitrack Editor has a video window that enables recording sound tracks and narration in Audition while previewing HD video. When you have finished creating your soundtrack, you can export it to a complete video and audio media file with Adobe Media Encoder.

Audition is a cross-platform, 64-bit native application that runs equally well on macOS or Windows computers. Thanks to combining two programs within a single, integrated application, Audition has multiple uses, including restoring audio, multitrack recording for musicians, mastering, sound design, broadcast, video-game sound, narration and voice-overs, file format conversion, small-scale CD production, and even forensics. All of these features are available in a clean, easy-to-use, straightforward interface whose workflow has benefited from over a decade of continuous development and refinement.

The 2018 release of Audition deepens the level of integration with Adobe Premiere Pro CC and Adobe After Effects CC for easy exchange of files and complete sequences. This greatly simplifies the process of creating a sound track.

The new "flat" interface is designed in-line with Adobe's other digital video and audio applications. There are new track management controls in the Multitrack Editor, the option to generate speech for temporary voice overs, new ITU Loudness Standard tools for broadcast delivery, a new Remix feature that allows you to change the duration of music seamlessly, and automated audio ducking to quickly set audio-level adjustments when mixing vocals and music.

Long-time Audition users will appreciate the many little extras that enhance work-flow and audio quality, whereas those new to Audition will welcome its depth and flexibility.

About Classroom in a Book

Adobe Audition CC Classroom in a Book, Second Edition is part of the official training series for Adobe graphics, audio, and video publishing software and was developed with the support of Adobe product experts. The lessons are designed to let you learn at your own pace. If you're new to Audition, you'll learn the funda-mental concepts and features needed to start mastering the program. If you've been using Audition for a while, you'll find that Classroom in a Book teaches basic to intermediate features, and includes tips and techniques for using the latest version of the application for a wide variety of projects.

Although each lesson focuses on providing step-by-step instructions to reach specific goals, there's room for exploration and experimentation. You can follow the book from start to finish, or you can read the lessons that match your particu-lar interests and needs. It's recommended that you read Chapter 2, "The Audition Interface" before reading other lessons, as this will give you the basic familiarity you need before exploring specific techniques.

Each lesson offers an introduction that explains what you can expect to learn from a chapter and concludes with a review section summarizing what you've covered.

What's in this book

This edition covers many new features in Adobe Audition CC and how to apply them optimally in real-world situations. It includes techniques for audio and music professionals who depend on the tools and other features in Audition to accomplish a variety of tasks, as well as for videographers who want to become more involved in the process of creating, editing, and sweetening audio intended for video productions.

The book is organized into three parts:

- The introductory chapters begin with how to get audio in and out of Audition on macOS and Windows, and then progresses to an overview of the Audition interface.

- The second part concentrates on audio editing in the Waveform Editor and explores editing, signal processing and effects, audio restoration, mastering, and sound design.

- The third section focuses on the Multitrack Editor, including editing, automation, creating music with sound libraries, and in-depth coverage of mixing. In this section, you'll learn about producing a soundtrack for video projects, as well as integration with Adobe Media Encoder.

Step-by-step exercises are included throughout. Audio files created specifically for this book are provided, so you can try out your new skills and get some practical, hands-on experience.

Even non-musicians will learn how to create music using sound libraries and loops, in conjunction with Audition's extensive tool set for sound creation and editing. You'll also learn how to do rough testing of your room acoustics prior to mixing, using the tools within Audition.

As you progress through the lessons, you'll discover many timesaving features in Audition, such as file conversion, automation, Multitrack and Waveform Editor integration, clip automation, time stretching, and more. All of these functions can help you meet deadlines more easily than ever before—and that alone is a good reason to become familiar with Adobe Audition's workflow, capabilities, and user experience.

Note: Chapter 17, "Mixing," is provided as a downloadable PDF. You'll find it with the lesson files on the Registered Products tab on your Account page at peachpit.com. See "Accessing the Lesson Files and Web Edition" later in this section.

Prerequisites

Before you begin, you should have a working knowledge of your computer and its operating system. Make sure that you know how to use the mouse (or other pointing device, such as a trackpad) and standard menus and commands, such as how to open, save, and close files. If you need to review these techniques, see the help files and other documentation included with your Windows or macOS system. It's also recommended that you read over the introduction to the Audition user's guide, which describes digital audio basics.

You'll also need the ability to get audio in and out of your computer. Virtually all computers include onboard audio capabilities (audio input for recording, plus internal speakers or a headphone jack for monitoring). Be aware that consumer-grade built-in components will not showcase what Audition can do to the fullest extent. Professional and "prosumer" audio interfaces are available at reasonable costs, and these are recommended not just for following the exercises in this book, but also for your future creative audio work.

Installing Adobe Audition

Check that your computer is set up correctly and that it meets the necessary operating system and hardware requirements. For full information on the system requirements for Audition, visit *helpx.adobe.com/audition/system-requirements.html*.

You will need an Adobe Creative Cloud license to install Adobe Audition. For installation instructions, visit *helpx.adobe.com/support/audition.html*.

Audition is a 64-bit native application and takes full advantage of modern processors and memory handling. As with most audio and video applications, having sufficient system memory is essential for a smooth experience. The minimum system requirement is 4 GB of memory, and 8 GB or more is highly recommended. For detailed information on system requirements, please visit *www.adobe.com/products/audition/tech-specs.html*.

Online content

Your purchase of this Classroom in a Book includes online materials provided by way of your Account page on peachpit.com. These include:

Lesson files

To work through the projects in this book, you will need to download the lesson files from peachpit.com. You can download the files for individual lessons or it may be possible to download them all in a single file.

Web Edition

The Web Edition is an online interactive version of the book, providing an enhanced learning experience. Your Web Edition can be accessed from any device with a connection to the Internet, and it contains:

* The complete text of the book
* Hours of instructional video keyed to the text
* Interactive quizzes

In addition, the Web Edition may be updated when Adobe adds significant feature updates between major Creative Cloud releases. To accommodate the changes, sections of the online book may be updated or new sections may be added.

Accessing the Lesson Files and Web Edition

If you purchased an eBook from peachpit.com or adobepress.com, your Web Edition will automatically appear under the Digital Purchases tab on your Account page. Click the Launch link to access the product. Continue reading to learn how to register your product to get access to the lesson files.

If you purchased an eBook from a different vendor or you bought a print book, you must register your purchase on peachpit.com in order to access the online content:

1 Go to www.peachpit.com/register.

2 Sign in or create a new account.

3 Enter the ISBN: 9780135228326

4 Answer the questions as proof of purchase.

5 The Web Edition will appear under the Digital Purchases tab on your Account page. Click the Launch link to access the product.

The Lesson Files can be accessed through the Registered Products tab on your Account page. Click the Access Bonus Content link below the title of your product to proceed to the download page. Click the lesson file links to download them to your computer.

Restoring default preferences

The user preferences store information about panel and command settings. Each time you quit Audition, the positions of the panels and certain command settings are recorded in the respective preferences file. Any selections you make in the Preferences dialog box are also saved in the preferences file.

Many lessons recommend restoring a particular set of preferences so that what you see onscreen matches the images and instructions in this book. However, one of Audition's great features is the ease with which you can customize a workspace to your needs, so feel free to adopt whatever layout you like. Just be aware that your screen may not match the images in the book exactly.

To reset user preferences to the default settings, hold down Shift while starting Audition.

Additional resources

Adobe Audition CC Classroom in a Book is not meant to replace the documentation that comes with the program or to be a comprehensive reference for every feature. For comprehensive information about program features and tutorials, please refer to these resources:

Adobe Audition CC Learn and Support: You'll find help and support information at *helpx.adobe.com/support/audition.html*, which you can reach while using Audition by choosing Help > Adobe Audition Help. Help is also available as a printable PDF document. Download the document at *helpx.adobe.com/pdf/audition_reference.pdf.*

Audition Tutorials: For a wide range of interactive tutorials on Audition CC features, visit *helpx.adobe.com/audition/tutorials.html*. A more limited set of tutorials is available within Audition itself by choosing Help > Audition Learn.

Adobe Creative Cloud Learning: For inspiration, new techniques, cross-product workflows, and updates on new features, go to the Creative Cloud tutorials page *helpx.adobe.com/creative-cloud/tutorials-explore.html*.

Adobe Forums: Tap into peer-to-peer discussions, questions, and answers on Adobe products at *forums.adobe.com*. Choose Help > Adobe Audition User Forums to join in discussions specifically about Audition.

Adobe *Create*: The online magazine, *Create*, offers thoughtful articles on design and design issues, a gallery showcasing the work of top-notch designers, tutorials, and more. Check it out at *create.adobe.com*.

Resources for educators: *www.adobe.com/education* and *edex.adobe.com* offer a treasure trove of information for instructors who teach classes on Adobe software. Find solutions for education at all levels, including free curricula that use an integrated approach to teaching Adobe software and can be used to prepare for the Adobe Certified Associate exams.

Also check out these useful links:

Adobe Audition CC product home page: *www.adobe.com/products/audition.html.*

Adobe Labs: At *labs.adobe.com* you can access early builds of cutting-edge technology, as well as forums where you can interact with the Adobe development teams building that technology and other like-minded members of the community.

Adobe Authorized Training Centers

Adobe Authorized Training Centers offer instructor-led courses and training on Adobe products. A directory of AATCs is available at *training.adobe.com/ trainingpartners.*

1 SET UP ADOBE AUDITION CC

Lesson overview

In this lesson, you'll learn how to do the following:

- Configure a Mac computer's onboard audio for use with Audition

- Configure a Windows computer's onboard audio for use with Audition

- Choose the appropriate sample rate for a project

- Configure Audition to work with Mac or Windows systems

- Test your configurations to make sure all connections are correct

 This lesson will take about 45 minutes to complete. There are no audio lesson files because you'll be recording your own files to test the interface connections.

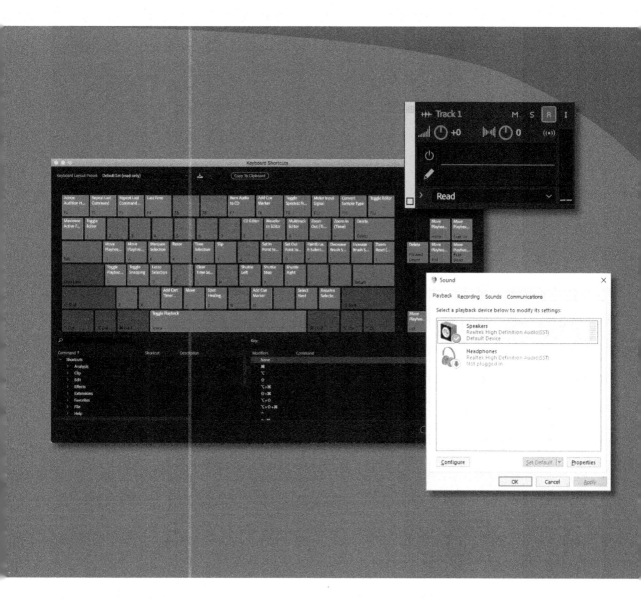

Before you can use Audition, you need to configure
your Mac or Windows computer and audio system to
work with the program.

Audio interface basics

Recording audio into a computer requires converting analog audio signals into digital data that your computer and Audition can recognize. Similarly, playback requires converting that digital data back to analog audio so you can hear it. The device that performs these conversions is usually called a *sound card* when it's built into the computer or an *audio interface* if it's an external piece of hardware. Both include analog-to-digital (A/D) and digital-to-analog (D/A) converters. In addition, software *drivers* handle communications between your computer and audio hardware.

This chapter concentrates on a computer's onboard audio capabilities, because the same concepts translate to more sophisticated (and higher-performance) audio interfaces. There are many brands and models of audio interfaces, so it's impossible to provide universally applicable lessons. Multiple sidebars in this chapter explain general audio interface characteristics to provide important background information for beginners.

Several lessons in this chapter are divided into versions for Windows and macOS computers. Read the content that's relevant to your system.

To make the best use of the lessons in this chapter, you'll need:

- An audio source, such as a portable music player (iPod, iPhone, Android, CD, and so on) with a 3.5mm minijack output, or other device with a suitable adapter to provide an output. Laptops may also have an internal microphone you can use; however, using a line-level device is recommended, and the lessons will reference that type of input. You can also use USB microphones that plug directly into a computer's USB port; however, note that they may introduce significant latency, as described later in this chapter, when used as class-compliant devices with Windows computers.

- Patch cable with a male-to-male 3.5mm plug to connect the audio source to your computer's audio input jack.

- Your computer's internal speakers for monitoring or earbuds/headphones with a 3.5mm stereo plug suitable for plugging into your computer's stereo output. You can also patch the output to a monitoring system if you have suitable cables.

Common audio interface connectors

The following are the most common input and output connectors found in computers and audio interfaces:

- **XLR jack.** This is compatible with microphones and other balanced-line level signals. Balanced lines use three conductors, which can be designed to minimize hum and noise pickup when they are carrying low-level signals.

- **¼-inch phone jack.** This is common with musical instruments and most professional audio gear. The jack can handle balanced or unbalanced signals; balanced line inputs can handle unbalanced lines as well. Headphone jacks also use ¼-inch phone jacks.

- **Combo jacks.** A combo jack can accept either an XLR or ¼-inch phone plug.

- **RCA phono jack.** A mainstay of consumer audio gear, RCA jacks are also found in some DJ audio interfaces and video equipment.

- **3.5mm / ⅛-inch minijack.** This is common for onboard computer audio, but rare for external interfaces except when included to interface with MP3 players and similar consumer devices. The 3.5mm / ⅛-inch minijacks sometimes provide headphone outputs as well.

- **S/PDIF (Sony/Philips Digital Interconnect Format).** This consumer digital interface typically uses RCA phono jacks but can also use an optical connector and (very rarely) XLR.

- **AES/EBU (Audio Engineering Society/European Broadcast Union).** This is a professional-level digital interface that uses XLR connectors.

- **ADAT (Alesis Digital Audio Tape) optical.** This optical connector carries eight channels of digital audio. It's used most commonly with interfaces for expanding the interface's inputs; for example, if you have an interface that lacks sufficient mic inputs but has an ADAT input, eight-channel mic preamps are available that send their outputs to an ADAT connector. This allows for easily adding eight mic inputs to an existing interface. Optical connectors are increasingly used for output to high-end consumer monitors, including TVs and surround sound systems.

macOS audio setup

Audition CC supports macOS X El Capitan 10.11, macOS Sierra 10.12, and macOS High Sierra 10.13. Updates to macOS are not synchronized exactly with updates to Adobe Audition. Although Audition likely will work on newer versions of macOS, it's important to check before updating.

To set input and output hardware:

1 Connect the audio source to the Mac's 3.5mm / ⅛-inch line input jack via the patch cord. If you're not using internal speakers, plug the headphones or monitoring system input into the Mac's line-level output or headphones jack.

2 Open Audition, and choose Adobe Audition CC > Preferences > Audio Hardware.

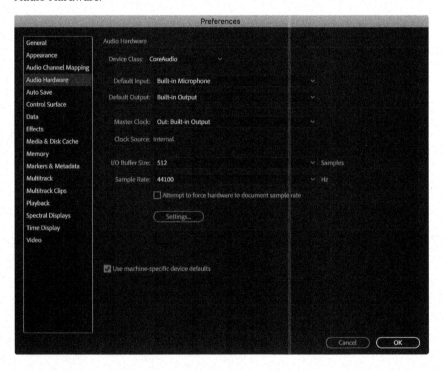

3 Don't change the Device Class or Master Clock preferences, because they will default correctly. The Default Input menu lists all available audio inputs. Choose Built-in [input]; in most cases, "input" will be "Line Input" or "Microphone."

4 The Default Output menu lists all available audio outputs. If you're using the built-in speaker, choose Built-In Output; for the line-level output, choose Built-In Line Output.

5 I/O Buffer Size determines the system latency. (See the sidebar "About latency [computer-based delay]" for more information.) Low values result in less delay through the system, whereas higher values increase stability. For now, choose 512 samples, which is a good compromise.

6 In the Sample Rate menu, choose 44100, which is the standard for CDs. The Sample Rate menu lists all available sample rates. (In theory, higher sample rates improve fidelity, but over 48000 the perceived difference is subtle at best.)

7 Click Settings to open the macOS Audio/MIDI Setup application, which automatically opens the Audio Devices window. Select Built-In Output, or select one of the line outputs you have installed.

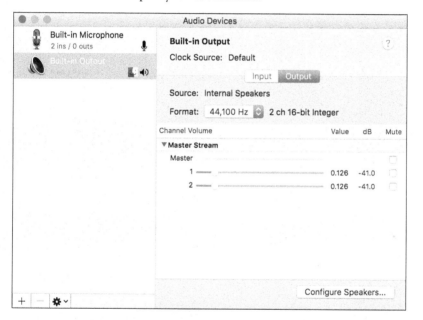

The settings will mimic what you set in Preferences (e.g., if you chose a 44.1 kHz sample rate, this will appear as the sample rate in the Format menu).

8 On the left, select Built-In Microphone or the line input you have installed. From the Format menu, choose:

- 2 ch (the number of channels)

- 24-bit Integer (the bit resolution; see the sidebar, "Bit resolution")

- 44.1 kHz (the sample rate; see the sidebar, "Common sample rates")

All macOS audio-related options are now set.

Note: The Audio MIDI Setup application accessed by clicking Audition's Settings button (Preferences > Audio Hardware) offers more information and flexibility than the macOS Sound preference pane (under System Preferences). There are level controls, the option to mute inputs, and the ability to click any input or output and examine its characteristics.

9 Close the Audio Devices window and quit Audio MIDI Setup.

● **Note:** The default hardware channel mapping defaults rarely need to be changed; however, you can remap if, for example, you were given a file in which the right and left channels were accidentally reversed: Map Audition's 1(L) channel to the Built-in Output 2, which connects to the physical right output.

10 Back in the Audition Preferences dialog box, select Audio Channel Mapping from the list on the left, to compare Audition's channels to your hardware inputs and outputs. For example, Audition's 1(L) channel will be mapped to Built-In Output 1 by default. Click OK to close this dialog box.

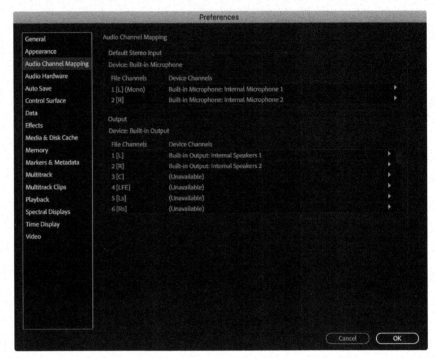

Bit resolution

Bit resolution expresses the accuracy with which the analog-to-digital converter measures the input signal. A good analogy is the relationship between pixels and image resolution: The more pixels in images of the same size, the more detail you'll see in the picture.

CDs use 16-bit resolution, which means that audio voltages are defined with an accuracy of approximately 1 part in 65,536. A 20- or 24-bit resolution provides a higher level of accuracy, but as with higher sample rates, higher bit resolution requires more storage. A 24-bit file is 50 percent larger than a 16-bit file if both are at the same sample rate. Unlike with higher sample rates, few dispute that 24-bit recording sounds better than 16-bit recording.

Recording music at 44.1 kHz with 24-bit resolution is a common trade-off among storage space, ease of use, and fidelity.

About latency
(computer-based delay)

Latency occurs in the conversion process from analog to digital and digital to analog, as well as in the computer: Even the most powerful processor can do only so many millions of calculations per second and sometimes can't keep up. As a result, the computer stores some of the incoming audio in a *buffer*, which is like a savings account for your audio input signal. When the computer is so busy elsewhere that it misses handling some incoming audio, it makes a "withdrawal" from the buffer instead.

The larger the buffer (measured in samples or milliseconds), the less likely the computer will run out of audio data when it's needed. A large buffer, however, also means that the input signal is being diverted for a longer period of time before being processed by the computer. As a result, the audio you hear coming out of the computer will be delayed compared to the input. For example, if you're monitoring your vocals, what you hear in your headphones will be delayed compared to what you're singing, and this can be distracting. Reducing the Sample Buffer value minimizes delay at the expense of system stability (you may hear clicking or popping with lower latency settings).

Windows audio setup

Unlike newer Mac systems, Windows systems typically have several drivers: legacy drivers (primarily MME and DirectSound) for backward compatibility and higher-performance drivers (WDM/KS or "Windows Driver Model/Kernel Streaming," which is a type of WDM driver). However, for Windows music applications, the most popular high-performance audio driver is ASIO (Advanced Stream Input/Output), created by software developer Steinberg. Virtually all professional audio interfaces include ASIO drivers, and many include WDM/KS drivers.

Unfortunately, ASIO is not part of the Windows operating system, so for these lessons you'll use the MME (Multimedia Extensions) protocol. It has relatively high latency but is stable and predictable. Experienced computer users can download the general-purpose ASIO driver ASIO4ALL, which is available free of charge from *www.asio4all.org*. It is the de facto ASIO driver for laptop owners who want to use ASIO with internal sound chips. Although you'll use MME for now, with a professional audio interface, use the ASIO or WDM/KS drivers provided with it, or as an alternative, ASIO4ALL.

Tip: If there's a microphone input and you're not using it, make sure it's not selected (or its fader is down) to prevent it from contributing any unwanted noise.

1   Windows motherboards typically have mic and 3.5mm / ⅛-inch line inputs. Connect the audio source to the computer's 3.5mm / ⅛-inch line input jack via the patch cord.

2   If you're not using internal speakers, plug the headphones or monitoring system input into the computer's line-level output.

Audition on macOS versus Windows

Using a program on macOS versus using it on Windows was once a hot topic, but over time, the operating systems and associated hardware have become more alike. Now, for all practical purposes, Audition operates identically on both platforms.

Each platform has strengths and limitations. For instance, macOS handles audio transparently, avoiding the multiple drivers found with Windows. Independent benchmarks show that all other factors being equal, however, Windows can apply more power to audio projects than macOS. With today's computers the situation is analogous to saying that a car capable of going 270 mph is more powerful than a car that tops out at 250 mph, when you probably won't drive over 90 mph anyway.

Ultimately, if there are macOS-only or Windows-only programs that are essential for what you do, that will tend to dictate the platform you will choose.

Windows 10 assignments

Although Audition exclusively supports 64-bit versions of Windows, it is compatible with Windows 7 and 8, as well as Windows 10, the current version. This exercise describes and depicts how to configure Audition to work with a typical Windows 10 system, but you'll find these steps are appropriate for the two earlier versions of Windows too and that the various versions' interface options look almost identical.

To set input and output hardware:

1   Connect the audio source to the system's 3.5mm / ⅛-inch line input jack via the patch cord. If you're not using internal speakers, plug the headphones or monitoring system input into the computer's line-level output or headphones jack.

2   Open Audition, and choose Edit > Preferences > Audio Hardware.

3 Click the Settings button to display the Windows Sound settings dialog box.

4 Make sure you are viewing the Playback tab. Select either Speakers or Headphones, depending on what you have plugged into the computer's output jack. After making your selection, if it's not already set, click the Set Default button to make this your default audio output.

5 With the recording device selected, click the Properties button, and choose the Advanced tab in the Properties dialog box.

6 Set the Default Format to 24 bit, 44100 Hz, and click OK.

▶ **Tip:** In the Sound Playback [selected device] Properties dialog box, you can use controls on the Levels tab to adjust the volume and balance, as well as mute the output.

7 Click the Sound dialog box's Recording tab.

8 Select Line In or one of the microphone inputs, and if it's not already selected, click Set Default.

▶ **Tip:** In the Sound Recording [selected device] Properties dialog box, you can use controls on the Levels tab to adjust the volume and mute the input.

9 With the input device selected, click the Properties button, and click the Advanced tab in the Properties dialog box.

10 Set the Default Format as follows, and then click OK:

- 2 Channel (the number of channels)

- 24 bit (the bit resolution; see the sidebar, "Bit resolution")

- 44100 Hz (the sample rate; see the sidebar, "Common sample rates")

11 Click the Sounds tab, and for Sound Scheme, choose No Sounds. It's distracting to hear system sounds while you're working with audio. Click OK.

The Audition Preferences dialog box will show the selected sample rate of 44100 Hz.

When producing professional music, it's common to use a sample rate of 44100 Hz. This has been a high-quality delivery standard for digital audio for many years. It's a good trade-off between quality and file size—which is a factor when delivering music for fixed-storage media like CDs.

When producing soundtracks for professional film and television production, it's common to use a higher sample rate of 48000 Hz, or even 96000 Hz.

When working on one type of audio or the other, use these settings to set up your audio recording and playback appropriately.

Audition settings for Windows audio

Now that the computer is configured properly for the audio inputs and outputs, you need to configure settings in Audition as well.

1 Continue from the last exercise in the Audition Audio Hardware preferences, or choose Edit > Preferences > Audio Hardware.

2 From the Device Class menu, choose MME.

3 From the Default Input menu, choose the default input device (Line In or Microphone) you specified previously; from the Default Output menu, choose the default output device (Speaker or Headphones) you specified previously. Do not change the Master Clock preference.

4 Choose a latency value of 200 ms, which is a "safe" value for most computers. Latency determines the delay audio experiences as it passes through the computer. Low values result in less delay through the system, whereas high values increase stability.

▷ **Tip:** The option to use machine-specific device defaults allows systems in a network environment to retain settings that relate to each individual hardware configuration.

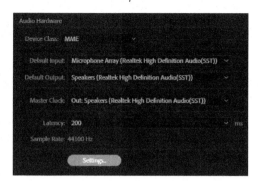

5 Select the Audio Channel Mapping preferences category (listed on the left) to correlate Audition's channels to the hardware inputs and outputs. For example, Audition's 1(L) channel will be mapped to Line 1. Click OK to close this dialog box.

● **Note:** The mapped defaults for channel mapping rarely need to be changed. However, you can remap if (for example) you were given a file in which the right and left channels were accidentally reversed: Map Audition's 1(L) channel to the Built-In Output 2, which connects to the physical right output.

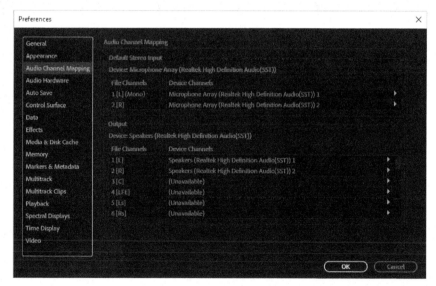

Common sample rates

The sample rate is the frequency with which the air pressure (which is effectively the volume) is measured each second.

An air pressure wave includes both a high pressure and a low pressure phase, and for this reason you need double the number of samples to capture a particular frequency.

For example, to record a 10 Hz signal (that is, 10 cycles per second), you would need to sample the air pressure 20 times a second.

The higher the frequency, the higher the perceived tone, so low sample rates fail to capture high tones that we would normally be able to hear.

High sample rates also reduce certain types of unwanted noise when audio is processed. Including more information in this way means larger file sizes, which is a trade-off you may need to consider carefully.

Different sample rates are typically used for different applications. Here are the most common sample rates used for professional audio:

- **32,000 (32 kHz).** Typically used for digital broadcast and satellite transmissions.
- **44,100 (44.1 kHz).** The sample rate for CDs and most consumer digital audio.
- **48,000 (48 kHz).** The most common sample rate used in broadcast video.
- **88,200 (88.2 kHz).** Some engineers claim this sounds better than 44.1 kHz, but it's rarely used.
- **96,000 (96 kHz).** Sometimes used in DVDs and other high-end audio recording processes.
- **176,400 and 192,000 (176.4 and 192 kHz).** These ultra-high sample rates generate much larger files and stress your computer more, yet offer no significant audio advantage.

Testing inputs

Because you specified default inputs and outputs in the previous lessons, Audition will default to using these for recording and playback. Now you'll test these connections to ensure that the inputs and outputs are set up properly.

1   Choose File > New > Audio File to create a new file in the Waveform Editor. A dialog box appears.

2 Name the file. Choose a sample rate of 44100 Hz (the standard for music audio files).

3 Choose the number of channels. Their inputs will default to whatever you specified in Preferences. If you choose Mono, only the first channel of an input channel pair will be recorded.

4 The bit depth represents the project's internal bit depth, not the bit resolution of your interface's converters. This resolution will be used to calculate changes in volume, effects, and the like, so choose the highest resolution, which is 32 (float).

5 Click OK to close the dialog box.

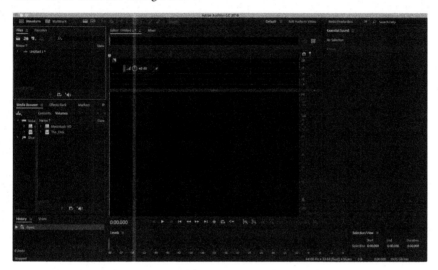

Your interface should display these panels. If not, follow the instructions in the sidebar, "Using workspaces."

At the bottom of the Editor panel, there are a series of transport and view zoom controls.

Using workspaces

If you have worked in your installation of Audition previously, it's possible your interface will be arranged differently than the screenshots in this book.

Audition uses preset workspaces, with various interface panels displayed to support various workflows, such as radio production or editing audio to video.

To match your installation of Audition to the workspace used in this lesson, choose Window > Workspace > Default. Then choose Window > Workspace > Reset To Saved Layout.

6   Click the Record button in the transport controls 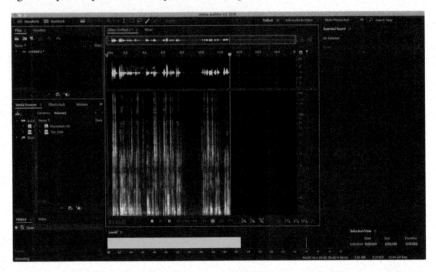, and then start playback
    from your audio source. If all connections are defined and all levels are set
    properly, you'll see a waveform being drawn in the Waveform Editor window.
    If your input device is a built-in microphone, say a few words to use your voice
    as a source. Record several seconds of audio, and then press the Record button
    again or press Spacebar to stop the recording.

7   Click the Move Playhead To Previous button [◄◄] in the transport controls, or
    drag the playhead in the Time Ruler at the top of the Editor panel (also called
    the *current time indicator [CTI]*) [▼] all the way to the left, to the beginning
    of the file.

8   Click Play [▶] at the bottom of the Editor panel, and you will hear what you
    recorded through your chosen output device (internal speakers, headphones,
    or monitoring system). Click the Stop button or press Spacebar to end playback.

9   Now let's test recording and playback in the Multitrack Editor. Choose File >
    New > Multitrack session. The New Multitrack Session dialog box appears.

10 Name the file. Browse to a convenient folder location. From the Template menu, choose None. The sample rate will default to the value you chose in Preferences.

11 As with the Waveform Editor, choose the highest resolution of 32 (float) for Bit Depth, and then, from the Master menu, choose the number of output channels (Stereo) for the Master Track.

12 Click OK to close the dialog box.

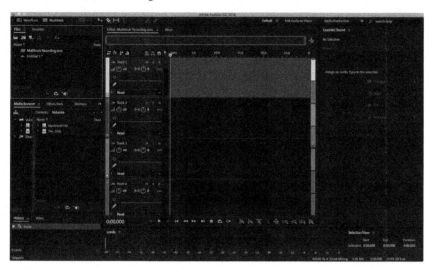

13 Arm a track by clicking the R (Record) button. Start playing your audio source; the channel's meter will indicate a signal.

Note that the input connects automatically to the default input you set earlier. If you open the Input menu (which displays Default Stereo Input by default), you can choose just one input for mono tracks or you can access the Audio Hardware preferences. This is useful if you have a multi-input audio interface and want to choose an input other than the default.

14 Click the Record button 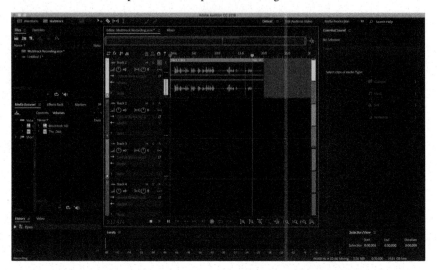 at the bottom of the Editor panel. If all connections are defined and all levels are set properly, you'll see a waveform being drawn in the Multitrack Editor window. Record several seconds of audio, and then press the Record button or Spacebar to stop the recording.

15 Click the Move Playhead To Previous button , or drag the playhead back to the beginning of the file.

16 Click Play at the bottom of the Editor panel to what you recorded through your chosen output device (internal speakers, headphones, or monitoring system). Click the Stop button or press Spacebar to end playback.

Using external interfaces

Professional interfaces usually have capabilities beyond those offered by built-in audio input and output hardware and, therefore, have their own control panels for routing signals, controlling levels, and so on.

Interfaces often have more than one set of stereo inputs and outputs. When you're choosing default inputs and outputs, you'll have a wider selection compared to using a computer's built-in sound capabilities.

With interfaces that provide multiple connection types (USB, FireWire, Thunderbolt, and so on), try them all on extended sessions to determine if one option works better than the other. You may find faster, more stable latency with one connection over another.

Windows USB interfaces can be *class-compliant*, meaning they don't need custom drivers. However, always use the custom ASIO or WDM drivers provided with an interface for maximum functionality and minimum latency.

With Windows computers, never use drivers called "emulated," such as "ASIO (emulated)." These result in the worst performance of all possible drivers.

Some interfaces include a feature called *zero-latency monitoring*. This means the input can be mixed directly to the output. Typically, you control the mixing by using an applet that appears onscreen, thereby bypassing any latency caused by going through the computer.

Audio interface/computer connections

There are several ways external audio interfaces communicate with a computer:

- **USB.** USB 2.0 can stream dozens of audio channels over a single cable that connects between the interface and a computer's USB port. USB 3.0 audio interfaces are less common, though they do exist and benefit from ten times the bandwidth. Virtually all USB 2.0 interfaces are compatible with USB 3.0. USB 1.1 interfaces are also available (although less popular now) for less-demanding applications and can typically stream six channels of audio, making them suitable for surround sound. Class-compliant interfaces are plug and play, but most professional interfaces use specialized drivers to improve speed and efficiency.

- **FireWire.** Like USB, FireWire also connects the interface to your computer with a cable. Although still common, FireWire has been eclipsed somewhat by USB for several reasons: Many laptops no longer include FireWire ports, most audio interfaces require specific FireWire chip sets, and the performance advantage FireWire once offered was more relevant when computers weren't as powerful. Some audio interfaces include FireWire and USB. It's less common for computers to have a Firewire connection, so check before you invest in the hardware.

- **PCIe card.** This plugs directly into a computer's motherboard, so it provides the most direct pathway to a computer. This option is less common because USB and FireWire offer more convenience (they connect externally and don't require you to physically open the computer to install the card). Also, there is nowhere to install a PCIe card in a laptop.

- **ExpressCard.** This is suitable for plugging into laptops that have ExpressCard slots but again is ceding its role to USB or FireWire interfaces.

- **Thunderbolt.** This relatively recent interface protocol, which carries data over a cable, is becoming more common; it's the only option, other than USB 3.0, on newer Mac computers. Thunderbolt provides PCIe-type performance and compatibility with existing audio interfaces, as well as with dedicated Thunderbolt interfaces.

Keyboard shortcuts

Audition has an intuitive system for discovering and assigning keyboard shortcuts. Choose Edit > Keyboard Shortcuts or press Alt-K (Windows) or Option-K (macOS) to open the Keyboard Shortcuts dialog box.

The Keyboard Shortcuts dialog box displays keys with shortcuts assigned. Here you can modify and add shortcuts, as well.

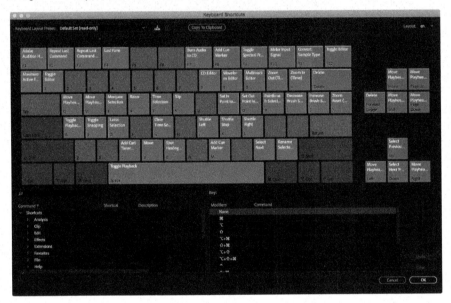

The Keyboard Shortcuts dialog box displays all keys that can be assigned shortcuts. Keys that have a shortcut assigned already have a color highlight and display their shortcut.

The 1 key, for example, toggles between the editors.

If you hold a modifier key or a combination of modifier keys—that's Ctrl, Alt, or Shift (Windows) or Command, Option, Shift (macOS)—the corresponding shortcuts are displayed.

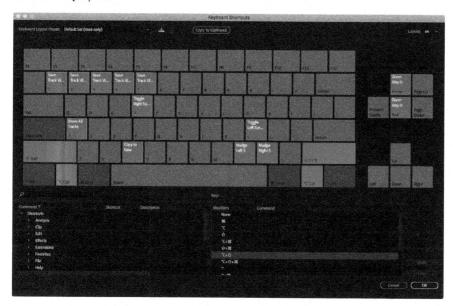

In this example, the Option and Shift keys are held down.

You can search for a shortcut by typing the name in the search box.

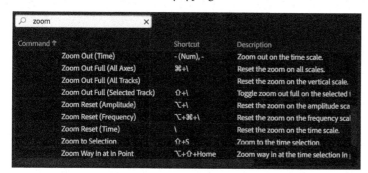

Any commands that match what you type will be listed.

To add a shortcut, select the command you would like to assign a shortcut to, click in the space to the right of the command under the Shortcut heading to display a text entry box, and type the shortcut you would like to use.

If you choose a shortcut that is already in use, Audition displays a warning. You then can choose whether to change the original assignment or to undo and pick another shortcut.

This book focuses on menu systems rather than keyboard shortcuts, so you can learn the full workflow more easily. However, learning keyboard shortcuts is often considered an important stage in the mastery of any application. In fact, Audition displays default keyboard shortcuts in its menus to make learning them easier.

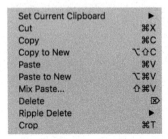

Any time you expect to perform an operation five times or more, consider assigning a keyboard shortcut for the task. Also, if you commit to learning one keyboard shortcut every time you sit down to work in Audition, you will quickly learn the shortcuts that you'll use regularly.

Review questions

1 What are the most popular driver protocols for macOS and Windows?

2 What is an unavoidable, negative byproduct of working with computer-based audio?

3 How can you minimize latency?

4 What are the advantages and disadvantages of high sample rates and high bit resolutions?

5 Although many external audio interfaces include ASIO drivers, the Windows operating system does not. How can you use ASIO with laptop sound chips?

Review answers

1 Core Audio for macOS and ASIO for Windows are the most popular driver protocols.

2 System latency causes a time delay between the output and what's being recorded at the input.

3 Change the number of sample buffers to alter latency. Use the smallest number possible, without the audio producing clicks or pops, to provide minimum latency.

4 High sample rates and bit resolutions have the potential to deliver better audio quality but create larger audio files and stress the computer more than lower rates and resolutions.

5 The free driver software, ASIO4ALL, provides ASIO drivers for sound hardware that was not designed for ASIO compatibility.

2 THE AUDITION INTERFACE

Lesson overview

In this lesson, you'll learn how to:

- Create custom workspaces for particular workflows
- Arrange panels for optimum workflow
- Use the Media Browser to find files on your computer
- Listen to files before loading them using the Media Browser's Playback Preview function
- Create shortcuts to frequently used folders
- Navigate to specific sections of a file in the Waveform Editor or a session in the Multitrack Editor
- Use markers to create points you can jump to immediately in the Waveform Editor or a session in the Multitrack Editor
- Use zooming to focus in on particular sections in the Waveform or Multitrack Editor

 This lesson will take about 60 minutes to complete. Please log in to your account on peachpit.com to download the lesson files for this chapter, or go to the "Getting Started" section at the beginning of this book and follow the instructions under "Accessing the Lesson Files and Web Edition." Store the files on your computer in a convenient location.

Your Account page is also where you'll find any updates to the chapters or to the lesson files. Look on the Lesson & Update Files tab to access the most current content.

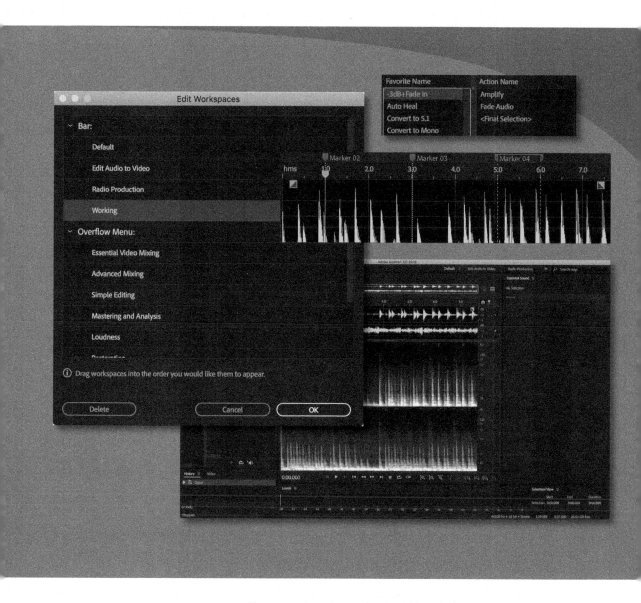

You can create custom workspaces with particular selections of windows and window arrangements in Audition, as well as choose various ways to navigate through the Waveform Editor and Multitrack Editor.

Two applications in one

Note: If you have not already downloaded the project files for this lesson to your computer from your Account page, make sure to do so now. See "Getting Started" at the beginning of the book.

A unique feature of Audition is that it combines the beautifully integrated functionality of two programs in a single piece of software:

• A Waveform Editor that can perform highly detailed and sophisticated editing

• A Multitrack Editor for creating multitrack music productions

Though these are separate (but connected) editors, it's helpful to think of them as modes, which change the way panels work (panels will be explained in a moment), and give access to different tools and options.

There are a number of ways to switch between the two editors. The simplest way is to click one of the two buttons at the top left of the Audition interface.

These two buttons have a clear function, but others are often simply a symbol you'll need to learn to recognize. Thankfully, if you hover your mouse over a button, its name and (if there is one) keyboard shortcut will appear in a tool tip. This is a great way to learn new tools and options.

The two interfaces are seamlessly connected, so audio can move freely between the two editing modes.

For example, audio in the Multitrack Editor can be transferred to the Waveform Editor for detailed editing, and changes will update automatically in the original multitrack session. Adjustments can be made to files brought into the Waveform Editor before making them the basis for a multitrack project.

Both editors have highly customizable workspaces that you can optimize—not just for editing or multitrack productions, but also for audio for video, sound library development, audio restoration, sound effects creation, and even forensics. This chapter concentrates on the Waveform Editor, but operations in the Multitrack Editor are similar or, in many cases, identical.

The editing/multitracking connection

Traditionally, multitrack recording programs and digital audio-editing programs were separate and optimized for their specific tasks. For example, multitrack recorders can have dozens of tracks (even over a hundred) and, therefore, require effects that minimize CPU power consumption because of the sheer number of tracks potentially incorporating effects. For the same reason, mixing and automation are extremely important for multitrack recorders. Digital audio "waveform" editors, on the other hand, deal with a limited number of tracks (usually just stereo audio), don't require mixing, and tend to have "mastering quality" effects that use a lot of CPU power.

Although Audition started as a digital audio editor with no multitracking capabilities, it now offers both. Audition doesn't just stick two isolated programs together, but instead integrates them. When working with a multitrack recording, you will often need to do detailed editing on a track. This would normally require exporting the file, opening it in a second program, editing it, and then reimporting it back into the multitrack recording software. With Audition, you just click the Waveform Editor, and all the tracks in the Multitrack Editor are already loaded and available.

This fluid movement between the two environments improves workflow. Another advantage is that the two sections have similar user interfaces, so you don't have to learn two separate programs. There is, however, a fundamental difference in the way audio files are treated when working in these two modes:

- Changes you make when working in the Waveform Editor modify the original audio file when you save. In this sense, the effects and adjustments you apply are referred to as *destructive* because you are making changes to the original media file. Once effects are applied in the Waveform Editor, they are written into the original audio file and their settings are no longer editable (although you can always undo prior to saving and always add more effects).

- Changes you make when working in the Multitrack Editor never modify the original audio files. Changes are handled in the same way as non-linear video editing systems work: You make changes to clips that link to media, rather than to the original media. When you save, you actually save a multitrack session file, which contains information about the effects and adjustments you applied. These effects and adjustments can always be edited, and as the original media is not changed, the workflow is described as *non-destructive*.

Audition workspaces

The Audition workspace is consistent with other Adobe video and graphics applications so you don't need to learn multiple user interfaces.

Audition offers multiple panels, and you can choose which panels make up a workspace. As with other Adobe applications, you can add or remove panels at any time. For example, you don't need the Video panel if you're not editing audio for video. Or, when you're creating a multitrack project, you may need the Media Browser panel open to locate files you want to use, but when mixing, you may decide to close it to create space for inserting other windows. You can save a particular panel arrangement as a *workspace*, which is a preset layout. You can position, rearrange, or resize panels individually, in groups, or while docked together.

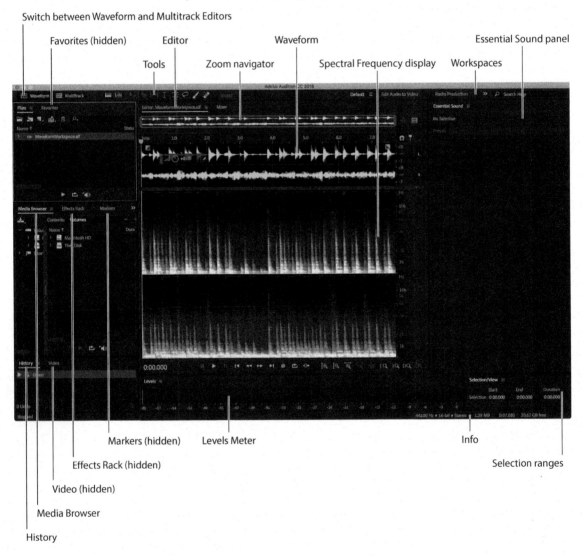

Switch between Waveform and Multitrack Editors

Favorites (hidden) Editor Waveform Essential Sound panel

Tools Zoom navigator Spectral Frequency display Workspaces

Markers (hidden) Levels Meter Info

Effects Rack (hidden) Selection ranges

Video (hidden)

Media Browser

History

Panels

Panels are the main elements in a workspace, and you can rearrange, resize, open, and close them to suit your particular needs.

1 With Audition open, choose File > Open, navigate to the Lesson02 folder, and open the file WaveformWorkspace.aif.

2 Choose Window > Workspace > Default.

3 To make sure Audition uses the stored version of the Default workspace, choose Window > Workspace > Reset To Saved Layout.

    Although it might be tempting to skip this step, consider: When you open Audition, it opens to the last workspace you were using. Modifications you made in your last work session, however, may no longer be relevant or helpful for your current work, so it's a good practice to go back to a clean slate, so to speak.

4 Click on the waveform in the Editor. When you click in a panel, a blue line outlines the panel.

Note: When you open Audition, it opens to the last workspace you were using. You can modify a workspace as much as you want, but you can always revert to the original version you created (as described later) by choosing Window > Workspace > Reset To Saved Layout.

Tip: To resize a panel in one direction, hover the mouse pointer over its edge until the cursor changes from a single arrow to a double arrow and drag. To resize a panel in two directions at once, hover over a corner until the cursor changes to a four-way arrow and drag. You can also resize the entire workspace by dragging any edge.

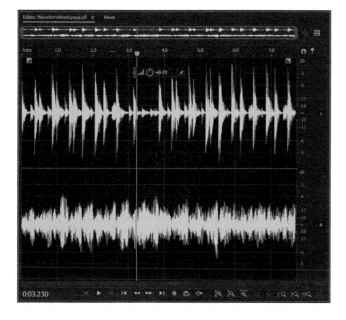

5 If you want to see more of the Editor panel, drag the left edge of the panel to the left to widen it.

6 Increase the panel's height by dragging the panel's lower edge down. This might cause the panels below the waveform to disappear or become narrow enough to be unusable. So, return the panel's lower edge to where it was, and then start to customize the workspace.

Every panel has a panel name at the top. Next to the name is the panel menu ▤.

Panel menus include common commands for closing, maximizing, or stacking the panel with other panels. They also often include commands that are unique to that particular panel.

The Files panel, for example, displays all the files and multitrack sessions you have opened, so the panel menu includes commands that relate to previewing and searching for files.

Close Panel
Undock Panel
Close Other Panels in Group
Panel Group Settings   ▶

Enable Auto-play
Enable Loop Preview
✓ Show Preview Transport
Match Case When Searching

Metadata Display...

If you close a panel, you can always reopen it by choosing it from the Window menu.

7 The Selection/View panel toward the lower right probably isn't needed right now, so open its panel menu and choose Close Panel to free up some more space. Note that the Levels panel expands to take up the space.

If you prefer, you can save space by gathering several panels together to create a panel group. The names of all the panels in the group are displayed across the top, and you then can click a panel name to bring that panel to the "front" of the group.

▶ **Tip:** With narrow groups containing multiple panels, not every panel will have a visible name. Click the double-arrows ⟩⟩ at the top-right corner of the group to see a menu listing all the panels it contains. Choose a panel name to display it.

8 You can drag a panel's name to move a panel to a different group or to create a new group: Drag the Favorites panel name to the middle of the Essential Sound panel. A blue *grouping zone* appears, letting you know you can drop the panel there.

▶ **Tip:** You can drag a panel's name to change its position among the other panels in the group.

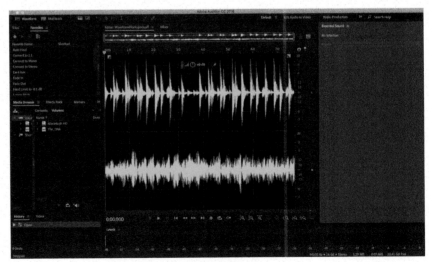

When you release the drag, the Favorites and Essential Sound panels form a panel group.

9 Drag the Media Browser panel name into the middle of the newly positioned Favorites panel. Now the Essential Graphics, Favorites, and Media Browser panels are grouped.

10 Drag the Levels panel name to the left edge of the Media Browser panel, until you see a blue bar with angled ends. This is an example of another type of drop zone used in Audition, the *docking zone*. Release to dock the Levels panel to the panel group containing the Media Browser panel.

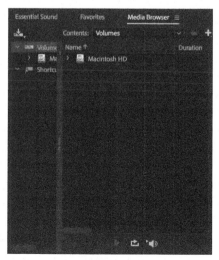

You can dock a panel to any edge of another panel. If you dock a panel to the left or right side of another panel, both panels shrink horizontally, so the width of the column of panels remains the same.

Notice that the design of the Levels panel has changed to display the levels vertically, rather than horizontally. Also, the other panels have all automatically resized to use the space left in the previous location of the Levels panel.

Note: There are narrow green drop zones on the four edges of the Audition interface. These are different from the blue drop zones because anything dropped into these green drop zones extends to the main application window's full length or height.

11 Click the Play button at the bottom of the Editor panel to see the new Levels design in action. Click the Stop button to stop playback.

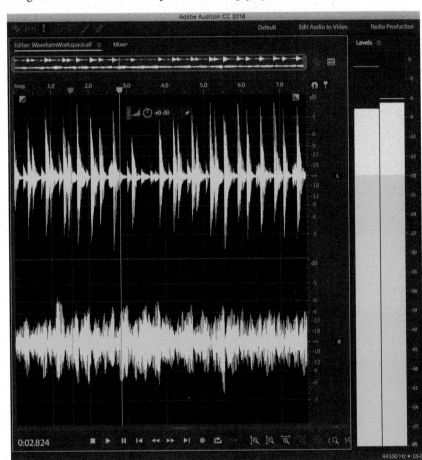

12 To create even more space, drag the right edge of the Editor panel further right, making the Levels panel narrower, until the levels numbers disappear.

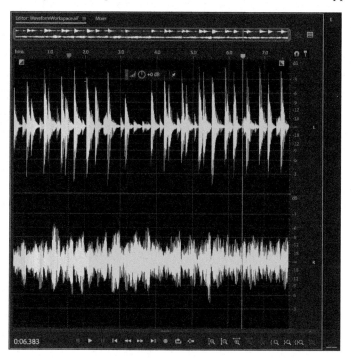

Adding a new panel

So far, you've rearranged existing panels within a workspace. However, you can also add new panels.

1 Choose Window > Diagnostics.

The Diagnostics panel provides a range of audio analysis and repair options.

When you chose the panel from the Window menu, Audition added it in its last location. In this case, that was almost certainly the default location, which is in the same group as the Effects Rack, Markers, and Properties panels.

2 If the Diagnostics panel appeared in another group, drag its panel name into the same group as the Effects Rack, Markers, and Properties panels.

3   Hover your mouse over the panel names in that group and turn the scrollwheel of your mouse. If you are using a trackpad, you can usually swipe with two fingers.

As you scroll or swipe, each of the panels in the group is displayed in turn, so you can confirm Diagnostics is in the group.

4   Drag the right edge of the group to the left to make the group narrower. At some point, most of the panel names will be hidden.

5   Click the double arrows » to display a list of panels in the group, and choose Effects Rack.

The Effects Rack panel is displayed.

All panels work in this way, meaning you can drag panels between drop zones to create new combinations in groups or even new groups.

Dragging and dropping panels into panel drop zones

When you drag a panel over another panel, blue drop zones appear that indicate where you can drop the panel. There are five main drop zones.

If the panel drop zone is in the panel center or panel name area (a *grouping zone*), Audition combines the arriving panel with existing panels in the group. As you discovered earlier, if the panel drop zone shows a bar with angled ends (*a docking zone*), the panel will land where the bar is and push the panel with the bar over to make room, creating a new group.

You can also drag whole groups into drop zones. To do this, you simply have to know where to drag from:

1   To expand the size of the group within the interface, combine the group containing the Effects Rack, Markers, Properties, and Diagnostics panels with the Files panel: Drag the area of blank space in the top-right corner of the group up into the Files panel (the *group gripper*). You'll know when you have clicked in the right spot, because your cursor will display tiny icons representing panels ⬚.

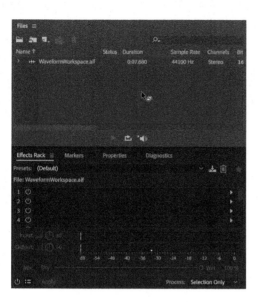

All the panels in the original group are combined with the Files panel.

2 Now that there are just two groups on the left side of the interface, drag the group boundary between the two to expand the group that now contains the Files, Effects Rack, Markers, Properties, and Diagnostics panel.

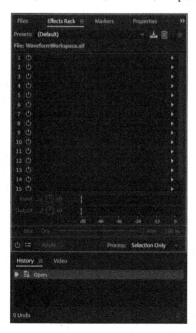

This flexible interface design can be a little confusing—especially as it is so easy to move panels around. Remember you can always reset the current workspace by choosing Window > Workspace > Reset To Saved Layout.

The panel menu

Every panel has a menu next to the panel name containing commands that relate to that panel. This is the panel menu. Some commands are standard to all panels, and there may be several additional commands that relate specifically to that panel. Standard commands include:

- Close Panel
- Undock Panel
- Close Other Panels In Group
- Panel Group Settings

Undocking allows you to "float" a panel outside of the main window. Here's how it works.

1 Click the panel menu for the Files panel.

Note: After undocking panels or groups, you can still dock them again by dragging them onto drop zones as you would any other panel or group.

2 Choose Undock Panel.

The panel becomes a separate window that you can resize and move independently from the Audition workspace. In fact, you can add other panels to it to create a floating panel group.

3 Just as you can undock single panels, you can undock entire panel groups. Click the Effects Rack panel menu, and choose Panel Group Settings > Undock Panel Group.

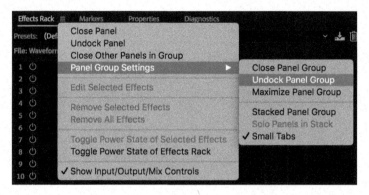

The whole group becomes a floating window you can position anywhere, including in front of the Audition interface. In addition, the Panel Group Settings submenu includes a couple other commands just for groups of panels, which you'll try out shortly.

▶ Tip: You can also undock a panel or panel group by dragging it completely out of the Audition workspace, or by Ctrl-dragging (Windows) or Command-dragging (macOS) it to another spot within the workspace.

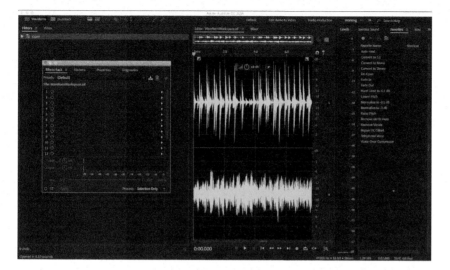

4   Move the entire floating panel group, containing the Effects Rack, Markers, Properties, and Diagnostics panels, back to its original location by dragging the top-right corner of the panel group into the top of the panel group containing the History and Video panels. Look out for the blue bar with angled ends before you release the group.

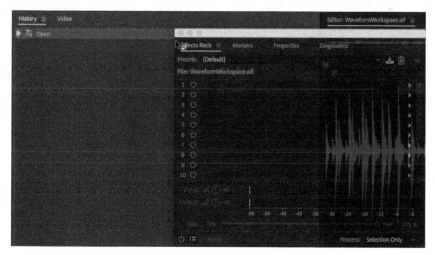

Multiple monitors

Floating windows are useful if you have multiple monitors with different screen resolutions, which cannot be spanned as a single display. By floating the panels you want on a second monitor, you can maximize the use of available screen space.

5   Drag the right edge of the group left to make it a little narrower. Aim to just be able to see all of the four panel names.

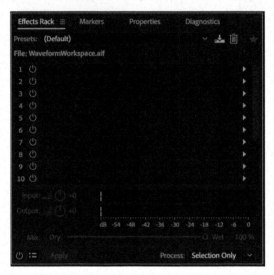

Note: The panel name is sometimes referred to as the panel tab. You'll even occasionally see that part of panels described as tabs in menus, help files, and tutorials. In the original design they looked like tabs, but the new flat user interface design changed that.

▶ **Tip:** If your keyboard has an Accent Grave key (`) you can hover over any panel and press this key to toggle maximizing the panel.

6   Open the panel menu for any of the panels in the group, and choose Panel Group Settings > Maximize Panel Group. The panel group expands to fill the entire Audition workspace.

Maximizing a panel group in this way is particularly useful when working with more complex panel contents, such as when you have a large number of audio files in the Files panel or a complex multitrack session with many tracks.

7   Double-click the currently active panel name.

The panel returns to its original size and position. You can double-click any panel name in this way to toggle between filling the interface and staying in a group.

You can also change the way the panels in a group are displayed and view them as a list of panels.

8 Click the same panel menu as in step 7, and choose Panel Group Settings > Stacked Panel Group.

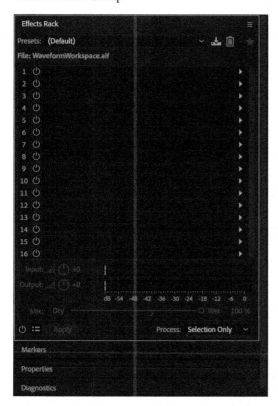

All of the panels in the group are now displayed in a vertical stack that you can scroll through. Each panel has its own horizontal heading you can click to display the contents, with the panel menu on the far right. Selecting a new panel collapses the last selected panel, but you can set stacked panels to stay expanded by choosing Panel Group Settings > Solo Panels in Stack in the panel menu.

9 Open the panel menu, and choose Panel Group Settings > Solo Panels In Stack to deselect it.

10 Click each of the panel headings in the stack; you will need to scroll down to see all of them.

Now all the panels are displayed, and a vertical navigation bar appears on the right enabling you to scroll through them.

Stacked panels are particularly useful if you are working on a small screen as they make more efficient use of the available screen area.

11 Click any of the panel menus in this group and choose Panel Group Settings > Stacked Panel Group, to deselect it.

Create and save custom workspaces

You can update the existing workspaces or easily create your own. First, practice creating a workspace based on the current layout:

1 Make any changes you would like to the current layout.

2 Choose Window > Workspace > Save As New Workspace.

   The New Workspace dialog box opens.

3 Name the workspace **Working**, and click OK.

   Your new workspace joins the list of current workspaces.

Tip: The workspace bar has a double arrow icon (similar to the one for panel groups); click it to display the overflow menu of available workspaces.

4 Click Edit Audio To Video in the list of workspaces at the top of the interface.

   The interface switches to the preset Edit Audio To Video layout.

5 Now try deleting the new workspace: Choose Window > Workspace > Edit Workspaces. The Edit Workspaces dialog box appears.

In the Edit Workspaces dialog box you can drag the workspace names to change the order in which they are displayed, as well as move them between the main list and the overflow menu.

6 Select the Working workspace you just created. Click Delete, and click OK.

7 To reset the Default workspace, click the Default workspace name to select it.

   This workspace already has some changes that you made before creating the new Working workspace.

8 Click the Default workspace panel menu, and choose Reset To Saved Layout.

   Now you should be in familiar territory with all the panels in their original locations.

Help files, live demonstrations, and online tutorials all usually presume you are working with the default workspace. To follow along with step-by-step guides, it's a good idea to begin by selecting and resetting the Default workspace.

Tools panel

The Tools panel has some unique attributes compared to the other panels.

The Tools panel defaults to being a toolbar: a thin strip of buttons along the top of the Audition interface. It incorporates:

- The Waveform Editor and Multitrack Editor selection buttons

- A series of tools for working on waveforms and multitrack audio clips

- The workspace selection buttons

- The searchable help box

The panel has no panel menu unless you undock it.

1 Right-click the blank space next to the tools in the Tools panel, and choose Undock Panel.

The resulting floating panel behaves like any other floating window. You can dock it with other panels, resize it, and position it wherever you like on the screen. In addition, the undocked Tools panel includes a Workspace menu that lists the available workspaces.

2 Open the Workspace menu in the Tools panel, and choose Reset To Saved Layout.

Note: The Status Bar at the bottom of the workspace is the one element that has a fixed location and cannot be floated or docked (however, you can choose whether to show or hide it by choosing View > Status Bar > Show). The Status Bar shows statistics about file size, bit resolution, sample rate, duration, available disk space, and so on.

Favorites panel

Similar to presets or macros, favorites are common, custom editing operations that are only a click or two away. You can perform almost any sequence of operations on audio, record them as a favorite, and then perform those same steps in a single action at any time later.

You can create new favorites, as well as remove, organize, and edit favorites. Although some workspaces default to including the Favorites panel, you can display it any time by choosing either Window > Favorites or Favorites > Edit Favorites. For now, this exercise focuses on basic favorite creation and editing. For advanced techniques involving favorites, see Chapter 4, which describes how to create and apply favorites with effects and more.

1   You should still have the WaveformWorkspace.aif file open and displayed in the Waveform Editor. If not, open it now by choosing File > Open, and browsing to the file in the Lesson02 folder.

2   Click the Favorites panel name to show the current list of favorites in the panel. If you're working on a small screen, you may need to resize the panel a little and drag the center divider across to see the full list of existing favorites.

Suppose a common operation your client needs on a regular basis is lowering a file's level by 3 dB and adding a fade-in over the first second, so you want to create a favorite that does both actions with one click.

3   To start recording this favorite, click the Record button ● in the top-left corner of the Favorites panel. If a dialog box appears that describes what a favorite is, click OK to dismiss it.

Floating over the top middle of the waveform display in the Editor panel, you'll find the HUD (heads-up display), which looks like a volume control.

4 Drag the HUD control to set it to −3 dB. When you release, the gain is reduced, the waveform updated, and is highlighted to show that it's selected. The HUD control reverts to 0 dB.

5 Drag the Fade In icon ◢ at the top-left corner of the waveform display to the right, to around the 1.0-second mark.

Tip: Dragging the Fade In or Fade Out icons left or right adjusts the timing of the fade. Dragging up or down changes the curve of the fade.

The waveform updates to show the result of the fade.

6 Click the Stop button ■ in the Favorites panel (this was the Record button in step 3).

7 A dialog box appears prompting you to name the favorite. Enter **-3dB+Fade In**, and then click OK. This adds the favorite to the list of favorites in the Favorites panel.

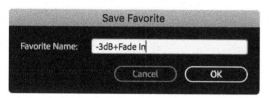

8 Now undo, to restore the waveform to the way it was before adding your edits. Press Ctrl+Z (Windows) or Command+Z (macOS) once to undo the fade-in, and then a second time to undo the gain change.

9 In the list of favorites, click -3dB+Fade In to select it, and then click the Favorites panel Play button ▶. The steps you recorded are performed again; the waveform will now be 3 dB softer and have a fade-in over the first second.

Tip: You can also select your newly created favorite from the Favorites menu.

10 You can reorder the list of favorites to place your most-used favorites near the top of the list. Click the Adjust Order button ▤ to the right of the Trash button, and then reorder your favorites by dragging and dropping them within the list.

11 Right-click the -3dB+Fade In favorite to display a context menu. Here you can choose to run, delete, and record favorites, as well as toggle the display of the step-by-step actions (this is enabled by default). Note that the new favorite consists of Amplify and Fade Audio.

Note: The Adjust Order button is a toggle. When the button is selected, the order reflects your customized order; when deselected, Favorites are arranged in alphabetical order.

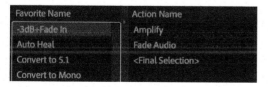

12 On the right side of the Favorites panel, right-click the Amplify action to display a context menu with advanced editing options, such as editing the selected action, capturing a particular time, and so on. Describing these in

detail is beyond the scope of this book, but this gives you an idea of the power of favorites. Choose Help > Adobe Audition Help for more information about editing Favorites.

13 Now suppose you decide that the -3dB+Fade In operation doesn't really need to be a favorite. Click it to select it, and then click the Trash button (to the right of the Play button). When asked if you're sure you want to remove the selected favorite, click Yes.

14 Quit Audition, and choose No when asked if you would like to save changes.

Explore the interface

Before you can get much work done, you need to know how to get around in an application's interface. There are three main types of navigation in Audition:

• Navigating to desired files and projects so you can open them, typically using the Media Browser

• Navigation related to playing back and recording audio within the Waveform Editor and Multitrack Editor

• Navigating visually within the Waveform Editor and Multitrack Editor (zooming in and out to specific parts of the file)

The following exercises let you practice each one.

Navigating to files and projects

Audition uses standard menu commands (such as Open, and Open Recent) to navigate your storage to find files, but enables you to open files in multiple ways. For example, you can open a file, which adds the file to the Files panel and opens it in the Editor, or you can Import a file, which adds the file to the Files panel but does not open it for editing.

You can also append an open audio file with the audio from another file. Give it a try:

1 Open Audition, choose the Default workspace, and reset the workspace.

2 Choose File > Open Recent > WaveformWorkspace.aif. If the file is not on the list, choose File > Open, navigate to the Lesson02 folder, and open the file WaveformWorkspace.aif.

3 Choose File > Open Append > To Current.

4 Navigate to the Lesson02 folder, choose String_Harp.wav, and in the dialog box, click Open to append the selected file to the end of the current waveform in the Waveform Editor.

Notice that the new audio extends the duration of the original audio. Although it is selected in the Editor panel, it is not added to the Files panel. Instead, it has modified the WaveformWorkspace.aif audio.

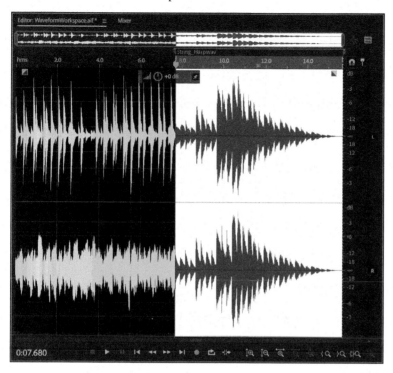

5   Choose File > Open Append > To New.

6   Navigate to the Lesson02 folder, choose String_Harp.wav, and then click Open.

This time the file you selected opens in a new Waveform Editor view. It does not replace the previously loaded file, and you can select either one using the Editor panel menu.

Because you chose to append to a new file, rather than to open the String_Harp. wav file, Audition created a new untitled audio file to contain the new audio.

7   Choose File > Close All, and then click No To All in the dialog box that appears. Leave Audition open in preparation for the next exercise.

● **Note:** You can choose Open Append > To New in the Multitrack Editor; however, this will simply open the file in the Waveform Editor, not the Multitrack Editor.

Navigating with the Media Browser

The Media Browser is an enhanced version of the browsing options offered in Windows and macOS. If you use Windows, you'll notice Media Browser works similarly to the standard Windows Explorer. If you use macOS, you'll find the Media Browser resembles the list view browser; selecting a folder in the left column opens its contents in the right column, like Finder's column view.

Either way, once you locate a file in the Media Browser, you can drag it into the Waveform Editor or Multitrack Editor window.

1 Choose Window > Workspace > Default.

2 Choose Window > Workspace > Reset To Saved Layout.

● **Note:** The Locations menu in the upper left, above the list of your computer's volumes, lets you select any drive. The contents of the selected drive appear immediately to the right in the Contents area.

3 Drag the Media Browser panel out of the group while holding Ctrl (Windows) or Command (macOS) to make it a floating window. This isn't strictly necessary but now you can more easily extend its size to see all the available options in the Media Browser. Resize the panel so you can see all of the options.

The left side of the Media Browser panel shows all the drives mounted to your computer. Clicking any of these drives displays its contents on the right. You can also click a drive's disclosure triangle to reveal its contents.

4 On the left, navigate to the Lesson02 folder. Click its disclosure triangle to expand it, and then click the Moebius_120BPM_F# folder.

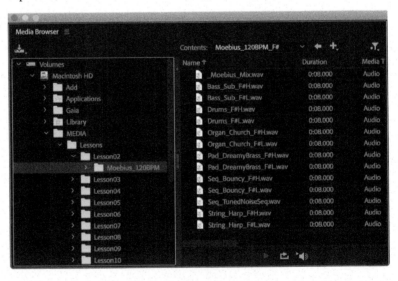

The contents of the folder are shown on the right. The attributes of each file, such as duration, sample rate, channels, and more, are displayed in a series of columns identified by headings. You may have to scroll right to see all of the information available.

5   You can change the column widths. Drag the divider line between two columns left or right to change the width.

6   You can rearrange the order of columns. Drag a column heading, such as Media Type, left or right to position it. This feature is helpful because you can drag the columns containing the information you need the most to the left side, so the data is visible even if the window isn't fully expanded.

7   You can add folders to a list of shortcuts to save you searching for them in the future. To create a shortcut for the Moebius_120BPM_F# folder, click it in the left column.

8   On the right side of the Media Browser panel, click the + symbol ◼, and choose Add Shortcut for "Moebius_120BPM_F#." You can also right-click the folder on the left side of the Media Browser panel, and choose Add Shortcut(s).

9   In the left column, close the Volumes disclosure triangle, and click the Shortcuts disclosure triangle to reveal your shortcut, which now provides one-click access to the designated folder.

10 Another Media Browser advantage is that you can listen to the files as you browse, thanks to the Preview Transport. If it's not visible, open the Media Browser panel menu, and choose Show Preview Transport. Click the Auto-Play button with the speaker icon; you'll be able to hear a file play as soon as you click it.

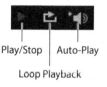

Play/Stop   Auto-Play

Loop Playback

> **Tip:** If enabled, the Loop Playback button causes the file to play until you either select another file or click the Stop button. If you don't want Auto-Play but want to play files manually, deselect Auto-Play and click the Play button (which toggles with the Stop button) to start playback.

Navigating within files and Sessions

Once you're in the Waveform Editor or Multitrack Editor, you'll want to be able to navigate within the Editor to locate or edit specific sections. Audition has several tools that you can use to do this.

1   In the Media Browser panel, navigate to the Lesson02 folder, and open the file WaveformWorkspace.aif using one of these methods:

•   Double-click the file.

•   Right-click the file, and choose Open File.

•   Drag the file into the Editor panel.

> **Tip:** You can also drag one or more files into the Files panel to work on them.

2 Choose the Default workspace, and use the Workspace panel menu to choose Reset To Saved Layout.

3 Resize the Editor panel as required to view all of the Transport and Zoom controls.

Transport controls   Zoom controls

4 Starting about a third of the way along the waveform, drag to about two-thirds of the way through the waveform to create a selection. The blue icon, with a red vertical line extending downward at the beginning of the selection in the timeline ruler (at the top of the waveform) is called the *playhead*.

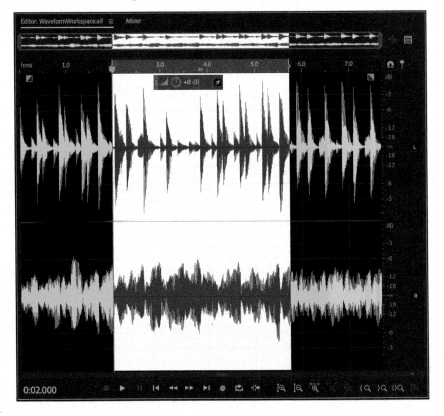

When you make selections in Audition, any adjustments or effects you apply are constrained to the selection. This allows you to make precise adjustments. The beginning of a selection is called an *In point*, and the end of a selection is called an *Out point*. These terms are commonly used in non-linear video editing, as well.

5 Click anywhere in the waveform to remove the selection.

Navigation via zooming

Zooming in Audition acts the same way as it does with a camera: Zoom out to see more of an object, and zoom in to see more detail. The Waveform Editor includes zoom buttons, and you can use the zoom navigator at the top of the Editor panel to precisely focus on part of your audio.

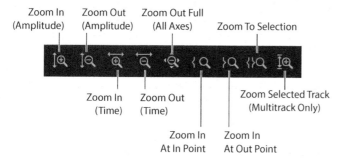

Zoom In (Amplitude) Zoom Out (Amplitude) Zoom Out Full (All Axes) Zoom To Selection

Zoom In (Time) Zoom Out (Time) Zoom Selected Track (Multitrack Only)

Zoom In At In Point Zoom In At Out Point

At the bottom of the Waveform Editor, you will find nine zoom buttons. If you want to position them elsewhere or float them in a window, you can open the Zoom panel from the Window menu. The Multitrack Editor includes these same zoom buttons.

1   Click twice on the leftmost button: Zoom In (Amplitude). Zooming in on amplitude lets you see low-level signals more easily.

▶ **Tip:** In the Waveform Editor panel, you can drag the horizontal divider between the Spectral Frequency Display and the Waveform Display to change the amount of space each takes up on screen.

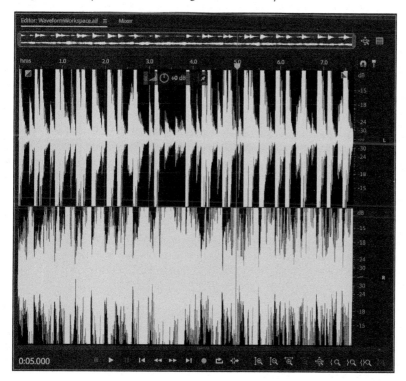

Notice that the amplitude scale on the right of the Editor panel scales as you zoom. It's easy to miss this change when zooming amplitude and, as a result, think your audio is louder than it really is.

2   Click twice on the next button to the right, the Zoom Out (Amplitude) button, to return to the previous amplitude zoom level.

3   Click eight times on the next button to the right, the Zoom In (Time) button, to see very short sections of time on the waveform.

4   Click twice on the next button to the right, the Zoom Out (Time) button, to zoom back out.

● **Note:** If you zoom in all the way using the Zoom In (Time) button, you can see and edit, individual audio samples.

5   Click once on the next button to the right, the Zoom Out Full (All Axes) button. This "shortcut" button zooms out the time and amplitude axes to their maximum size so you can see the complete waveform.

6   Make a selection: As in the previous exercise, click about a third of the way from the beginning, and then drag to about a third of the way from the end.

7   Click the fourth button from the right, the Zoom In At In Point button to shift the waveform display so the In point is in the center of the Editor panel.

8   Click the third button from the right, the Zoom In At Out Point button, to shift the waveform display so the Out point is in the center of the Editor panel.

9   Click the rightmost button, the Zoom To Selection button, to make the selection fill the window. Click anywhere in the waveform to deselect the selection.

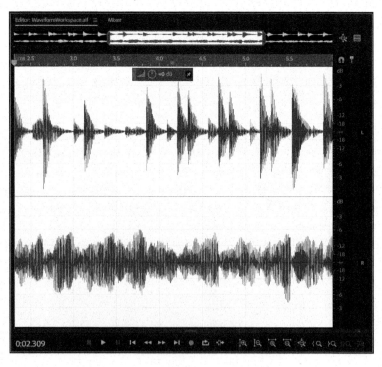

10 Click the Zoom Out Full button (the fifth button from the left in the Zoom toolbar) to return both axes to zoomed out full.

11 At the top of the window the zoom navigator shows a global overview of your audio file. Drag the left or right side handles of the navigator to zoom in or out of an area.

The area between the side handles is what you'll see in the Waveform Editor panel. Note that you can drag the zoom navigator between the handles to move the zoomed area left or right (earlier or later).

12 Hover anywhere over the waveform or the zoom navigator and scroll to zoom in and out horizontally.

13 Now hover over the dB scale on the right side of the Waveform Editor panel and scroll to zoom in and out vertically.

14 To reset the zoom to see the entire audio waveform again, click the Zoom Out Full button.

Navigation with keyboard shortcuts

Keyboard shortcuts can help tremendously with navigation. Once you've memorized important shortcuts, it takes less effort to press a couple of keys than to locate a specific area on the screen, move the pointer to it, access a menu, choose an item, and so on.

Audition even lets you create your own keyboard shortcuts for the various commands. Choose Edit > Keyboard Shortcuts, or press Alt+K (Option+K), and then follow the onscreen directions to add and remove shortcuts. For more information on keyboard shortcuts, see Chapter 1, "Set up Adobe Audition CC."

For now, try out some common keyboard shortcuts for navigation in this exercise:

1 Continuing from the previous exercise, click the zoom navigator, click the right handle, and drag left until the waveform in the Editor panel shows about 2.0 seconds of audio.

Notice the timeline ruler along the top of the Editor panel shows hours, minutes, and seconds.

2 Press the Page Up key on your keyboard, and then press the Page Down key. The playhead alternates between the left and right sides of the Waveform Editor, respectively.

▶ **Tip:** If you are working on a Mac keyboard without Page Up and Page Down keys, you can hold the fn key to turn the Up and Down arrow keys into Page Up and Page Down keys.

3 Press the Page Up and Page Down keys repeatedly. The zoomed-in area in the zoom navigator moves left and right in even intervals. Whenever you press Page Up, the playhead will always "stick" to the left side of the Waveform Editor, and when you press Page Down, the playhead will always "stick" to the right side.

4 Hold down Ctrl (Windows) or Command (macOS), and press the Page Up and Page Down keys repeatedly. The zoomed-in area moves as in the previous step, but the playhead remains in its current position.

5 Press the plus (+) key at the top of your keyboard to zoom in, and press the minus (−) key to zoom out. Pressing and holding these keys zooms continuously. (Although to type a plus sign you have to hold the Shift key, you do not have to do so for the shortcut to work.)

Navigation with markers

You can place markers (also called *Cue markers*) in the Waveform Editor and Multitrack Editor panels to indicate specific places you want to navigate to immediately. For example, in a project in the Multitrack Editor, you might place markers at the start of each scene in a film soundtrack, so you can jump back and forth between them. In the Waveform Editor, you might place markers to indicate places where edits are required.

Markers are saved with Multitrack Editor session files and audio files, so you can use them as a persistent reference.

1 If it's not open already, navigate to the Lesson02 folder, and open the file WaveformWorkspace.aif.

2 Choose Window > Workspace > Default.

3 Choose Window > Workspace > Reset to Saved Layout.

4 Choose Window > Markers to open the Markers panel. You may need to resize the Markers panel, or undock it and resize it, to see all of the controls.

Here, the Markers panel is docked in its default location, with the Media Browser, Effects Rack, and Properties panels.

5 Click in the waveform toward the beginning, around 1.0 second.

6 Press M to add a marker at the playhead location and add the marker to the list of markers in the Markers panel.

7 Click in the waveform at around 3.0 seconds. Click the Add Cue Marker button in the Markers panel. This also adds a marker at the location of the playhead, as well as in the list of markers in the Markers panel.

8 You can also mark a selection. Drag along the waveform between around 5.0 seconds and 6.0 seconds to create a selection. Press M to mark the selection. Note that the Markers panel shows a different symbol to indicate that this *Range marker* is marking a selection.

9 You can convert the Range markers to an individual Cue marker at the selection start. Right-click either the start or end of the Range marker, and then choose Convert to Point. You will then see a single marker around 5.0.

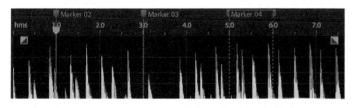

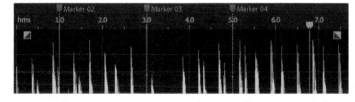

10 You can navigate between markers in several ways. Double-click any marker in the Markers panel list to jump the playhead to that marker. With Range markers, the playhead will jump to the marker at the range's beginning.

Another method for marker navigation involves the Transport controls, as you'll learn in the next exercise. Leave this project open in preparation for it.

> **Tip:** To set a default marker name, open the Markers panel menu, and choose Default Marker Name. This is a shortcut to the Markers & Metadata area in the Preferences dialog box, where you'll find the Default Name For New Cue Markers option. From now on, new markers will have the name you specify.

> **Tip:** To rename a marker, right-click its icon in the Waveform Editor and choose Rename Marker. Or, click the marker name in the Markers panel, click again after a slight pause (don't double-click), and type a new name. Renaming using either method renames both instances of the marker.

Navigation with the Transport controls

The Transport controls offer several navigation options, including navigation using markers.

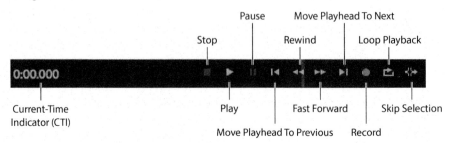

Note: If a file contains no markers, Move Playhead To Next jumps to the end of the file and Move Playhead To Previous jumps to the beginning.

Tip: The Fast Forward button to the right of the Rewind button works similarly to the Rewind button but moves the playhead forward in the file. You can right-click either button to set the speed.

Note: The Rewind, Fast Forward, Move Playhead To Next, Move Playhead To Previous, and, of course, Stop buttons can all be invoked during playback.

1 Continuing from the previous exercise, click the Move Playhead To Previous button at the bottom of the Editor panel. The playhead moves to the previous marker.

2 Click the Move Playhead To Previous button again. The playhead moves again to an earlier Marker. Click the Move Playhead To Previous button until the playhead moves to the beginning of the file.

3 Click the Move Playhead To Next button four times. The playhead steps to each of the markers until it reaches the end of the file.

4 To move the playhead backward in the file without dragging the playhead or using markers, click and hold the Rewind button until the playhead is in the desired location. You'll hear audio during the scrolling process. Rewind back to the beginning.

5 Click the Play button . Audition plays the file.

6 As soon as the playhead passes the first marker, click the Move Playhead To Next button. The playhead jumps to the second marker and continues playback. Click the Move Playhead To Next button again, and the playhead jumps to the third marker.

7 Right-click the Play button and choose Return Playhead To Start Position On Stop. With this option selected, clicking Stop will return the playhead to where it started. With this option deselected, the playhead will stop at the position it was at when you clicked the Stop button.

8 Right-click the Play button again, and deselect Return Playhead To Start Position On Stop.

9 Quit Audition, and choose No when asked if you would like to save changes to the file.

Review questions

1 What is the difference between a group and a panel?

2 What is a drop zone?

3 What is a floating window?

4 In addition to locating files, name two major advantages of using the Media Browser.

5 What is the purpose of a marker?

Review answers

1 A group contains more than one panel.

2 A drop zone indicates where a panel or group will dock when it's dragged to that zone.

3 A floating window exists outside of an Audition workspace and can be dragged anywhere on your screen.

4 You can listen to the files you locate as well as see their attributes before you open them in Audition.

5 A marker indicates a place in a file or Multitrack Editor session that the playhead can jump to directly, speeding up navigation.

3 WAVEFORM EDITING

Lesson overview

In this lesson, you'll learn how to do the following:

- Select a portion of a waveform for editing

- Cut, copy, paste, mix, and silence audio

- Learn to eliminate unwanted sounds

- Use multiple clipboards to assemble final audio from individual clips

- Add new sounds to an existing piece of music using Mix Paste

- Create loops with music files

- Fade audio regions to create smooth transitions and remove pops and clicks

 This lesson will take about 75 minutes to complete. Please log in to your account on peachpit.com to download the lesson files for this chapter, or go to the "Getting Started" section at the beginning of this book and follow the instructions under "Accessing the Lesson Files and Web Edition." Store the files on your computer in a convenient location.

Your Account page is also where you'll find any updates to the chapters or to the lesson files. Look on the Lesson & Update Files tab to access the most current content.

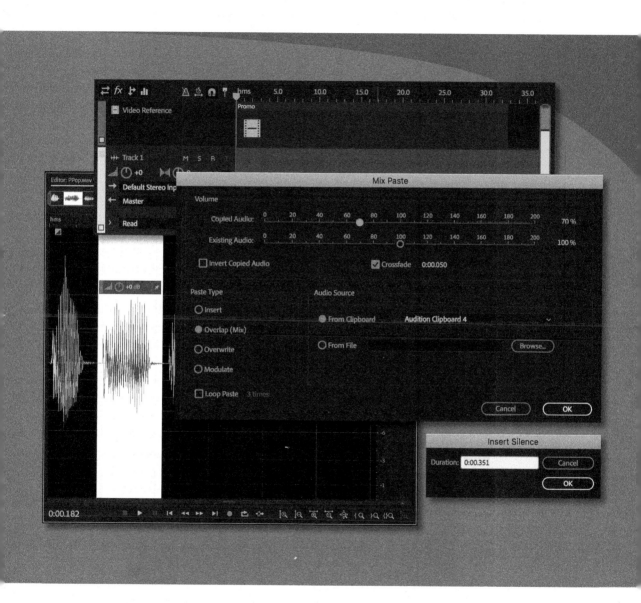

Audition makes it easy to cut, paste, copy, trim, fade, and apply other processes to audio files. You can also zoom in to make extremely precise edits, while seeing a zoomed-out version in the overview window at the top.

Open a file

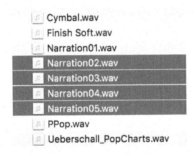

In Adobe Audition, you can open multiple files, which are then stacked behind each other in the main Waveform view. You can choose individual files from the Editor panel menu.

Note: If you have not already downloaded the project files for this lesson to your computer from your Account page, make sure to do so now. See "Getting Started" at the beginning of the book.

1 Start Audition. Choose File > Open, navigate to the Lesson03 folder, select the file Narration01, and click Open.

2 Choose the Default workspace, and reset the workspace by going to Window > Workspace > Reset to Saved Layout.

3 To open multiple files simultaneously, choose File > Open, and select Narration02, and then Shift-click Narration05. Four files are selected.

Tip: To select noncontiguous files, you can hold Ctrl (Windows) or Command (macOS) as you click each file you want to open.

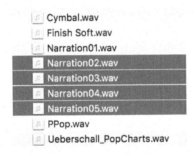

4 Click Open. Audition loads the selected files.

5 Open the Editor panel menu to see a list of the files you loaded. Choose any of these files to open it in the Waveform view. Or, choose Close to close the current file in the list (that is, the one visible in the Editor panel).

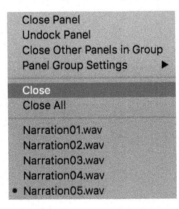

Tip: Double-clicking the background of the Files panel is effectively the same as choosing File > Open.

6 Now double-click the background of the Files panel to open the file Finish Soft. wav from the Lesson03 folder, and keep Audition open in preparation for the next exercise.

Video files

1 Choose File > New > Multitrack Session. The New Multitrack Session dialog box appears.

2 In the Session Name field, name the file **Audio for Video**. Choose None from the Template menu, 44100 Hz from the Sample Rate menu, 16 from the Bit Depth menu, and Stereo from the Master menu.

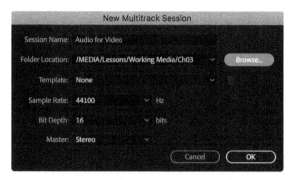

3 Click Browse, and navigate to a convenient location to store the new multitrack session. You might find it easiest to create a new folder in the Lessons folder for this purpose; call it **Working Media**. Click Choose when you have chosen your location.

4 Click OK in the New Multitrack Session dialog box.

5 In the Media Browser panel, or in Explorer (Windows) or Finder (macOS), open the Lesson12 folder, and then open the folder Audio for Video File and drag the file Promo.mp4 into the beginning of Track 1. This creates a video track automatically, and opens the Video panel where you can see the video.

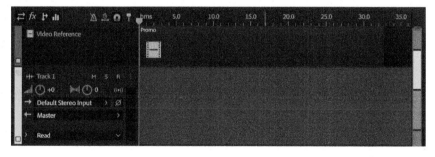

Note: Audition can recognize almost any type of common video format, but Audition is not a video editor and cannot edit the preview video. Any video edits need to be done in a program like Adobe Premiere Pro prior to loading the file into Audition. You can, however, move a video's start point within the video track of the Multitrack Editor.

Tip: You can right-click the Video panel and choose from five scaling options and three resolutions. Best Fit Scaling is usually the optimal choice, because the video size will conform to the size of the panel. When you're working with video, Audition can create a separate video preview track at the top of the workspace. If you import video that also includes an audio track, the audio will likewise be imported into Audition and placed in the audio track immediately below the video track.

Tip: It can be quite difficult to line up a file with the very start of the multitrack session. To make it easier, you can drop the file farther, and then drag the resulting segment left. You can also drop a file onto the track header, with the various track controls, to automatically align the file with the start of the track.

6 You may need to resize the Video panel to see the entire video image. (Note: The video file is provided courtesy of HarmonyCentral.com.)

The example video clip has no audio, and so nothing appears on the audio tracks in the multitrack session. If you open a video file with audio channels, they will be added to the multitrack session at the same time.

Don't forget video for audio

The phrase "audio for video" recognizes the reality that most of the time audio is added to existing video. However, if you have some degree of control over the audio *and* video process, sometimes it makes more sense to compose the music first and then lay video on top of the audio.

This is particularly true for videos that aren't critically dependent on timing. Kiosk videos, some ads, trailers, and promos are often fairly flexible in the way that video needs to be presented, and cutting it to the audio can simplify matters considerably.

But does the music matter that much? Some studies have indicated that people who were shown videos with identical video quality but differing audio quality judged those videos with better sound as having better *video* quality. If you can come up with a great piece of music, sometimes it's worth taking the video-for-audio route.

Select regions

To begin editing your audio, you need to start by choosing a file and specifying which parts of that file you want to edit. This process is called *selection*.

1 Open the Editor panel menu to see a list of recent files loaded into Audition. Choose Finish Soft.wav (or just reopen the file from the Lesson03 folder), and it will load into the Editor panel.

2 Click the Play button to listen to the file from start to finish.

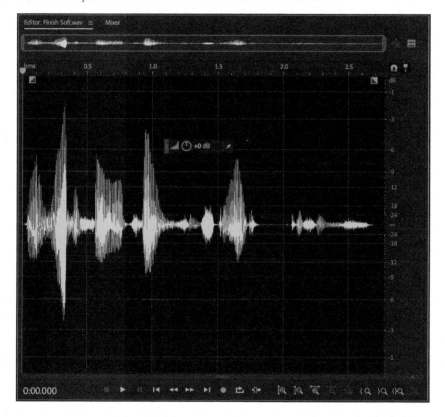

3 Notice that the words "to finish" are softer than the other words. The difference is visible in the waveform, as well as being clearly audible. Sometimes when you're recording narration, a drop in volume can occur at the end of phrases. You can fix this in Audition.

Note: When you
select a region, the
heads-up display (HUD)
with a small volume
control relocates to the
middle of the selection
automatically—unless
you have moved the
HUD previously, in
which case it will stay
where you put it. You
can toggle this behavior
by clicking the small pin
icon on the HUD.

4   Drag from the beginning to the end of the words "to finish." You've now *selected*
those words for editing, as indicated by a white background.

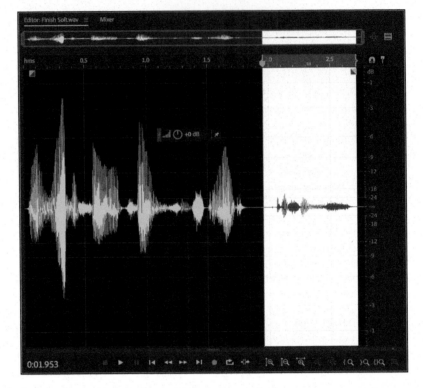

You can fine-tune the selection by dragging the region's right or left border,
either in the Waveform view or Timeline.

5   Drag upward on the HUD's volume control to increase the volume level to +6
dB. When you release the mouse, the HUD reverts to showing +0dB. This is
because the HUD applies relative changes each time you use it. As soon as an
adjustment is applied, the HUD returns to +0 and a new change will be based
on the current level.

6　To preview the change, click Play, and then click anywhere in the waveform to remove the selection. Move the playhead to the beginning, and click Play to hear the change in the context of the whole file.

If the level is good, you're done. If not, choose Edit > Undo Amplify, or press Ctrl+Z (Windows) or Command+Z (macOS). Then you can vary the level and audition the results again, as you did in the previous step.

7　When you're satisfied with the level, click anywhere in the waveform to deselect the region. Audition retains any volume changes, because they occur as soon as you change the level, and they will stay unless you undo the edit. Keep Audition open in preparation for the next exercise.

Note: You can show or hide the HUD by selecting or deselecting Show HUD in the View menu, or toggle it on and off by pressing Shift+U.

Tip: Double-click anywhere within a file to select the entire file. This also returns the playhead to the beginning of the file.

Cut, Copy, and Paste

Cutting, deleting, and pasting audio regions are particularly useful for narration audio files if you want to remove distracting sounds, tighten up spaces, increase spaces between words and phrases, or even rearrange the dialogue, if needed. In this exercise, you'll edit the narration file Narration05.wav so it flows logically and doesn't have unwanted sounds. Here's what the narration says:

"First, once the files are loaded, select the file you, uh, want to edit from the drop-down menu. Well actually, you need to go to the File menu first, select open; then choose the file you want to edit. Remember; you can (clears throat) open up, uh, multiple files at once."

You'll get rid of the uhs and throat clearing, and rearrange the narration to say:

"Go to the File menu first; select open; then choose the file you want to edit. Remember that you can open up multiple files at once. Once the files are loaded, select the file you want to edit from the drop-down menu."

1　Choose the file Narration05.wav using the Editor panel menu, or double-click the file in the Files panel. If the file isn't present, reopen it from the Lesson03 folder. A shortcut is to choose File > Open Recent, and then choose Narration05.

2 Play the file until you reach the first "uh." Stop the Transport, and drag across the "uh" to select it. You may need to zoom in to make a precise selection.

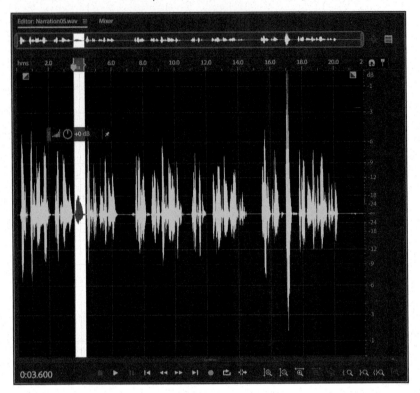

● **Note:** There's a difference between Edit > Cut and Edit > Delete. Cut removes the region but places it in the currently selected clipboard so it can be pasted elsewhere if desired. Delete also removes the region but does not place it in the clipboard, and leaves whatever is in the clipboard intact.

3 To hear what the file will sound like after you delete the uh, click in the Time Ruler at the top of the waveform several seconds prior to the region, and then click the Skip Selection button ▣ at the bottom of the Editor panel. Click the Transport Play button; the file will play up to the region's start, and then seamlessly skip to the region's end and resume playback. If you hear a click, refer to the sidebar "About zero-crossings."

4 Choose Edit > Delete to delete the "uh."

When you invoke this command (Delete), you may not see any visual difference when zoomed out, because the adjustments are often very minor. However, Audition is indeed moving the region boundaries as defined by the command; you can verify this by zooming in to the waveform so you can see the results with more accuracy.

5 Now you'll remove the unwanted throat clearing. If you trim right up to the throat-clearing boundaries, when you click the Skip Selection transport button you'll hear a gap. Instead, select a region that starts somewhat before and ends slightly after the actual throat clearing to tighten that gap. This time instead of choosing Edit > Delete, press Backspace (Windows)/Delete (macOS).

6 Now delete the second uh that's in the audio, being careful not to cut off too much of the beginning of the word "multiple."

Deleting this "uh" results in too tight a transition between the words before and after the "uh" (You also have to be careful not to cut off too much of the beginning of the word "multiple").

7 Undo your last cut. Instead of deleting the "uh," you'll insert silence to produce a better result. To do this, select the "uh" and choose Edit > Insert > Silence.

The Insert Silence dialog box appears, displaying the length of the silence to be inserted, which will match the region you selected. You could edit this, but for now click OK.

About zero-crossings

When you define a region and the boundary occurs where the level is anything other than zero, this may result in a click on playback.

If the boundary occurs on a *zero-crossing* (a place where the waveform transitions from positive to negative, or vice versa) there is no rapid level change and no click.

After making a selection, Audition can automatically optimize the region boundaries so they fall on zero-crossings. Choose Edit > Zero Crossings and select one of several options:

- **Adjust selection inward.** Moves the region boundaries closer together so each falls on the nearest zero-crossing

- **Adjust selection outward.** Moves the region boundaries farther apart so each falls on the nearest zero-crossing

- **Adjust left side to left.** Moves the left region boundary to the nearest zero-crossing to the left

- **Adjust left side to right.** Moves the left region boundary to the nearest zero-crossing to the right

- **Adjust right side to left.** Moves the right region boundary to the nearest zero-crossing to the left

- **Adjust right side to right.** Moves the right region boundary to the nearest zero-crossing to the right

8   If the silent gap between words is too short or too long, define part of the
    silence as a region. With Skip Selection enabled, start playback to test whether
    you've deleted the right amount. Lengthen or shorten the silence as needed, and
    then choose Edit > Delete to shorten the gap.

Now that you've fixed some of the verbal glitches, let's change the sentence struc-
ture into a more coherent narration. Keep this file open; if you need to interrupt
this lesson, choose File > Save As, and save the file as **Narration05_edit**.

Use multiple clipboards

You're probably familiar with a computer's clipboard. In a word processing program, you typically copy a sentence to the clipboard and then paste it from the
clipboard to somewhere else in the text. The clipboard in Audition works similarly.
Audition, however, offers *five* separate clipboards, so you can temporarily store up
to five pieces of audio for pasting later. You'll put that feature to good use rearranging some phrases in the Narration05 file.

1   Continuing to work with the Narration05.wav file, select the part of the file,
    towards the beginning, that says, "Once the files are loaded, select the file you
    want to edit from the drop-down menu."

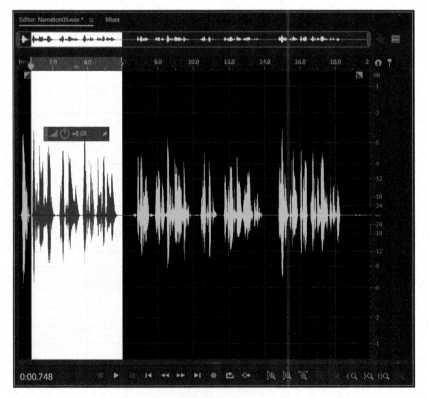

2 Choose Edit > Set Current Clipboard > Clipboard 1 (it will likely already be selected). You can also select this clipboard by pressing Ctrl+1 (Windows) or Command+1 (macOS).

3 To remove the phrase and store it in Clipboard 1, choose Edit > Cut, or press Ctrl+X (Windows) or Command+X (macOS) to place the phrase in Clipboard 1. The (Empty) label will no longer appear next to the Clipboard 1 name.

4 Select the part of the file that says, "Go to the file menu first; select open; then choose the file you want to edit."

5 Press Ctrl+2 (Windows) or Command+2 (macOS) to make Clipboard 2 the current clipboard. (You could also choose Edit > Set Current Clipboard > Clipboard 2.)

Clipboard 2 Selected When you select a clipboard, the clipboard name is displayed at the bottom left corner of the Audition interface.

6 Choose Edit > Cut to place the phrase in Clipboard 2.

7 Select the part of the file that says, "Remember; you can open up multiple files at once."

8 Press Ctrl+3 (Windows) or Command+3 (macOS) to make Clipboard 3 the current clipboard.

9 Choose Edit > Cut to place the phrase in Clipboard 3. Keep the Narration05 file open.

Now you have a separate clip for each phrase, which will make rearranging the phrases easier. The goal is to end up with:

"Go to the file menu first; select open; then choose the file you want to edit. Remember; you can open up multiple files at once. Once the files are loaded, select the file you want to edit from the drop-down menu."

1 Select all the leftover bits of audio in the Narration05 file (or simply press Ctrl+A [Command+A]), and press the Delete key. This clears all the audio and places the playhead at the file's beginning.

2 Clipboard 2 contains the introduction you want. Press Ctrl+2 (Windows) or Command+2 (macOS) to select that clipboard, and then choose Edit > Paste or press Ctrl+V (Windows) or Command+V (macOS).

3 Disable Skip Selection ![icon], return the playhead to the beginning of the file, and then click Play to confirm you have the desired audio.

4 Click in the Waveform to deselect the pasted audio. Otherwise, subsequent pasting will replace the selected region.

5 Click where you want to insert the next phrase. For this lesson, you'll place it at the end of the existing audio.

6   Clipboard 3 has the desired middle section for this project. Press Ctrl+3
    (Windows) or Command+3 (macOS) to select that clipboard, and then choose
    Edit > Paste or press Ctrl+V (Windows) or Command+V (macOS).

7   Repeat steps 4 and 5.

8   Clipboard 1 has the desired ending for this project. Press Ctrl+1 (Windows) or
    Command+1 (macOS) to select that clipboard, and then choose Edit > Paste or
    press Ctrl+V (Windows) or Command+V (macOS).

Play the file to hear the rearranged audio.

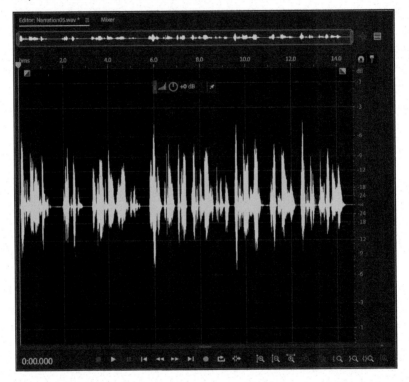

For further practice, you can:

•   Tighten up spaces between words by selecting a region and pressing Ctrl+X
    or Backspace (Windows); or Command+X or Delete (macOS), or by choosing
    Edit > Cut.

•   Add more space between words by placing the playhead where you want
    to insert silence (don't drag; just click the desired point in the timeline) and
    choosing Edit > Insert > Silence. When the Insert Silence dialog box appears,
    enter the desired duration of silence in the format minutes:seconds.hundredths
    of a second.

When you're done, choose File > Close All, and click No To All when asked if you
would like to save any files.

Mix paste

As well as adding or removing sections of audio, Audition allows you to merge one section of audio with another. Combining sections of audio this way does not extend or shorten the audio—the two are combined into one. The technique is called a *mix paste*.

Let's add a cymbal to a piece of music.

1 Navigate to the Lesson03 folder, and open the files Ueberschall_PopCharts.wav and Cymbal.wav.

2 Press Ctrl+A (Command+A) to select the entire cymbal sound.

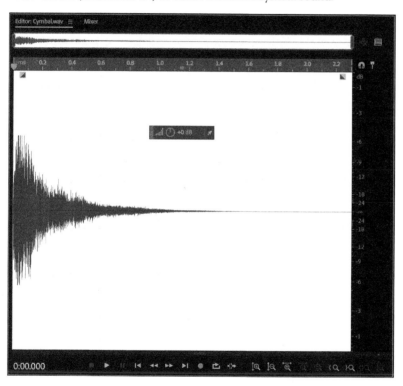

3 Press Ctrl+C (Command+C) to copy the cymbal sound to the current clipboard.

4 From the Editor panel menu, choose the Ueberschall_PopCharts.wav file.

5 Play the start of the music to get familiar with the content, then position the playhead at the start of the audio.

6 Choose Edit > Mix Paste.

The Mix Paste dialog box appears where you can adjust the levels of the copied audio and existing audio, as well as choose a Paste Type. Because you want the cymbal to be mixed with the existing audio, choose Overlap (Mix).

Note: Pop Charts is a commercially available sound library from Ueberschall that you can use to create your own royalty-free sound tracks and needle-drop music. You can find it and more at www.ueberschall.com/en/products.

Note: Mix Paste offers several other options. Insert opens up space in the file for what you're pasting, Overwrite replaces the audio for the duration of what you're pasting, and Modulate causes the pasted audio to change the existing audio's waveform as well as mix the two files together. Also note that you can choose the audio source, which can be from the clipboard or another file altogether.

Tip: The reason for adjusting the mix of the pasted and existing audio is to avoid distortion. If you try to mix two audio files that are already at 100% or maximum volume, for example, you would need to reduce each one by at least 50% to avoid distortion, because otherwise the mixed levels would exceed the maximum available headroom.

7 To prevent the cymbal sound from being too overbearing, set the Copied Audio volume to about 70%, and then click OK.

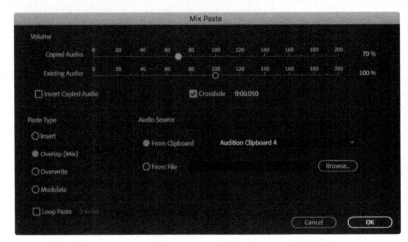

8 Play the file to hear the cymbal mixed with the original audio. Then choose File > Close All (don't save anything) to clear out all current files in preparation for the next exercise.

Create a loop

Many elements in music are repetitive. A *loop* is a piece of music that lends itself to repetition, such as a drum pattern. Many companies offer sound libraries of loops that are suitable for creating sound tracks. You can create your own loops, as well, by extracting a loop from a longer piece of audio. Give it a try.

1 Choose File > Open, navigate to the Lesson03 folder, and open the file Ueberschall_PopCharts.wav.

2 Click the Transport's Loop Playback button, or press Ctrl+L (Windows) or Command+L (macOS).

3 Select a region that makes musical sense when looped. You can move the region boundaries during playback. If you have a hard time finding good loop points, set a region to start at 7.742 seconds and end at 9.673. You'll need to zoom in to set these times accurately, or you can type them directly into the Selection/View panel as Start and End values.

To change numbers in Audition, you can click to select them and type new numbers; or simply drag them left or right.

4 Once you've located and selected a suitable loop, choose Edit > Copy To New, or press Shift+Alt+C (Windows) or Shift+Option+C (macOS) to copy your loop to a new file that appears in the Editor panel.

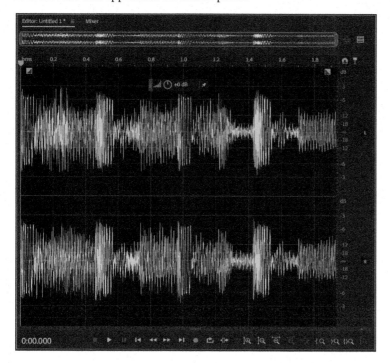

▶ **Tip:** You can save an individual selection several ways. Choose File > Save Selection As to save the selection immediately to disk without having it appear as a file in the Editor panel or be accessible in the Editor panel menu. However, note that it will be saved to the current clipboard, as well. You can also cut or copy a selection (which, of course, is saved to the current clipboard), and then choose Edit > Paste To New. This creates a new file that's accessible in the Editor panel menu.

Note: In the Spectral Frequency view described in Chapter 5, frequency information is also displayed in the Status Bar.

You can switch between this loop and the original file from which it came using the Editor panel menu.

5 With the loop displayed in the Editor panel, choose File > Save As, or press Shift+Ctrl+S (Windows) or Shift+Command+S (macOS), and navigate to where you want to save the loop. Now you have a loop you can use in other pieces of music.

Showing waveform data under the cursor

Sometimes it's helpful to know the exact characteristics (time, channel, and amplitude) of the part of the waveform that's directly under the cursor. You can display this data in the Status Bar.

1 Right-click in the Status Bar, which is the thin strip at the very bottom of the Audition window.

44100 Hz • 16-bit • Stereo   5.21 MB   0:30.966   18.29 GB free

2 Choose Data Under Cursor from the context menu.

3   Pass the cursor over the waveform to see a readout of the channel, amplitude, and time in the Status Bar. Note that this is not actually measuring the waveform, but instead showing the data represented by the cursor's position.

L: -20.22 dB @ 0:08.346

Add fades

Audio may have unintended noises, such as hums or hisses, that are masked when the main content, such as a narration, is playing but are audible when it stops. Other unintended noises can also occur, like p-pops (a popping sound that happens from the sudden burst of air associated with plosive sounds, such as "b" or "p"), clicks, mouth noises, and so on. Audition has advanced techniques for removing noise and restoring audio, but for simple problems, a fade is often all you need.

1   Choose File > Open, navigate to the Lesson03 folder, and open the file PPop.wav.

2   Zoom in and move the playhead to the start of the file in the Waveform Editor panel. Note the spike at the beginning that corresponds to the pop.

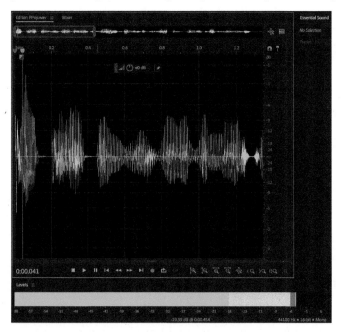

3   Click the small, square Fade In button in the upper-left corner of the waveform and drag to the right. You can see the fade attenuating the spike. Dragging the Fade In button up or down alters the fade's shape (up for convex, down for concave). A concave fade is an ideal choice here, because it gets rid of the most objectionable part of the pop but still leaves the "p" sound.

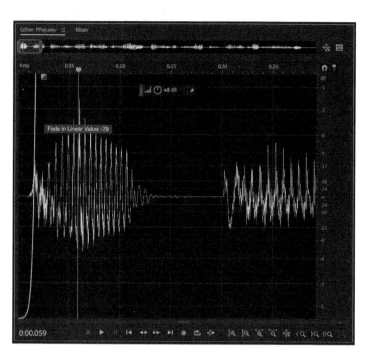

You may need to zoom in further to precisely adjust the fade.

4 There's also another, less objectionable pop at 0.20 seconds. Although you could cut this file to the clipboard, create a new file, add a fade-in, and paste it back into place, an easier solution is simply to select the pop sound as a region and use the HUD's volume control to drop the level by 8 or 9 dB.

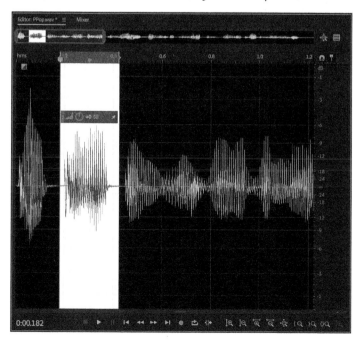

5 Suppose you want to shorten the file to end with "that can happen" instead of "that can happen when recording narration." Zoom in and go to the end of the file. Locate the part that says "when recording narration," select it as a region, and then press the Delete key.

However, now "happen" doesn't end elegantly and there may be an audible artifact at the end. You'll use the Fade Out button to reduce this.

Tip: If a file doesn't begin or end on a zero-crossing and you hear a click, adding a very slight fade time will reduce or eliminate the click. Use a convex fade for this application.

6 Click the Fade Out button and drag left to 2.8 seconds. Then drag down to about −30 and release the mouse button to make the fade "stick."

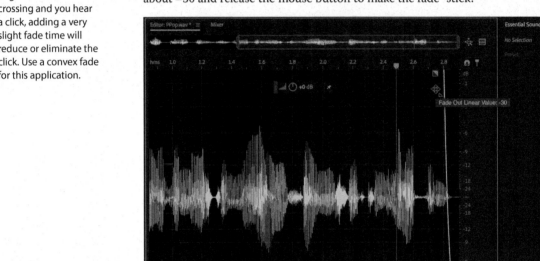

7 Play the file to hear that the artifact at the end is either minimized or gone, depending on the specific characteristics of the fade you added.

8 Go to File > Close All, and choose No To All when asked if you would like to save.

Review questions

1 What is the easiest way to change the level for a selection?

2 Why is it important to have selection boundaries on zero-crossings?

3 How many clipboards does Audition offer?

4 What's the most effective way to eliminate a p-pop?

Review answers

1 Make a selection, and use the heads-up display (HUD) to change the level.

2 Cutting and pasting with selections bounded by zero-crossings tends to minimize clicks.

3 Audition has five individual clipboards that can hold five independent pieces of audio.

4 Placing a fade-in on top of a p-pop lets you determine how much of the pop to minimize and the extent to which you want to minimize it.

4 EFFECTS

Lesson overview

In this lesson, you'll learn how to do the following:

- Use the Effects Rack to create combinations of effects

- Apply effects to audio

- Adjust parameters in various effects to process audio in specific ways

- Use the Preview Editor to see how a waveform will be altered by an effect before you apply the effect

- Simulate guitar amp and effects setups with Guitar Suite effects

- Load third-party plug-in effects on Windows or macOS computers

- Apply single effects rapidly without the Effects Rack by using the Effects menu

- Create and save favorite combinations of effects and other settings that you can apply immediately to audio

 This lesson can take several hours to complete, depending on how deeply you want to explore the various processors. Please log in to your account on peachpit.com to download the lesson files for this chapter, or go to the "Getting Started" section at the beginning of this book and follow the instructions under "Accessing the Lesson Files and Web Edition." Store the files on your computer in a convenient location.

Your Account page is also where you'll find any updates to the chapters or to the lesson files. Look on the Lesson & Update Files tab to access the most current content.

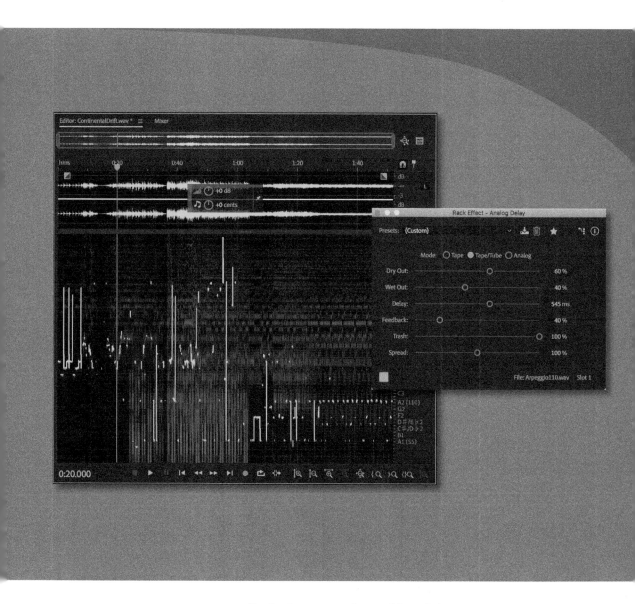

Use signal processors to "sweeten" the audio in multiple ways: fix tonal balance, alter dynamics, add ambience or special effects, and much more. Draw from the extensive collection of effects included in Audition or use third-party, plug-in processors.

Effects basics

Effects, also called *signal processors*, can "sweeten" audio as well as fix problems (such as too much treble or bass). They are the audio equivalent of video effects, like contrast, sharpen, color balance, light rays, pixelate, and so on. In fact, sometimes audio engineers even use similar terms, such as "brightness," to describe increased treble.

Adobe Audition includes a wide range of effects. Most can work with the Waveform and Multitrack Editors, but some are available only in the Waveform Editor. There are three main ways of working with effects:

- **The Effects Rack** allows you to combine up to 16 effects, which you can enable or disable independently. You can add, delete, replace, or reorder effects. The Effects Rack is the most flexible way of working with effects.

- **The Effects menu** allows you to select an individual effect from the Effects menu bar and apply it to the currently selected audio. When you need to apply only one specific effect, using this menu can be quicker than using the Effects Rack. Some effects available in the Effects menu are not available in the Effects Rack.

- **The Favorites menu** provides a quick way to work with effects. If you come up with a particularly useful combination of effects settings, you can save it as a *favorite*. Favorites can also include changes to amplitude or fades. You can access favorites from the Favorites menu or the more flexible Favorites panel (as described in Chapter 2, "The Audition Interface"). Selecting a favorite applies that preset instantly to the currently selected audio. Note that you cannot change any parameter values before applying the effect, but you can use the Preview Editor to see how the waveform will be altered by the effect prior to applying it.

This chapter begins with effects available in the Effects Rack. The second section discusses the Effects menu and the remaining menu-only effects. The final section describes how to work with presets, including favorites.

Using the Effects Rack

Begin by choosing Window > Workspace > Default, and then reset the workspace by choosing Window > Workspace > Reset To Saved Layout.

1 Choose File > Open, navigate to the Lesson04 folder, and open the file Drums110.wav.

2 Click the Transport Loop Playback button so the drum pattern will play continuously. Click the Play button to listen to the loop, and then click the Stop button.

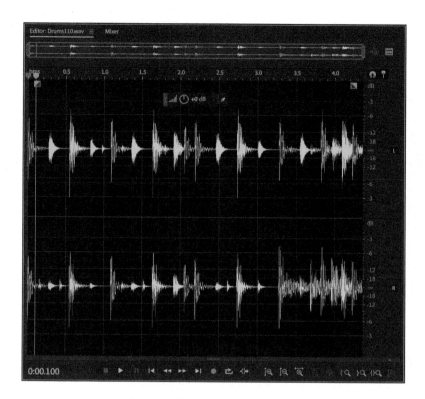

3 Click the Effects Rack panel name to bring it to the front of the frame. Resize the panel as necessary to be able to see several, or even all 16 "slots," called *inserts*; each can hold an individual effect and also includes a Master Power On/Off button 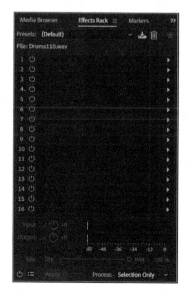. A toolbar is located above the inserts, and meters with a second toolbar are below the inserts.

Note: Although you can't see any graphical connection among effects in the Effects Rack, they are in series, meaning that the audio file feeds the first effect input, at the top of the stack, the first effect output feeds the second effect input, the second effect output feeds the third effect input, and so on until the last effect output goes to your audio interface. Effects do not have to go into consecutive inserts. You can leave empty inserts between effects, and then place effects in these inserts later.

4 To add an effect to an insert, click the insert's right arrow and choose an effect from the menu. For the first effect, choose Reverb > Studio Reverb. The Rack Effect – Studio Reverb effect window opens.

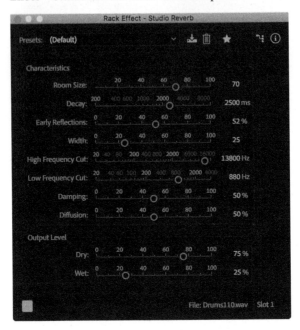

Inserting an effect turns its Power button to On (green) and opens the effect's window. Move the window to one side for now, so you can see the Effects Rack.

5 For a second effect, choose Delay and Echo > Analog Delay. Once again, move the window to one side so you can see the Effects Rack.

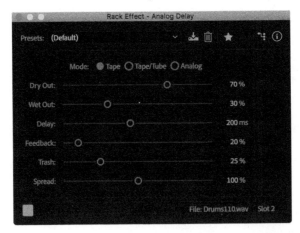

6   Turn Off (bypass) the Analog Delay effect by clicking its Power button. Press the spacebar to begin playback, and then turn the Studio Reverb effect's Power button on and off to hear how reverb changes the sound.

7   Click the Studio Reverb window to bring it to the front. If it's not visible, you can always double-click the effect in the Effects Rack. Press the spacebar again to stop playback.

8   When playback is stopped, you can choose an effect's preset. Open the Studio Reverb's Presets menu, and choose Drum Plate (Large). Begin playback.

You'll hear a more pronounced reverb sound.

9   Click the Analog Delay effect window to bring it to the front, and then turn on its Power button.

You'll hear an echo effect, but it's not in time with the music.

10   To make the delay follow the rhythm, click in the Delay parameter's numeric field, type **545** in place of 200, and then press Enter (Return). The echoes are now in time with the music. (Later in this chapter you'll learn how to choose rhythmically correct delay times.)

Keep this audio file open as you continue.

> **Tip:** Each effect dialog box has an additional Power button in the lower-left corner to make it easy to bypass/compare the processed and unprocessed sound. Clicking this Power button also toggles the Power button for the effect in the Effects Rack.

Removing, editing, replacing, and moving an effect

Rather than stepping through a structured exercise, try the various bulleted options that follow to see how they work. After each action, restore the project to its previous state by choosing Edit > Undo [*name of action*] or pressing Ctrl+Z (Windows) or Command+Z (macOS):

- To **remove a *single* effect**, click the name of the effect in the Effects Rack and press Backspace/Delete. *Or,* click the insert's right arrow and choose Remove Effect from the menu.

- To **remove *all* effects** in the rack, right-click anywhere on an effect insert slot, and choose Remove All Effects.

- To **remove *some* effects** in the rack, Ctrl-click (Windows) or Command-click (macOS) each effect insert containing an effect you want to remove to select them. Then right-click anywhere in any selected effect, and choose Remove Selected Effects.

- To **edit an effect** when its window is hidden or you have closed it, double-click the effect in the Effects Rack. You can also click the insert's right arrow and choose Edit Effect from the menu, or right-click anywhere on an effect in the Effects Rack and choose Edit Selected Effect.

- To **replace an effect** with a different effect, click the insert's right arrow and choose a different effect from the menu.

- To **move an effect** to a different insert, click the name in the effect's insert and drag to the desired destination insert. If an effect already exists in that insert, Audition will push the existing effect down to the next insert below.

Bypassing all or some effects

You can bypass individual effects, groups of effects, or all effects in the Effects Rack by doing *any* of the following:

- Click the Master Power button in the lower-left corner of the Effects Rack's panel ▆ to bypass *all* enabled rack effects. When powered back on, only effects that had been enabled prior to bypassing are turned back on. Bypassed effects remain bypassed regardless of the Master Power button setting.

- Right-click any effect's insert, and choose Toggle Power State of Effects Rack.

- To bypass some effects, Ctrl-click (Windows) or Command-click (macOS) each effect's insert you want to bypass, right-click any of these inserts, and then choose Toggle Power State of Selected Effects.

"Gain-staging" effects

Sometimes inserting multiple effects in series causes certain frequencies to "add up" and produce audio levels that may exceed the available headroom. For example, a filter that emphasizes the midrange could create distortion by increasing levels above acceptable limits.

To adjust the Input levels (the level going into the effects), or Output levels (the total level coming from the effects), use the controls (with associated meters) in the lower part of the Effects Rack.

1   Remove the existing effects from the Effects Rack using any of the methods described earlier. You can also select each effect and press Backspace/Delete to remove it.

2   In any effect insert in the Effects Rack, click the right arrow, and choose Filter And EQ > Parametric Equalizer.

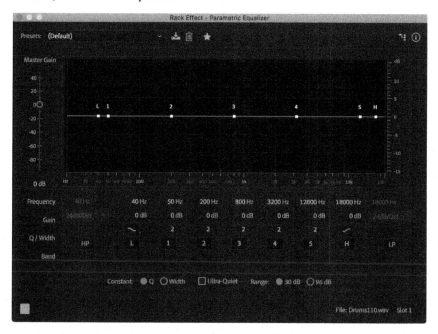

You'll explore the Parametric Equalizer effect in detail later in this chapter. For now, try a simple but powerful adjustment.

3 When the Parametric Equalizer window opens, click the small box labeled 3 in the middle of the Equalizer (EQ) graph and drag it to the top of the graph. Close the Parametric Equalizer window; you don't need it taking up space.

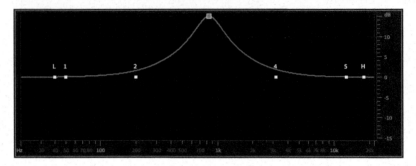

4 *Caution: Turn your monitoring levels very low,* and then press the spacebar to start playback. The excessive levels will trigger the Output meter's red overload indicators to the meter's right. The red marking indicates that the signal is so loud it is distorting—the signal is greater than the system's capacity.

Tip: Once triggered, the red distortion indicators stay lit so if distortion occurs while you're not looking at the screen, you'll know that distortion occurred. Click anywhere in the Output meter to reset the red distortion indicators. To reset the Effects Rack Input or Output knobs to +0 dB, Alt-click (Windows) or Option-click (macOS) a knob.

Tip: You can toggle the display of the meters and controls in the Effects Rack panel by clicking the button to the right of the master on/off switch in the lower-left corner.

5 Turn up your monitoring level enough to hear the distortion. The Effects Rack Input and Output level controls default to +0 dB gain, which means neither the signal coming into the Effects Rack, nor the signal leaving it, is amplified (increased) or attenuated (decreased). However, the massive EQ boost from the Parametric Equalizer effect is overloading the output.

6 Reduce the Input level until the peaks no longer trigger the red distortion indicators after the meters have been reset (see the tip on resetting the indicators). It's generally good practice to keep the Output control at +0 dB and compensate for the excessive levels by trimming the Input level. This may require reducing the Input to −8 dB or lower.

Keep this project open for the next lesson.

Altering the effect's wet/dry mix

An unprocessed signal is called *dry*. A signal with effects applied is called *wet*. Sometimes you want a blend of the wet and dry sounds rather than all of one or the other. The Mix slider adjusts the mix of wet and dry sound, which is an easy way to make an effect more subtle.

1 With the Drums110.wav file still open and the levels set properly to avoid the distortion created by the Parametric Equalizer effect, drag the Mix slider (located below the meters) to the left to increase the amount of dry, unprocessed sound in the mix. Listen carefully to the impact on the sound.

2 Drag the slider to the right to increase the amount of wet, filtered sound.

Applying effects

Inserting an effect doesn't change the original file. Instead, the original audio plays *through* the effect. This is called a *non-destructive* process using a real-time effect, because the original file remains unaltered.

However, you may want to *apply* the effect to the file, or a selected part of a file, so that saving the file (with File > Save) saves the processed version, replacing the original.

1 Close the Drums110.wav file without saving. You can close the file by selecting it in the Files panel and pressing Backspace/Delete. With the program open, choose File > Open Recent, and choose the file Drums110.wav again.

Closing a file without saving changes then re-opening it is a way to be certain you have a "clean" unmodified version of the file to work on.

2 In any effect's insert in the Effects Rack, click the right arrow, and choose Reverb > Studio Reverb.

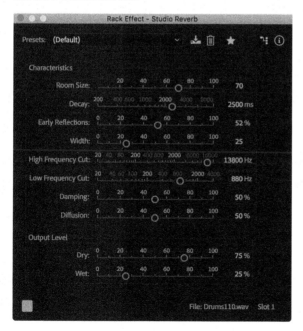

Note: You can insert additional effects into the Effects Rack to change the sound further, and then apply those effects. The file will reflect the changes caused by all the effects you've applied, but the changes will become permanent only when you save the file (using either Save or Save As). At that point, Audition permanently embeds the effects in the file.

3   In the Studio Reverb window, choose the preset Drum Plate (Small) from the Presets menu.

4   The Process menu, located in the toolbar at the bottom of the Effects Rack panel, allows you to apply the effect to the entire file or just a selection. For this exercise, choose Entire File.

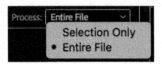

5   Click the Apply button. This not only applies the effect to the file to process it, but also removes the effect from the Effects Rack so the file isn't "double processed" by having the effect embedded in the file and also processed in the Effects Rack.

You can combine and preview up to 16 effects in the Effects Rack, and when you click Apply, the combination of effects and settings are merged into the waveform, clearing the Effects Rack.

6   Close the file without saving by choosing File > Close All.

Effect categories

The Effects Rack and Effects menu have several categories. Each category is a group of effects with a common theme. The best way to learn about each effect, including detailed information about the options and choices you might make, is to read the online Help.

You can access the online Help by choosing Help > Adobe Audition Help. Choosing this command will open an Internet browser with the Audition Help on-screen.

In the Audition Help, you can search for an effect, or choose User Guide > Effects Reference. From there you can choose one of the categories discussed below and obtain more detail on each effect.

You'll be using a number of effects in the course of these exercises, particularly those effects that make more advanced results easier to achieve. Still, mastery may come only when you have invested the time in deepening your understanding of each effect, and each effect category.

In the following sections, some effects described are available in both the Effects Rack and the Effects menu, while others are available exclusively in the Effects menu.

You will find a number of audio files you can experiment with in the Lessons > Lesson 04 folder.

The following sections explore some of the most significant effects in each category.

Amplitude and Compression effects

Amplitude and Compression effects change levels and alter dynamics. In broad terms, this means the effects in this category change the amplitude of your audio, the speed at which the audio gets louder or quieter, or the way compression is applied.

Amplify

Amplify can make a file louder or softer. When you're increasing amplitude to make a file louder, choose an amount of amplification that is low enough so that the file remains undistorted.

Channel Mixer

The Channel Mixer alters the amount of left and right channel signal present in the left and right channels. Two possible applications are converting stereo to mono and reversing the left and right channels.

Converting stereo to mono is a common enough operation that the Channel Mixer preset named All Channels 50% performs this conversion. When working in the Multitrack Editor, you'll discover there's a Sum to Mono button for every track.

DeEsser

The DeEsser reduces vocal sibilants ("ess" sounds). De-essing is a three-step process: Identify the frequencies where sibilants exist, define that range, and then set a threshold, which if exceeded by a sibilant, automatically reduces the gain within the specified range. This makes the sibilant less prominent while maintaining the clarity of the speech.

Dynamics processing

With a standard amplifier, the relationship between the input and output is linear. In other words, if there's a gain of 1, the output signal will be the same as the input signal. If there's a gain of 2, the output signal will have twice the level of the input signal, whatever the input signal level may be.

The Dynamics Processor effect changes the relationship of the output to the input. This change is called *compression* when a large input signal increase produces only a small output signal increase and *expansion* when a small input signal increase produces a large output signal increase. Both can be present at the same time by expanding signals within one range of levels and compressing signals in a different range of levels. The Dynamics Processor's graph shows the input signal on the horizontal axis and the output on the vertical axis.

Compression can make a sound subjectively louder and is the tool that makes TV commercials SO MUCH LOUDER THAN EVERYTHING ELSE. Expansion is less

Note: If you're not familiar with the concept of audio compression, the name can be a little misleading. Rather than compressing the overall signal, compression compresses the range between the quiet and loud parts of the audio. In practice, compression effects increase the amplitude of audio overall, or at specific frequencies, while also limiting the maximum attenuation (or amplitude). The combination of a gain increase plus a limited signal results in a compressed range that is (usually) perceptually louder.

common; one application is to expand objectionable low-level signals (like hiss) to reduce their levels further. There are uses for both as special effects.

The easiest way to become familiar with dynamics processing is to load various presets, listen to how they affect the sound, and correlate what you hear to what you see on the graph.

1 If you have any files open, choose File > Close All.

2 Choose File > Open, navigate to the Lesson04 folder, and open the file Drum+Bass+Arp110.wav.

The audio has a range of levels and a mix of instruments.

3 In an Effects Rack insert, click the right arrow button, and then choose Amplitude and Compression > Dynamics Processing.

4 Enable looping on the Transport, and then start playback.

5 Choose the 3:1, Expander < 10 dB preset.

The blue line indicates the new relationship between the input signal (the original audio) and the output signal (the result of the effect).

With this preset, as the input signal (along the bottom edge) changes from −100 dB to around −40 dB, the output (along the right edge) changes from −100 dB to only −95 dB. As a result, the Dynamics Processor has compressed 60 dB of input dynamic range into 5 dB of change at the output. But from around −40 dB to 0 dB, the output changes from −95 dB to 0 dB. Therefore, the Dynamics Processor has expanded 40 dB of input dynamic range into 95 dB of output dynamic range.

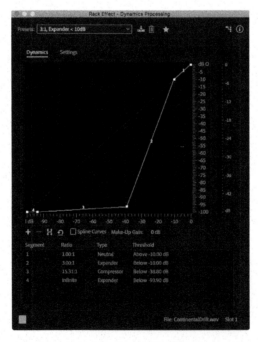

Notice the small square control points on the blue line. You can drag those directly to manually adjust the blue line, which represents the relationship between the input and output signals.

Each blue line has a tiny segment number, and the area below the graph provides the following information about each segment:

- The segment number

- The relationship between output and input expressed as a ratio

- Whether the segment is an Expander, a Compressor, or Neutral

- The Threshold (range of levels) where the expansion or compression takes effect

6 Try a few other presets. Note that you will need to turn down the Effects Rack's Output level when you're using some of the more aggressive presets to avoid distortion.

7 Try creating your own dynamics processing: Begin by choosing the (Default) preset, which provides neither compression nor expansion.

8 Drag the little white square in the upper right down slowly to around −10 dB. Listen to how this brings down the peaks and makes the sound less dynamic.

9 Create a less abrupt change. Click in the middle of segment 1 (where the segment crosses −15 dB) to create another square. Drag it up a little bit to around −12 dB.

10 Now try expansion to reduce low-level sounds. Click the line at −30 dB and −40 dB to create two more squares. Drag the one at −40 dB all the way down to −100 dB. This effect makes the drums sound more percussive.

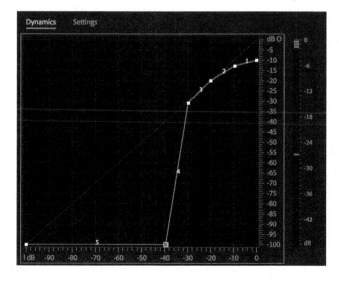

Note: There's no
need to close effect
windows to playback,
access menus or
controls, or even apply
other effects. Your only
limitation is space on
your computer screen.

11 Look at the Effects Rack's Output meter as the audio plays. Bypass the dynamics processing, and you'll see that the original signal is actually a little louder because the compression you applied has reduced the peaks. To compensate for this, click in the Dynamics Processor's Make-Up Gain parameter located just below the curve's horizontal axis to select the value. Increase the gain by +4 dB.

12 Bypass and enable the Dynamics Processor by toggling the Power button for the effect on the Effects Rack ▣. Because you added Make-Up Gain, the processed signal is now a little bit louder.

13 Stop playback, click the Effects Rack insert with the Dynamics Processor, and press Backspace/Delete (no need to close the effect window, as it will close when you delete the effect).

Note: Basic
compression and
expansion can solve
many audio problems
that need dynamics
control. The Dynamics
Processor is extremely
sophisticated, however,
and the Settings panel
within the effect
allows for further
customization. Refer to
the Audition online Help
for detailed information
on other Dynamics
Processor parameters.

Hard limiter

Like an engine's governor that limits the maximum number of RPMs, a *limiter* restricts an audio signal's maximum output level. For example, if you don't want an audio file to exceed a level of –10 dB, yet there are some peaks that reach –2 dB, set the limiter's Maximum Amplitude to –10 dB, and it will "absorb" the peaks so they don't exceed –10 dB. This is different from simple attenuation (which lowers the levels of *all* signals), because now levels below –10 dB remain untouched.

Levels above –10 dB will be limited with an essentially infinite ratio, so *any* input level increase produces no output level above –10 dB. It's a little like flattening only the highest peak of a mountain range, leaving the rest of the range untouched.

This limiter also has an Input Boost parameter, which can make a signal subjectively louder. Here's why: If you set the Maximum Amplitude to 0, you can increase the level of an input signal that already reaches the maximum headroom, because the limiter will prevent it from distorting by clamping its output to 0. Listen to how this affects a mix.

1 With the Drums+Bass+Arp110.wav still loaded, click an Effects Rack insert's right arrow button, and choose Amplitude and Compression > Hard Limiter.

You can use sliders, drag
on the blue numbers,
or click and type new
numbers to update
the setting.

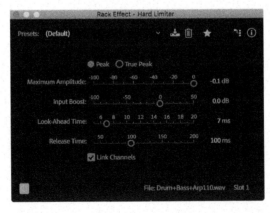

2   Enable looping on the Transport, and start playback.

3   The default Maximum Amplitude numeric is −0.1. This ensures that the signal won't hit zero, so the output won't trigger the red zone in the Effects Rack panel's Output level meters.

4   Raise the Input Boost above 0 while observing the Output level meters in the Effects Rack.

Even if you add lots of boost, like 10 dB, the output still doesn't go above −0.1, and the Output meters never register red peaks.

5   The Release Time sets how long it takes for the limiter to stop limiting after a signal no longer exceeds the maximum amplitude. In most cases, the default is fine. With a fair amount of input boost, shorter Release settings might produce a choppy effect, even though they limit the signal more accurately.

6   The Look-Ahead Time setting allows the limiter to react to fast transients. With Look-Ahead Time at 0, the limiter has to react *instantly* to a transient, which is not possible: It has to know a transient exists before it can decide what to do with it. Look-Ahead alerts the limiter when a transient is coming, so the reaction can be instantaneous. Longer settings cause a slight delay through the effect, although in most cases this doesn't matter. The default setting is fine, but experiment with increasing the Look-Ahead Time slider if the transients sound mushy.

7   Stop playback after you've finished experimenting with these settings.

Single-Band Compressor

The Single-Band Compressor is a "classic" compressor for dynamic range compression and is an excellent choice for learning about how compression works.

As explained in the "Dynamics processing" section, compression changes the relationship between the output signal to the input signal. The two most important parameters are Threshold (the level above which compression starts to occur) and Ratio, which sets the amount of change in the output signal for a given input signal change. For example, with a 4:1 ratio, a 4 dB increase in input level produces a 1 dB increase at the output. With an 8:1 ratio, an 8 dB increase in input level produces a 1 dB increase at the output. In this lesson, you'll hear how compression affects the sound.

1   If the Drums+Bass+Arp110.wav file is not open, close any other files and open it. Also, delete any currently loaded effects.

Note: Release Time is an important common control available in a number of effects. It controls the time for which an effect will be applied after it is triggered by a threshold set elsewhere in the effect.

Note: It's easy to overdo hard limiting. Past a certain amount of input boost, the sound will become unnatural. The level at which this occurs varies depending on the input signal source. With solo instruments and vocals, you can usually apply more boost than with complex material.

2 In any Effects Rack insert, click the right arrow, and choose Amplitude and Compression > Single-Band Compressor.

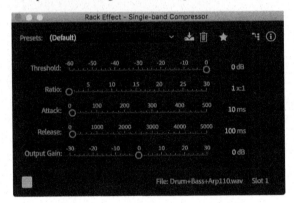

3 Enable looping on the Transport, and start playback.

4 Assuming the Default preset is loaded, move the Threshold slider over its full range. You won't hear any difference because the Ratio defaults to 1:1, so there's a linear relationship between the output and input.

5 With Threshold at 0, move the Ratio slider over its full range. Again you won't hear any difference, because all audio will lie below the Threshold; there's nothing above the Threshold that can be affected by the Ratio slider. This shows how the Threshold and Ratio controls interrelate, and explains why you usually need to go back and forth between these two controls to dial in the right amount of compression.

6 Set the Threshold slider to –20 dB and the Ratio slider to 1. Slowly increase the Ratio slider by moving it to the right. The farther you move it to the right, the more compressed the sound. Leave the Ratio slider at 10 (meaning 10:1).

7 Experiment with the Threshold slider. The lower the Threshold, the more compressed the sound; below about –20 dB with a Ratio of 10:1, the sound is so compressed it becomes unusable. Leave the Threshold slider at –10 dB for now.

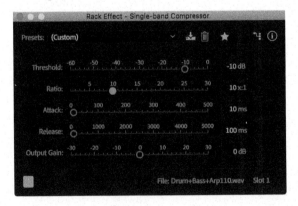

8   Look at the Effects Rack panel's Output meter. When you bypass the Single-Band Compressor, note that the meters are more animated and have more pronounced peaks. Enable the Single-Band Compressor; the signal's peaks are less dynamic and more uniform.

9   Note the maximum peak level in bypassed mode. Then, with the Single-Band Compressor enabled, adjust its Output Gain control to around 2.5 dB, so its peaks match the same level as when bypassed. Now when you compare the bypassed and enabled states, you'll hear that despite having the same peak levels, the compressed version sounds louder. The reason is that reducing peaks allows for increasing the overall output gain without exceeding the available headroom or causing distortion.

It's possible to make this difference even more pronounced. Attack sets a delay before the compression occurs after a signal exceeds the threshold.

10 Use the default Attack time of 10 ms; this lets through percussive transients up to 10 ms in duration before the compression kicks in and retains some of a signal's natural percussiveness.

11 Now set the Attack time to 0, and again observe the Output level meters. With 0 Attack time, the peaks have been reduced even further, which means the Single-Band Compressor Output Gain can go even higher.

12 Set the Single-Band Compressor Output Gain to 6 dB. When you enable/bypass the Single-Band Compressor, the peak levels are the same but the compressed version sounds a lot "bigger."

13 Set the release time subjectively for the smoothest, most natural sound, which will usually be between 200 and 1000 ms. The Release setting determines how long it takes for the compression to stop compressing once the signal falls below the threshold.

14 Keep Audition open and loaded with the same file.

Tube-Modeled Compressor

The Tube-Modeled Compressor has the same control complement as the Single-Band Compressor but offers a slightly different, somewhat less crisp sonic character. You can use the same basic steps as in the previous exercise to explore the Tube-Modeled Compressor. The one obvious difference is that the Tube-Modeled Compressor has two meters: The one on the left shows the input signal level, and the one on the right shows how much the gain is being reduced to provide the specified amount of compression.

Multiband Compressor

The Multiband Compressor is a variation on the Single-Band Compressor. It divides the frequency spectrum into four bands, each with its own compressor, so you can compress some frequencies more than others.

Dividing the signal into four bands also embodies elements of equalization (described later), because you can alter a signal's frequency response.

If you think adjusting a Single-Band Compressor is complex, a Multiband Compressor with four bands isn't just four times as complex—it's even more so, because all the bands also interact with each other. One of the best ways to become familiar with the Multiband Compressor controls is to load multiple presets, and then see and hear the results.

Each band has an S (Solo) button; click one to hear what that band alone is doing.

Speech Volume Leveler

The Speech Volume Leveler incorporates three processors—leveling, compression, and gating—to even out level variations with narration, as well as reduce background noise with some signals.

Delay and echo effects

Adobe Audition has three echo effects with different capabilities. All delay effects store audio in memory and then play it back later. The time that elapses between storing and playing the audio is the delay time.

Delay

The Delay effect simply repeats the audio, with the repeat's start time specified by the delay amount.

Stereo audio has separate delays for the left and right channels, whereas mono audio has a single set of controls.

Analog Delay

Before digital technology, delay used tape or analog delay chip technology. These produced a grittier, more colored sound compared to digital delay. The Analog Delay in Audition provides a single delay for stereo or mono signals and offers three delay modes:

- Tape (slight distortion)
- Tape/Tube (crisper version of tape)
- Analog (more muffled)

Timing a delay

With rhythmic material, correlating delay to the rhythm creates a more "musical" effect. Use the formula 60,000/tempo in bpm (beats per minute) to determine the echo for a quarter note. For example, the drum loop tempo is 110 bpm, so the echo time for a quarter note is 60,000/110 = 545.45 ms. An eighth note is half that or 272.72 ms, a 16th note is 136.36 ms, and so on. The Lesson04 folder includes a file called Period vs. Tempo.xls, courtesy of Craig Anderton. Enter a tempo in this spreadsheet to see the number of milliseconds and samples that correspond to particular rhythmic values.

Analog Delay simply repeats the audio with the start time of the repeat specified by the delay amount. Unlike the Delay effect, Analog Delay includes separate controls for Dry and Wet levels instead of a single Mix control.

1   Choose File > Close All. Don't save any changes. Choose File > Open, navigate to the Lesson04 folder, and open the file Drums110.wav.

2   In any Effects Rack insert, click the right arrow, and then choose Delay and Echo > Analog Delay.

3   Set Dry Out to 60%, Wet Out to 40%, and Delay to 545 ms. Feedback determines the number of repeats as they fade out. Start playback. No Feedback (a setting of 0) produces a single echo, values moving toward 100 produce more echoes, and values above 100 produce "runaway echoes." (Watch your monitor volume!)

4   With feedback at 40, set the Trash control (which increases distortion and boosts low frequencies, adding warmth) to 100. Change the different modes (Tape, Tape/Tube, Analog) to hear how each affects the sound. Vary the feedback, being careful to avoid excessive, runaway feedback.

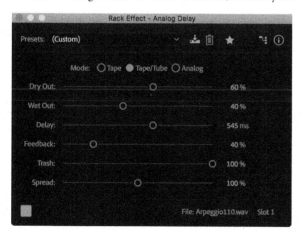

5   Spread at 0% narrows the echoes to mono and at 200% produces a wide stereo effect. Play with the various controls, and you'll hear anything from dance mix drum effects to '50s-style sci-fi movie sounds. Keep Audition open for the next lesson.

Echo

The Echo effect allows for tailoring the echoes' frequency response by inserting a filter in the delay's feedback loop, where the output feeds back to the input to create additional echoes. As a result, each successive echo processes each echo's timbre to a greater degree. For example, if the response is set to be brighter than normal, each echo will be brighter than the previous one.

Filter and EQ effects

Equalization (or EQ) is an extremely important effect for adjusting tonality. For example, you can brighten muffled narration by boosting the treble or make tinny, thin-sounding voices sound fuller by increasing the low frequencies. Equalization can also help differentiate among different instruments; for example, bass guitar and a drum kit's kick drum both occupy the low frequencies and can interact in a way that makes each one less distinct. To solve this problem, some engineers might emphasize the bass's highs to bring out pick and string noise, whereas others boost highs on the kick to bring out the "thwack" of the beater.

Adobe Audition has five equalizer effects:

* Parametric Equalizer

* Graphic Equalizer

* FFT (Fast Fourier Transform) Filter

* Notch Filter

* Scientific Filter

Each is used for different purposes that can adjust tonality and solve frequency-response-related problems.

Parametric Equalizer

The Parametric Equalizer offers nine stages of equalization. Five stages have a *parametric* response, which can boost (make more prominent) or cut (make less prominent) specific ranges (*bands*) of the frequency spectrum. Each parametric equalization stage has three parameters.

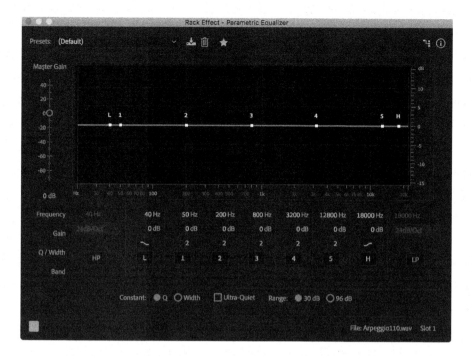

Caution: In the following exercise, keep monitor levels down as you make adjustments. The Parametric Equalizer is capable of high amounts of gain at the selected frequencies.

The bottom edge of the Parametric Equalizer graph indicates frequency, while the right edge indicates attenuation. The blue line indicates the adjustment the effect will apply; a flat line at 0 dB signifies no adjustment.

1 Choose File > Open, navigate to the Lesson04 folder, and open the file Drum+Bass+Arp110.wav.

2 In any Effects Rack insert, click the right arrow, and then choose Filter And EQ > Parametric Equalizer. Start playback.

3 There are five numbered control points. Each represents a parametric stage. Drag up on number 3 to boost response, or drag down to cut the response. Drag left to affect lower frequencies or right to affect higher frequencies. Listen to the way this changes the sound.

4 In the area below the graph, there are settings for each control point, with the Frequency, Gain, Q/Width, and the number of the control point. The number is also an enable/disable button.

Drag up, or right on the selected stage's Q/Width parameter to narrow the range affected by the boost or cut, or drag down, or left to widen the range. Try clicking the stage's number to toggle that stage on or off.

5 Load the Default preset to restore the EQ to having no effect. The L and H squares control a *low shelf* and *high shelf* response, respectively. This starts boosting or cutting at the selected frequency, but the boost or cut extends outward toward the extremes of the audio spectrum. Past a certain frequency, the response hits a "shelf" equal to the maximum amount of cut.

6 Drag the H square up slightly. This increases the treble. Now drag it to the left, and you'll hear that the boost now affects a wider range of high frequencies. Similarly, click the L box to hear how this affects the low frequencies. In the Parameter section for the low and high shelf sections, you can click the Q/Width button to change the steepness of the shelf's slope.

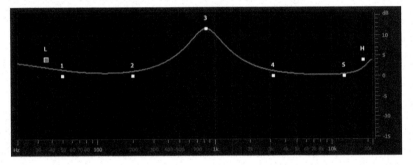

7 Reload the Default preset so the EQ has no effect. There are two additional stages, Highpass and Lowpass, which you enable by clicking the HP and LP buttons, respectively. Click those buttons now.

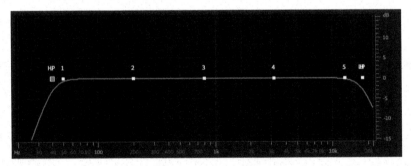

A Highpass response progressively reduces response below a certain frequency (called the *cutoff frequency*); the lower the frequency is below the cutoff, the greater the reduction. A Highpass filter is helpful for removing subsonic (very low-frequency) energy.

8 Drag the HP box to the right to hear how it affects low frequencies.

9 You can also change the filter slope's steepness, in other words, the rate of attenuation compared to frequency. In the HP panel that displays its parameters, click the Gain menu and choose 6 dB/octave. Note how this creates a gradual curve. Then choose 48 dB/octave to produce a steep curve.

10 Similarly, listen to the way the Lowpass filter affects the sound by dragging the LP box left or right, and choosing different curves from the Gain menu. Keep this project open for the next lesson.

The strip along the bottom of the screen has three additional options.

- **Constant:** Changes the way Q is calculated (the width of the curve). Q is a ratio compared to frequency. Constant Width means the Q is the same regardless of frequency. Q is the most commonly chosen option.

- **Ultra-Quiet:** Reduces noise and artifacts but requires much more processing power and can usually be deselected.

- **Range:** Sets the maximum amount of boost or cut to 30 dB or 96 dB. The more common option is 30 dB.

All of these responses are available simultaneously.

Graphic Equalizer (10/20/30 Bands)

A Graphic Equalizer can boost or cut with a fixed bandwidth at various fixed frequencies. It gets its name because moving the sliders creates a graph of the filter's frequency response.

There are three versions of the effect, each with more frequency bands and, therefore, more subtlety in the adjustments.

FFT Filter

The FFT Filter is an extremely flexible filter that lets you "draw" the frequency response. The default settings are a practical point of departure. FFT (Fast Fourier Transform) is a highly efficient algorithm commonly used for frequency analysis.

Notch Filter

The Notch Filter is optimized to remove very specific frequencies in an audio file, like a particular resonance or AC hum. However, Audition also has a filter optimized specifically for removing hum, which you'll try out in Chapter 5, "Audio Restoration."

Scientific Filter

Scientific Filters are commonly used for data acquisition, but they have audio applications as well. For example, they can help you create extremely steep slopes, narrow notches, ultra-sharp peaks, and other highly precise filter responses.

The trade-off is that this precision can compromise other aspects of filtering (for the technically minded, these include phase shift and delay through the filter). These trade-offs resemble the trade-offs inherent in analog filter technology, however, and some people prefer this kind of sonic "character."

Modulation effects

Unlike some of the previous effects, modulation effects aren't designed to solve problems as much as add spice to sounds in the form of special effects. These effects tend to produce very specific sounds, and the presets included are a good place to start. With most of these effects, you'll usually begin with a preset and make adjustments to achieve the desired result.

Chorus

> **Tip:** The Chorus effect works optimally with stereo signals, so if your source is mono, convert it to stereo for the best results. To do this, choose Edit > Convert Sample Type, and from the Channels menu, choose Stereo. Then click OK.

Chorus can turn a single sound into what seems like an ensemble. This effect uses short delays to create additional "voices" from the original signal. These delays are modulated so that the delay varies slightly over time, which produces a more animated sound.

Flanger

Like Chorus, Flanger uses short delays, but they're even shorter to create phase cancellations that result in an animated, moving, resonant sound. This effect was popularized in the '60s due to its psychedelic properties.

Chorus/Flanger

Chorus/Flanger offers a choice of Chorus or Flanger; each is a simpler version of the dedicated Chorus and Flanger effects but with the convenience of combining the two.

Phaser

The Phaser effect is similar to Flanger but has a different, and often more subtle, character because it uses a specific type of filtering called an *allpass* filter instead of delays to accomplish its effect.

Noise reduction/restoration

Noise reduction and noise restoration are such important topics that these processors are covered in detail in Chapter 5, "Audio Restoration", which describes the many options Adobe Audition offers for audio restoration. These include the ability to remove noise, delete pops and clicks, minimize the sound caused by scratches in vinyl records, reduce tape hiss, and more.

Reverb effects

Reverberation imparts an acoustic space's characteristics (room, concert hall, garage,) to audio. Two common reverb processes are convolution reverb and algorithmic reverb. Audition includes both.

Convolution reverb is generally the more realistic sounding of the two. It loads an *impulse,* which is an audio signal (typically in WAV file format) that embodies the characteristics of a particular, fixed acoustic space. The effect then performs convolution, a mathematical operation that operates on two functions (the impulse and the audio) to create a third function that combines the impulse and the audio, thus impressing the qualities of the acoustic space onto the audio. The trade-off for realism is a lack of flexibility.

Algorithmic reverb creates an algorithm (mathematical model) of a space with variables that allow for changing the nature of that space. It's therefore easy to create different rooms and effects with a single algorithm, whereas with convolution reverb, you would need to load different impulses for fundamentally different sounds. All Audition reverbs other than the convolution reverb use algorithmic reverb technology.

Each type of reverb is useful. Some engineers prefer algorithmic reverbs because it's possible to create idealized reverb spaces; others prefer convolution reverb due to its "real" feel.

Convolution reverb

The convolution type of reverb can produce extremely realistic reverberation effects, and can also be useful for sound design. However, it is a CPU-intensive process.

The effect allows you to load an impulse file, which gives enormous flexibility as there are many impulse files based on real-world locations readily available for download.

Studio Reverb

The Studio Reverb is an algorithmic reverb that's simple, effective, and works in real time so it's easy to hear the results of changing parameters.

1 If you have any files open, choose File > Close All. Then choose File > Open, browse to the Lesson04 folder, and open Drums110.wav. In any Effects Rack click an effect insert, click an effect insert's right arrow, and choose Reverb > Studio Reverb.

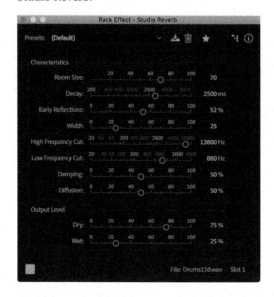

2 With the Default preset selected, vary the Decay slider.

3 Drag the Decay slider all the way to the left, and then vary the Early Reflections slider. Increasing early reflections creates an effect somewhat like a small acoustic space with hard surfaces.

4 Set Decay to about 6000 ms and Early Reflections to 50%. Adjust the Width control to set the stereo imaging, from narrow (0) to wide (100).

5 Move the High Frequency Cut slider more to the left to reduce the high frequencies for a darker sound or more to the right for a brighter sound.

6 Move the LF Cut slider to the right to reduce low-frequency content, which can tighten up the low end and reduce muddiness, or more to the left if you want the reverb to affect lower frequencies.

7 Experiment with the Damping setting. The difference between Damping and High Frequency Cut is that Damping applies progressively more high-frequency attenuation the longer a sound decays, whereas High Frequency Cut is constant.

8 Vary the Diffusion control. At 0% the echoes are more discrete. At 100% they're blended together into a smoother sound. In general, high Diffusion settings are common with percussive sounds; low Diffusion settings are used with sustaining sounds (voice, strings, organ, and so on).

9 Experiment with the Output level options, which vary the amount of dry and wet audio.

Reverb

When you call up the Reverb effect, you'll likely see a warning alerting you that this is a CPU-intensive effect and advising you to apply the effect before playback.

The Reverb effect is a convolution reverb, though unlike with the Convolution Reverb effect, you can't load an impulse file.

Full Reverb

Full Reverb is a convolution-based reverb and is the most sophisticated of the various reverbs. It is also the most impractical to use because of the heavy CPU loading. You cannot adjust parameters other than the level controls for dry, reverb, and early reflections levels during playback, and even then, the level control settings take several seconds to take effect. If you stop playback and adjust them, however, the change occurs immediately on playback.

Surround Reverb

The Surround Reverb effect is primarily intended for 5.1 sources, but it can also provide surround ambience to mono or stereo sources.

If you're producing a 5.1 mix for film or television, you may find this reverb particularly useful for bringing mono or stereo audio sources to life in a constructed surround sound environment.

Special effects

The Special category includes effects that simply don't fit into any of the other categories. Besides the effects discussed in the sections that follow, the Special category includes the Loudness Radar meter, created by TC Electronic, which does not alter sound but gives valuable diagnostic information when producing a mix for broadcast television. It's discussed in Chapter 6, "Mastering."

Distortion

Distortion occurs by clipping a signal's peaks, which creates harmonics. The Distortion effect in Audition can create different amounts of clipping for positive and negative peaks to produce asymmetrical distortion, which can produce a more jagged sound, or link the settings for both peaks to produce symmetrical distortion, which tends to sound somewhat smoother.

Vocal Enhancer

The Vocal Enhancer effect is one of the easiest effects to use because it has only three options. The effect is most often applied to add clarity to speech, using the Male or Female option. The Music option reduces frequencies that might interfere with speech. It's a useful quick fix for a video mix where background music is used with vocals.

Guitar Suite

The Guitar Suite emulates a guitar signal processing chain to produce impressive results.

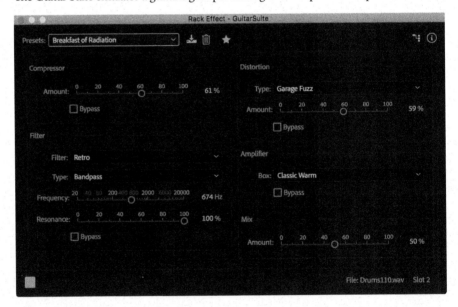

There are four main processors, each of which you can bypass or enable individually:

- **Compressor:** Because a guitar is a percussive instrument, many guitar players use compression to even out the dynamic range and produce more sustain.

- **Filter:** This shapes the guitar's tone.

- **Distortion:** This is a condensed version of the Distortion effect processor.

- **Amplifier:** A large part of a guitar's sound is the amplifier through which it plays: The number of speakers and the size of each, as well as the type of box, have a major effect on the sound. Fifteen types are available, including a box for bass guitar.

Mastering

Think of the Mastering effect as a quick way to master material that doesn't require you to create an *à la carte* set of mastering processors within Audition.

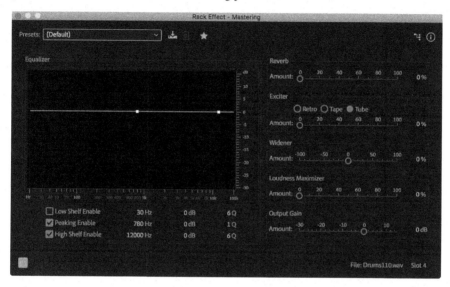

The suite includes the following effects:

- **Equalizer:** Includes a low shelf, high shelf, and parametric (peak/notch) stage. Its parameters work similarly to the same parameters in the Parametric Equalizer effect. The Equalizer also includes a real-time graph in the background that shows the current frequency response spectrum. This helps with making EQ adjustments; for example, if you see a huge bass bump in the low end, the bass probably needs to be reduced.

- **Reverb:** Adds ambience if needed.

- **Exciter:** Creates high-frequency "sparkle" that's unlike conventional treble-boosting EQ.

- **Widener:** Widens or narrows the stereo image.

- **Loudness Maximizer:** A dynamics processor that increases the average level for a louder sound without exceeding the available headroom.

- **Output Gain:** Can be adjusted to control the effect output and therefore compensate for any level changes due to adding various processes.

Now, let's walk through working with the Mastering suite.

1   Choose File > Open, navigate to the Lesson04 folder, and open the file DeepTechHouse.wav. Play the file. Note that there are two problems: The bass booms a bit too much, and the high end lacks definition.

2   In any Effects Rack insert, click the right arrow, and then choose Special > Mastering.

3   Load the preset Subtle Clarity. Toggle the Power button to enable/bypass the preset's effect. Listen to the result; this preset does indeed produce more clarity.

4   Now fix the bass. Select Low Shelf Enable; a small point appears toward the left, which you can drag to change the shelf characteristics.

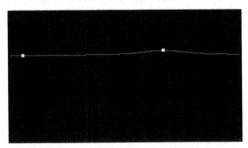

5   Drag the Low Shelf control point right, to around 240 Hz. Then drag down to about –2.5 dB. Enable/bypass the Mastering effect, and you'll hear that when Mastering is enabled, the low end is tighter and the high end is more defined.

6   The Reverb parameter is set to 20% in the preset; move it left to 0%, and the sound will be a little dryer. A value of 10% seems to work well for this tune. Note that the Mastering reverb effect is not intended to provide big hall effects, but instead adds ambience when used subtly.

7   Drag the Exciter's slider to the right, and the sound will become way too bright. A little bit of the Exciter effect goes a long way. (Most of the preset's additional clarity is due to the slight, upper-midrange boost around 2033 Hz working in conjunction with the Exciter, which affects the highest frequencies.) Because the song is already fairly bright, disable the Exciter effect by dragging its slider all the way to the left.

8   Adjust the Widener to taste; end on a setting around 60%.

9   For this song, set the Loudness Maximizer to 30 to provide a useful boost without adding a distorted or unnatural sound. Because the Loudness Maximizer will prevent the level from exceeding 0, you can leave the Output Gain at 0.

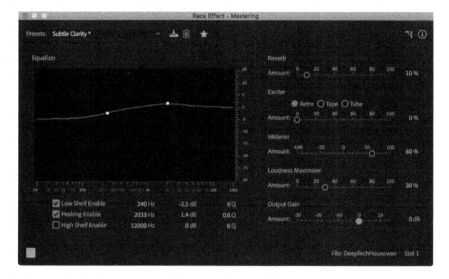

10 Toggle the Power button to enable/bypass the effect and listen to the difference. The mastered version has more sparkle, the bass is in proper proportion with respect to level, the stereo image is wider, and there's been a subjective overall level boost.

Note: The sonic difference among the three characters of Retro, Tape, and Tube becomes most noticeable with dull material and high Exciter amounts.

Tip: It might seem logical to set the Widener for the widest possible stereo image to create a more dramatic sound. However, emphasizing the extreme left and right areas of the stereo spectrum can deemphasize the center, thus unbalancing a mix. If you listen closely and move the slider between 0 and 100, you'll usually find a sweet spot that provides maximum width without altering the mix's fundamental balance.

Note: The Loudness Maximizer can increase the apparent loudness for a more "punchy" sound. However, as with the Exciter, you can have too much of a good thing. Excessive maximization can lead to ear fatigue, as well as make the music less interesting by reducing dynamics.

Stereo imagery effects

Audition includes three effects for altering a stereo image: Center Channel Extractor, Stereo Expander, and Graphic Phase Shifter. The latter is an esoteric tool that you will likely not need to use when you're doing typical audio projects, so concentrate on the Center Channel Extractor and Stereo Expander for now.

Center Channel Extractor

With stereo signals, some sounds are traditionally mixed to center, particularly the vocals, bass, and kick drum. Reversing the phase of one channel cancels out any material panned to center while leaving any signals panned left and right alone. This is commonly used for karaoke to remove the vocals. By filtering the channel that's out of phase to emphasize voice frequencies, bass and kick aren't affected that much.

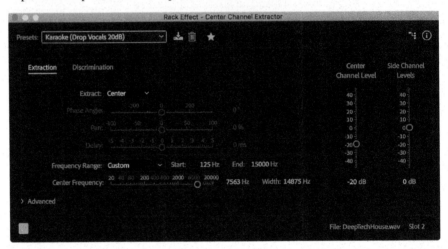

The Center Channel Extractor is a sophisticated implementation of this principle that allows for boosting or cutting the center channel and includes precise filtering to help apply the effect where it's wanted.

Stereo Expander

The Stereo Expander is a more sophisticated version of the Widener in the Mastering effect suite. The Stereo Expander has the same goal: expand the stereo image outward to make the difference between the left and right channels more obvious and dramatic. Unlike with the Widener, however, you can also shift the center channel left or right with the Stereo Expander. This lets you weight the stereo image more toward the left or right.

Time and Pitch effects

The Automatic Pitch Correction and Pitch Shifter effects enable you to make precise corrections or adjustments to audio pitch. Automatic Pitch Correction is designed for vocals and corrects the pitch of notes so that they are in tune. Pitch Shifter transposes audio upward or downward in pitch without affecting the tempo.

Automatic Pitch Correction

Pitch correction is intended for vocals whose pitch is slightly out of tune. This effect analyzes the vocal to extract the pitch, calculates how far off a note is from the correct pitch, and then corrects the note by raising or lowering the pitch to compensate.

Be careful when applying this effect; many vocalists deliberately sing some notes a little flat or sharp to add interest or tension to a vocal. Correcting these can remove a vocal's human quality.

Pitch Shifter

The Pitch Shifter can transpose an audio file up or down in pitch, but unlike some pitch-shifting algorithms, it does so without changing tempo. Note that the greater the amount of transposition, the lower the fidelity.

Some audio signals transpose more elegantly than others. For example, isolated, low-frequency sounds don't handle transposition particularly well.

Third-party effects (VST and AU)

In addition to using the built-in Audition effects, you can load effects (plug-ins) made by third-party manufacturers. Audition is compatible with the following formats:

- **VST (Virtual Studio Technology)** is the most common Windows format and is also supported by macOS. However, you need separate plug-in versions for macOS and Windows. For example, you can't buy a particular VST plug-in for macOS and use it with Windows.

- **VST3** is an updated version of VST2 that offers more efficient operation and other general improvements. Although not quite as common as standard VST, it's gaining in popularity.

- **AU (Audio Units)** is specific to macOS, was introduced with OS X, and is the most common format for macOS.

On either platform, plug-ins are installed in specific hard drive folders. You need to let Audition know where to find these plug-ins. The information in the following sections applies to both Windows and macOS unless otherwise specified.

Note: Many free, legal plug-ins in a variety of formats are available on the Internet. These range from poorly coded effects made by beginning programmers to plug-ins that are every bit as good as—and sometimes better than—commercially available, professional products.

The Audio Plug-In Manager

The Audio Plug-In Manager provides several functions:

- It scans your computer for plug-ins so Audition can use them and creates a list showing the name, type, status, and file path (where the plug-ins are located on your computer).

- It allows you to specify additional folders that contain plug-ins and then re-scan these added folders. Most plug-ins install to default folders, and Audition scans these folders first. Some plug-ins may install into a different folder, however, or you might want to create more than one folder of plug-ins.

- It lets you enable or disable plug-ins.

Check it out.

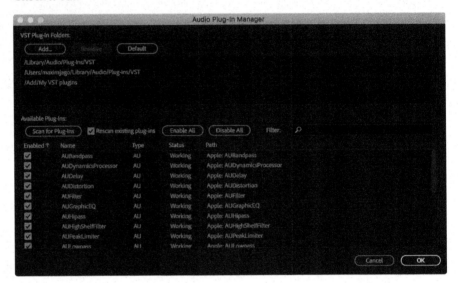

1   Choose Effects > Audio Plug-In Manager.

Note: Although rare, some plug-ins may be incompatible with Audition. This could be due to a nonstandard implementation, an older plug-in that was not updated, a bug within the plug-in that shows up only with particular programs, or a proprietary plug-in that's not intended to work universally. If Audition encounters a plug-in it cannot load, the scanning process stops. If scanning doesn't resume after a minute or so, click Cancel. Audition will enter the incompatible plug-in in the list of plug-ins, but it will be disabled. Run the scan as many times as necessary until the process completes.

2   Click Scan for Plug-Ins. Audition must inspect your hard drive, so this can take a while.

When scanning is complete, you'll see the plug-in listing and status, which usually indicates the manager is done. However, if needed, also complete the following steps.

3   To add an additional folder with plug-ins, click Add and navigate to the folder.

4   Select the check box to the left of the plug-in's name to enable or disable a particular plug-in.

5   Click Re-Scan Existing Plug-Ins to re-scan the existing plug-ins.

Note that you can enable or disable all plug-ins by clicking the appropriate button.

6   When you're finished with the Plug-In Manager, click OK.

Using VST and AU plug-ins

VST and AU plug-ins appear as part of the same menu that opens when you click the right arrow for an Effects Rack insert. For example, in Windows you'll see entries for VST and VST3 effects along with the other entries for Modulation, Filter and EQ, Reverb, and the like; macOS adds another entry for AU effects.

Click the effect you want to insert, as you would with any of the effects included with Audition.

Using the Effects menu

You can process any audio selected in the Waveform or Multitrack Editor by choosing the desired effect from the Effects menu. Unlike with the Effects Rack, you can apply only one effect at a time.

This section covers effects that are available exclusively from the Effects menu. Any effects you can also access from the Effects Rack work the same way when opened from the Effects menu, with three exceptions:

* The Invert, Reverse, and Silence effects are applied to the audio as soon as you select them. You can use the Undo command to undo the effects.

* Most effects chosen via the effects categories (Amplitude and Compression, Delay and Echo, and so on) have an Apply and Close button. Clicking Apply applies the effect to the selected audio.

* Unlike in the Effects Rack, editing is destructive (although the changes aren't made permanent until you save the file). However, you can still preview changes before applying them, because most effects applied via the Effects menu have Play ▶ and Loop 🔁 buttons in addition to a Power on/off button ⬛. Loop repeats the selected portion of the audio (or all of the audio if you haven't made a selection) when you click Play.

Invert, Reverse, and Silence effects

Invert changes the signal's polarity (commonly called *phase*) and produces no audible difference. Reverse flips an audio selection so that the beginning occurs at the end and the end at the beginning. Silence replaces the selected audio with silence.

1   Choose File > Open, navigate to the Lesson04 folder, and open the file NarrationNeedsHelp.wav.

2 Play the file to hear what it sounds like, and then select the part at the beginning that says, "Most importantly, you need to maintain good backups of your data."

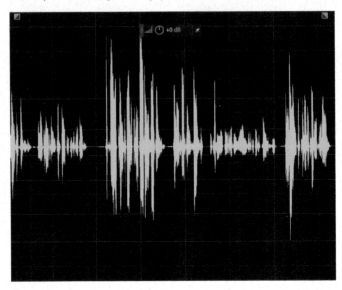

3 Choose Effects > Invert. Note that the positive and negative sections are flipped, so the positive peaks are now negative and vice versa. However, if you play this, you'll hear no audible difference.

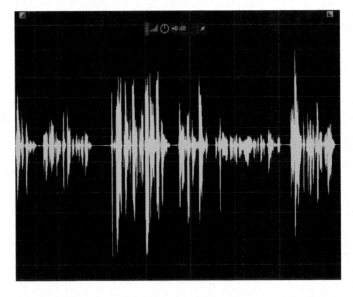

4 Choose Effects > Reverse. Play the selection, and you'll hear reversed speech.

5 Choose Effects > Silence to convert the audio to silence.

6 Close the file without saving it.

Match Loudness effect

It's often helpful to match levels among different pieces of music. This is particularly important for broadcasting, where some governments impose regulations defining maximum volume levels.

However, there are many ways to measure level. A signal's peak is one indication of level, but so is a signal's average level. A drum hit has a high peak level but a low average level because after the hit, the amount of energy decays rapidly. On the other hand, a sustained sound, such as a distorted guitar, has a high average level but low peak level.

As a result, the International Telecommunications Union (ITU) has developed standard measurement protocols—the most recent being LUFS (Loudness Units referenced to Full Scale). Loudness units are based on the human perception of amplitude.

One application of Audition is to match levels to the broadcasting standard of -23 LUFS.

1 Choose Effects > Match Loudness. The Match Loudness panel opens.

You may need to resize the panel to see all of the controls and information. If you are working on a smaller screen, consider undocking the panel by holding Ctrl (Windows) or Command (macOS) while you drag the panel name away from the group.

2 In Explorer (Windows) or Finder (macOS), browse to the Lesson04 folder. Drag the files ContinentalDrift.wav and DeepTechHouse.wav directly into the upper half of the Match Loudness panel. Audition analyzes the signal and displays readings that relate to different ways to measure loudness.

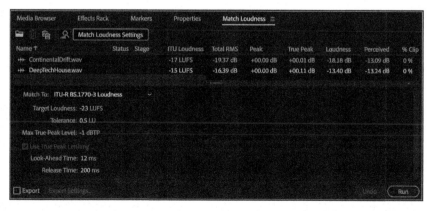

If the information is not displayed, click the Compute Loudness button ![icon].

3 Click the Match Loudness Settings button to display the fully editable settings. It's unlikely you will ever change these settings, other than to choose a preset in the Match To menu.

4 Choose ITU-R BS.1770-3 Loudness if it is not already active.

5 For the Loudness parameter, the target is set to **−23 LUFS**. Leave the Look-Ahead Time and Release Time at their default values (12 ms and 200 ms, respectively).

6 Click Run. Audition adjusts both files to an ITU Loudness level of −23 dB. The other readings will change to reflect the changes in overall level.

7 Click the Editor panel menu, and choose ContinentalDrift.wav. Listen to about a minute of it.

8 Click the Editor panel menu, select DeepTechHouse.wav, and again, listen to about a minute of it. Note how the subjective levels over time for the two files are very similar.

● **Note:** You can export the matched waveforms by selecting Export, then clicking Export Settings and selecting the desired options in the Export Settings dialog box prior to clicking Run. For more information on exporting files, refer to Chapter 17, "Mixing and Output."

Additional Amplitude and Compression effects

Three items on the Effects > Amplitude and Compression submenu are not available in the Effects Rack:

• **Normalize:** Allows you to automatically adjust the audio level to a peak amplitude you specify. You can apply the adjustment to a whole audio file or a selection, which makes it useful for leveling out sections of inconsistent level.

• **Fade Envelope:** Reduces amplitude over time using precisely designed curves.

• **Gain Envelope:** Allows you to boost or reduce amplitude over time with precisely designed curves.

Many of these adjustments can be achieved manually but applying the effect can save time by incorporating several changes into a single process.

Diagnostic, Noise Reduction, and Restoration effects

Diagnostic, Noise Reduction, and Restoration effects will be covered in Chapter 5 along with the real-time, non-destructive noise reduction and restoration tools. The effects selected from the Effects menu produce the same sonic results but are destructive, DSP-based processes. The Loudness Radar Meter in the Special menu is covered in Chapter 6, "Mastering."

Doppler Shifter effect

The Doppler Shifter effect (found in the Special menu) is an unusual effect that changes pitch and amplitude to make signals sound "three dimensional" as they circle around you, whiz by from left to right, and do other effects that alter spatial placement.

Note that opening the Doppler Shifter effect automatically opens the Preview Editor so you can see the effect the Doppler Shifter has on the processed waveform.

Manual Pitch Correction effect

The Manual Pitch Correction effect is one of three effects that are available only from the Time and Pitch submenu of the Effects menu.

While viewing the effect settings, the HUD displays an additional control for pitch along with the standard volume control. Drag this control down to lower pitch; drag up to raise pitch.

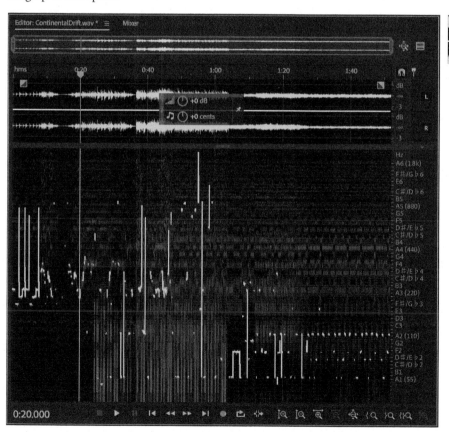

Below the waveform display, the Spectral Pitch Display is enabled, allowing you to make adjustments while interacting with a real-time readout of pitch data.

Pitch Bender effect

The Pitch Bender can change a file's pitch over time. This effect doesn't stretch time to compensate for pitch changes, so it takes less time to play through sections with higher pitches and more time to play through sections with lower pitches. The Pitch Bender allows for drawing an envelope for smooth changes.

Stretch and Pitch effect

The Stretch and Pitch effect is the third effect in the Time And Pitch category that's available only from the Effects menu. It offers high-quality time stretching and pitch adjustment.

Presets and favorites

When you create a particular effect you like, or even a complete Effects Rack configuration with multiple effects, you can save it as a *preset* for later recall. The preset creation process is similar for both individual effects and the Effects Rack.

Audition also allows you to save more elaborate combinations of adjustments as *favorites*. Favorites may include not only effects settings, but fades and amplitude adjustments. Favorites can be created in either the Multitrack or the Waveform Editor, but can be applied only in the Waveform Editor.

Create a single-effect preset

Here's how to create and save a preset for the Amplify effect that boosts gain by +2.5 dB.

1 Choose File > Open, navigate to the Lesson04 folder, and open the file Arpeggio110.wav.

2 Choose Effects > Amplitude And Compression > Amplify. Enter **+2.5 dB** in the Left and Right Gain numeric fields.

3 Click the Save Settings As A Preset button  to the right of the Presets menu. The Save Effect Preset dialog box opens.

4   Enter a name for the preset, such as **+2.5 dB increase**, and click OK. The preset
    name then appears on the Presets menu.

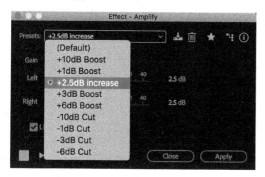

Create a preset using multiple effects

When you've created a combination of effect settings in the Effects Rack that you
expect to use a lot, you can save it as a preset.

1   When the effect settings are as desired, click the Save Effects Rack As A Preset
    button ![icon] in the upper right corner of the Effects Rack, to the right of the
    Presets menu. The Save Favorite dialog box opens.

2   The Save Effect Preset dialog opens. Enter a name for the preset and click OK.
    The preset name then appears on the Presets menu in the Effects Rack.

Delete a preset

To delete a preset, choose it from the Presets menu, and then click the Delete
Preset button ![icon] to the right of the Save Effects Rack As A Preset button.

Create a favorite using a variety of adjustments

Favorites can include more than effects settings. They can include fades and amplitude adjustments.

1   Start recording a favorite by doing one of the following:

    •   In the Favorites panel, click the Record A New Favorite button.

    •   Choose Favorites > Start Recording Favorite.

2   Apply the sequence of effects, fades, and/or amplitude adjustments you want to
    include in your favorite.

3   When you're finished, do one of the following:

    •   In the Favorites panel, click the Stop Recording button.

    •   Choose Favorites > Stop Recording Favorite.

4   Give the new favorite a name in the Save Favorite dialog box and click OK.

Creating and deleting effects-only favorites

The procedure for creating a single-effect favorite is very much the same as for creating a preset, but you can do it only in the Waveform Editor.

1   Once you've got the settings the way you want them in the effect dialog box, click the Save Current Effect Settings As A Favorite button ⭐ toward the upper-right corner of the effect's window.

2   Give the favorite a name in the Save Favorite dialog box and click OK.

    The new favorite will be listed in the Favorites panel.

Creating a favorite that uses a combination of effects is also similar to creating a preset, and this works in both the Waveform and the Multitrack Editors.

1   When combination of effects in the Effects Rack is configured as desired, click the Save Current Effects Rack As A Favorite button ⭐ toward the upper-right corner of the Effects Rack.

2   Give the favorite a name in the Save Favorite dialog box and click OK.

    The new favorite will be listed in the Favorites panel.

When a favorite has outlived its usefulness, visit the Favorites panel to delete it.

1   In the list of favorites in the Favorites panel, click the name of the favorite you want to delete. The favorite is selected.

2   Click the Delete Selected Favorites button 🗑 at the top of the Favorites panel.

3   Click Yes in the alert box that opens. The favorite is removed from the list.

Apply a favorite

You have to be using the Waveform Editor to apply a favorite.

1   Open the clip you want to process in the Waveform Editor.

2   In the Editor panel, select a portion of the clip or make no selection to process the entire clip.

3   Do one of the following:

   •   Choose Favorites > [favorite settings].

   •   Open the Favorites panel and click the favorite of your choice.

The saved settings will immediately be applied to the selected audio.

Review questions

1 What are the advantages of the Effects Rack, the Effects menu, and favorites?

2 Is it possible to expand the roster of effects available to Audition?

3 Why is gain-staging important with the Effects Rack?

4 What is the difference between dry and wet audio?

Review answers

1 The Effects Rack allows you to make complex effects chains, the Effects menu includes additional effects and can apply single effects rapidly. Favorites allow you to apply settings (or combinations of settings) to audio immediately upon choosing the favorite.

2 Audition can load third-party VST, VST3, and for the Mac, AU effects as well.

3 Effects can increase gain, thus causing distortion within the Effects Rack. By adjusting levels going into and out of the rack, it's possible to avoid distortion.

4 Dry audio is unprocessed, whereas wet audio has been processed. Many effects let you alter the proportion of the two types of audio.

5 AUDIO RESTORATION

Lesson overview

In this lesson, you'll learn how to do the following:

- Remove hiss, such as tape hiss or preamp noise

- Reduce the level of clicks and pops automatically

- Minimize or even remove constant background noises, including hum, air conditioning, ventilation system noise, and the like

- Remove undesired artifacts, such as someone coughing in the middle of a live recording

- Do highly effective manual click and pop removal

- Use restoration tools to completely modify a drum loop

 This lesson will take about 45 minutes to complete. Please log in to your account on peachpit.com to download the lesson files for this chapter, or go to the "Getting Started" section at the beginning of this book and follow the instructions under "Accessing the Lesson Files and Web Edition." Store the files on your computer in a convenient location.

Your Account page is also where you'll find any updates to the chapters or to the lesson files. Look on the Lesson & Update Files tab to access the most current content.

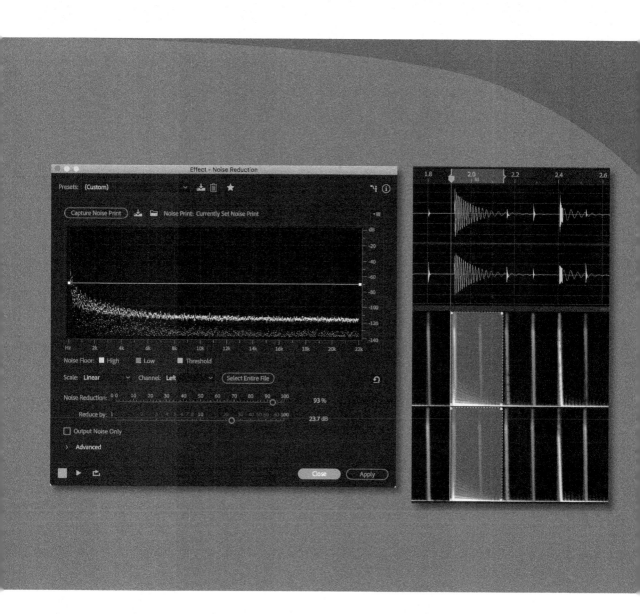

Audition offers tools for reducing hiss, hum, clicks, pops, and other types of noise. Plus, you can also remove undesired artifacts by defining sections to be removed based on amplitude, time, and frequency.

About audio restoration

● **Note:** If you have not already downloaded the project files for this lesson to your computer from your Account page, make sure to do so now. See "Getting Started" at the beginning of the book.

Sometimes you'll work with audio with hum, hiss, or other artifacts that needs restoration, such as music from vinyl records or cassette. Audition has multiple tools for solving these problems, including specialized signal processors and graphic waveform editing options.

However, audio restoration involves trade-offs. For example, removing the crackles from vinyl recordings may remove part of the sound that occurs during the crackles. So you may have to reconcile solving a problem with the infamous "law of unintended consequences."

Nonetheless, as the exercises in this lesson demonstrate, it's possible to use Audition to clean up audio significantly while retaining sound quality.

Reducing hiss

▶ **Tip:** The Mastering And Analysis workspace is a good choice for these lessons. It includes the Frequency Analysis panel, which displays the current audio level at a range of frequencies.

Hiss is a natural byproduct of electronic circuits, particularly high-gain circuits. Analog tape recordings always had some inherent hiss, but so do mic preamps and other audio signal sources. Audition provides two ways of reducing hiss (also see the section "Reducing noise"); we'll start with the easiest option.

1 With Audition open to the Waveform Editor, choose File > Open, navigate to the Lesson05 folder, and open the file Hiss.wav.

2 Click the Transport Play button, and you'll hear obvious hiss, especially during quiet sections. Click the Transport Stop button.

▶ **Tip:** When you're mixing music that will be mastered, don't trim a file up to the beginning; leave some of the track before the music begins. This can provide a noise floor reference if noise reduction is needed.

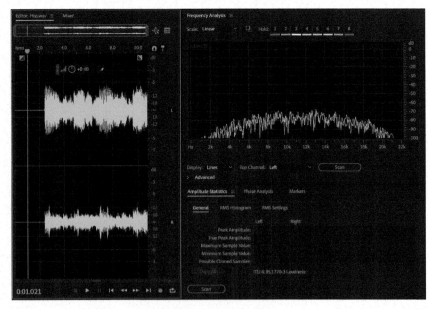

3 Select the first 2 seconds of the audio file, which contain only noise (the *noise floor*). Choose Effects > Noise Reduction/Restoration > Capture Noise Print. Audition will take a *noise print* (like a noise "fingerprint") of this signal and subtract audio with only these hiss characteristics from the audio file. If an alert appears, click OK to dismiss it.

4 Choose Effects > Noise Reduction/Restoration > Hiss Reduction (process).

5 Click the Capture Noise Floor button. A curve appears that shows the noise's spectral distribution.

While playing the beginning of the file, if you have the Frequency Analysis panel open, you'll notice the curve is similar in the two graphs.

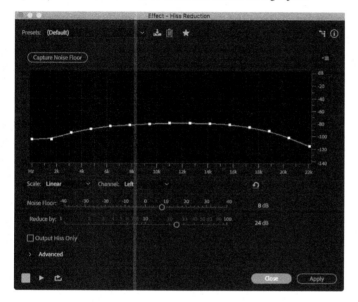

6 Extend the audio selection in the Waveform Editor to around 5 seconds, and click the Transport Loop button (if it's not already selected). This also turns on the Hiss Reduction dialog box's Loop button.

7 Click the Hiss Reduction dialog box's Play button. You'll hear less noise. You generally want to use the minimum acceptable amount of noise reduction to avoid altering the rest of the signal; reducing hiss may also reduce high frequencies.

8 Move the Reduce By slider to the left and the hiss will return. Move it right to 100 dB, and although there will be no hiss, the transients will lose some high frequencies.

9 Move the Reduce By slider to find a compromise setting between noise reduction and high-frequency response. For now, leave it at 10 dB.

10 The Noise Floor slider tells Audition where to draw the line between the noise floor and the signal. Move the slider farther to the left, and you'll hear more

▶ **Tip:** You typically adjust the Reduce By parameter first to set the overall amount of noise reduction, and then adjust the Noise Floor parameter to determine the noise reduction characteristics. Re-tweaking each slider, however, can optimize the sound further. Also, note that selecting Output Hiss Only will play only what's being removed from the audio. This can help determine whether any desirable audio is being removed along with the hiss.

noise. Now move the slider to the right; you'll hear less noise and also a reduced high-frequency response. Leave the slider set to 10 dB for now as a good compromise setting.

11 Revisit the Reduce By slider and move it to 20 dB. The hiss is gone, but there's a little less "snap" to the transients compared to the 10 dB setting. You'll need to decide which quality is more important to you, but for now choose 15 dB as a compromise setting.

12 Click the Transport Stop button. Deselect the Transport Loop button, click once within the Waveform Editor to deselect the loop. Doing so means any effects will be applied to the entire duration.

13 Click the Transport Play button. Enable and disable the Hiss Reduction dialog box's Power State button to hear the file with and without noise reduction. The difference is significant, especially at the beginning and end where there's no signal to mask the hiss. Stop playback.

14 Click the Hiss Reduction dialog box's Close button.

15 Even if there's no noise floor, Audition can still help remove noise. While still in the Waveform Editor, choose File > Open, navigate to the Lesson05 folder, and open the file HissTruncated.wav.

16 Choose Effects > Noise Reduction/Restoration > Hiss Reduction (process).

17 Click the Transport Play button. Despite not capturing a noise print, you can verify that there's less noise by clicking the Hiss Reduction dialog box's Power State button to listen to the enabled and bypassed states.

18 Move the Reduce By slider to around 20 dB, which is a typical amount for noise reduction. Now vary the Noise Floor slider for the best compromise between hiss reduction and high-frequency response; –2 dB is a good choice.

19 Click the Hiss Reduction dialog box's Power State button to listen to the enabled and bypassed states. Although the noise reduction doesn't have quite the finesse you can achieve by working with a noise print, it still makes a huge improvement without any significant audio degradation.

20 Close the Hiss Reduction dialog box, stop playback, and then close the two files in preparation for the next exercise. Don't save any changes when asked.

Reducing crackles

Crackles can consist of the little ticks and pops you hear with vinyl recordings, occasional digital clocking errors in digital audio signals, mouth noises that happen during narration, a bad physical audio connection, and so on. Although it's difficult to remove these completely without affecting the audio, Audition can help attenuate lower-level clicks and crackles.

1 Choose File > Open, navigate to the Lesson05 folder, and open the file Crackles.wav.

2 Make sure the Transport Loop button is selected and click the Play button. You'll hear clicks and crackles, especially during the quiet parts between drum hits in the beginning.

3 Choose Effects > Noise Reduction/Restoration > Automatic Click Remover.

4 Move the Threshold slider to 0. The Threshold slider sets the sensitivity to clicks. With it at 0, the processor will interpret almost anything as a click and you'll hear the program sputter as it tries to make an excessive number of real-time calculations. Lower values "trap" more clicks, but may also reduce lower-level transients you want to keep. Conversely, moving the Threshold slider to a setting of 100 lets through too many clicks. Choose a setting of 20 to reduce most clicks while minimally affecting the audio quality.

5 Click the Transport Stop button, and then move the Complexity slider to 80; this slider sets how complex a click Audition will process. This is not a real-time control, so you need to adjust it, play the audio, adjust, play, and so on. Higher settings allow Audition to recognize more complex clicks but require more computation and may degrade the audio somewhat.

6 Click the Transport Play button. Because this is a computation-intensive process, during real-time playback Audition may not be able to process a click prior to playing it back. The only way to be certain how processing will affect the sound is to click the Apply button; click it now. This closes the Automatic Click Remover dialog box.

7 Click the Transport Play button. Although the clicks are lower in volume, the removal process affects the audio, so try revising the setting again. Choose Edit > Undo Automatic Click Remover or press Ctrl+Z (Windows) or Command+Z (macOS).

8 Choose Effects > Noise Reduction/Restoration > Automatic Click Remover; the settings will be as you left them. If Complexity is dimmed, click the Automatic Click Remover dialog box's Play button and then the Stop button. Move the complexity slider to 35, and click Apply again.

Note: There's not a lot of difference between minor Complexity setting variations. For example, if you had chosen 40 or 30 instead of 35, you probably wouldn't notice any difference compared to a setting of 35.

Tip: When comparing before-and-after versions of audio files, you can also click between the steps in the History panel.

9 Click the Transport Play button. The new setting produces better results than the original default value of 16 or the higher value of 80 that you tried. To compare the repaired sound with the original, choose Edit > Undo Automatic Click Remover, and then choose Edit > Redo Automatic Click Remover. Click the Transport Stop button when you're done comparing the two.

10 Close the file, without saving it, ready for the next exercise.

Reducing pops and clicks

Pops, such as the sounds that happen when a vinyl record has a scratch, tend to be more severe than crackles. As with crackles it's difficult to remove severe pops, but Audition can reduce their severity very well.

1 Choose File > Open, navigate to the Lesson05 folder, and open the file MajorPops.wav.

2 Make sure Transport Loop is selected and click Play. This is the same file used in the previous lesson, but note how the clicks and pops are far more severe.

3 Choose Effects > Noise Reduction/Restoration > Click/Pop Eliminator (process). This effect initiates the Visual Edit Preview function, so you can see how processing will affect the original file. If Default is not the current preset, choose it from the Presets menu.

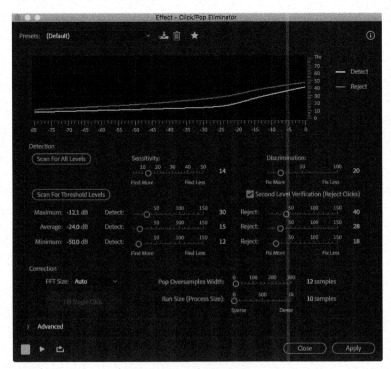

4   Click the Advanced disclosure triangle; Detect Big Pops should be selected. If not, select it and choose the default setting of 60.

5   Click Scan For All Levels.

The Click/Pop Eliminator is a sophisticated effect with multiple adjustments, but fortunately, it's fairly intelligent and knows how to adjust its settings for most material.

6   Click the Transport or Click/Pop Eliminator dialog box's Play button. The pops are still present but sound more muffled. This is an improvement, but you can do better.

7   Set the Run Size slider to around 100 samples, and set the Pop Oversamples Width slider to 50.

These settings allow Audition to process more severe pops with longer durations. For crackles and very short clicks, these sliders can be set to lower values.

8   Play the results, and you'll hear that the most severe pops are gone. Compare the original waveform to the lower waveform in the Visual Edit Preview, and you'll see that the pops are no longer present.

9   Click Apply.

10 Close the file, without saving it, ready for the next exercise.

Reducing broadband noise

Although you can reduce hiss with the Hiss Reduction effect, there are other types of noise you'll want to reduce as well, such as hum, air conditioning noise, and ventilation sounds. If these sounds are relatively constant, Audition can reduce or remove them using the Noise Reduction process. This can also reduce hiss and allow for more detailed editing compared to the Hiss Reduction option.

1   Choose File > Open, navigate to the Lesson05 folder, and open the file BroadbandHum.wav. This file contains not just hum, but harmonics from the hum and other artifacts.

2   Click the Transport Play button to hear the hum that was caused by a bad electrical connection (this kind of hum can also occur with unbalanced audio cables and high-gain circuits). Pay special attention to the very beginning of the audio.

3 Select the first second of the audio file (zoom in if necessary), which contains only hum.

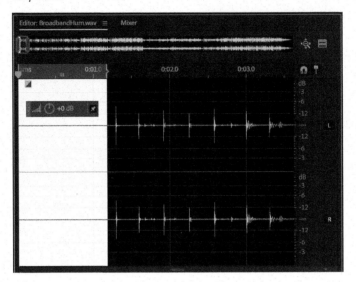

4 Choose Effects > Noise Reduction/Restoration > Noise Reduction (process).

5 Click the Capture Noise Print button. A curve appears that shows the noise floor's spectral distribution.

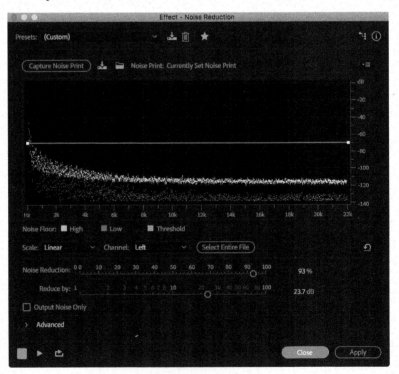

6 Select about the first 20 seconds of the file, and click the Transport Loop button if it is not already selected.

7 Click the Noise Reduction dialog box's Play button. The hum will be gone during silent sections.

8 Move the noise reduction slider to 0.0 and listen closely. You may hear a slight artifact immediately after a drum sound decays, because noise reduction doesn't apply as much reduction when the sound is being masked, and it takes some time to return to full reduction when audio is no longer present. Return the Noise Reduction slider to 100% to remove these artifacts.

9 Set the Reduce By slider, which sets the amount by which the noise will be reduced, to 15 dB. Settings between 10 and 20 dB are a good compromise between affecting the audio and reducing the noise.

10 Click the Advanced disclosure triangle for more options if you still hear a tiny bit of hum after a drum sound decays.

11 Vary the Spectral Decay Rate parameter between 0 and 100%. This parameter determines how long it takes for the noise reduction to return to maximum when the audio goes from signal to silence. A setting of 100% lets through a lot of hum, but 0% may produce a change that is too abrupt. Choose 20%, which is a good compromise value, thus eliminating the hum at the end of the drum sounds.

12 Toggle the Noise Reduction dialog box's Power State button, and you'll hear the effectiveness of the noise reduction process.

13 Click Close in the Noise Reduction dialog box (do not click Apply).

14 Close the file, without saving it, ready for the next exercise.

▶ **Tip:** When working with the effects that must be processed, it is often helpful to select a section of the audio to test the result without waiting to render the result for the whole file. Once you're happy with the settings, you can undo, and run the settings for the whole file.

De-humming a file

The previous exercise showed how to reduce broadband noise. However, Audition also includes a DeHummer function that's optimized specifically for reducing hum and is simpler to adjust if the only problem is hum.

1 Choose File > Open, navigate to the Lesson05 folder, and open the file Hum.wav.

2 Start playback, and you'll hear really bad hum superimposed in the audio. This kind of hum is commonly introduced by electrical interference.

3 Choose Effects > Noise Reduction/Restoration > DeHummer.

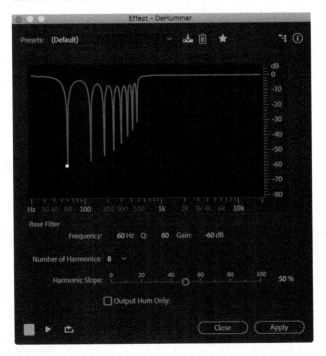

▶ **Tip:** Always use the minimum setting for Number Of Harmonics that still produces acceptable results. Also, note that aside from North America and parts of South America, most of the world uses an AC line frequency of 50 Hz. To remove hum at this frequency, under Base Filter set the Frequency value to 50 Hz.

4 Select the Default DeHummer preset, and start playback; the hum is gone, but so is part of the audio because it sounds a little less full.

5 Chose 3 from the Number Of Harmonics menu. This still gets rid of the hum, because its main component is the hum's 60 Hz fundamental, with just two harmonics.

6 Click Apply, and the hum is gone from the file.

7 Close the file, without saving it, ready for the next exercise.

Removing artifacts

Sometimes particular sounds will need to be removed, like a cough in the middle of a live performance. In Audition, you can use the Spectral Frequency Display to accomplish this. It allows for editing based on not just amplitude and time (as with the standard Waveform Editor), but also frequency.

Open the Spectral Frequency Display (if it's not already visible) by pressing Shift+D, by clicking the Show Spectral Frequency Display button ▦ at the top left of the Audition interface, by dragging up on the divider handle at the bottom of the waveform display, or by choosing View > Show Spectral Frequency Display.

This exercise shows you how to remove a cough in a performance by Argentinian classical guitarist Nestor Ausqui.

1   Choose File > Open, navigate to the Lesson05 folder, and open the file Guitar WithCough.wav.

2   Click the Transport Play button, and you'll hear a cough in the background at around 9.9 seconds.

3   Choose View > Show Spectral Frequency Display. Because you'll be doing detailed work, make the Waveform Editor window as large as possible by dragging the horizontal and vertical dividers.

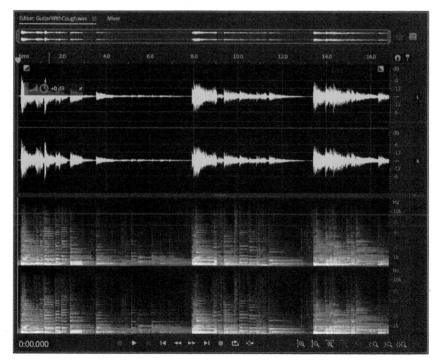

4 Zoom in and look closely at the spectrum at around 9.9 seconds. Unlike the linear bands of audio in various frequencies you see in the rest of the file, there's something that looks almost like a cloud; that's the cough.

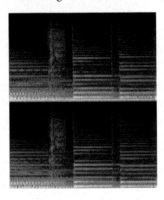

Tip: To decrease or increase the brush size, press [(Left Bracket) or] (Right Bracket), respectively.

Note: You'll need to change the brush's Size value depending on the zoom level of the Spectral Frequency Display.

Tip: To drag in a straight line, hold down the Shift key while dragging.

5 Click the Spot Healing Brush tool button ![icon] in the top toolbar, or press the B key to select the brush. Your cursor changes to a circle when hovering over the Spectral Frequency display.

6 When you select the Spot Healing Brush tool, a Size parameter appears next to the Spot Healing Brush tool's toolbar button. Adjust the size so that the circular cursor is as wide as the cough, but no wider; you don't want to remove any of the good audio.

7 In one channel, drag the circular cursor over the area with the cough; the same area will be selected automatically in the other channel. The area over which you dragged will be ghosted in white. Be careful to drag over only the cough.

Tip: The size of the cursor and its placement are critical to removing the cough. If the cough isn't gone, undo and try a different brush size, or change its placement. For example, it's usually more important to make sure you include all of an artifact's attack (the start of the sound) rather than its decay (the part of the sound that trails off to zero level). You can also try using this process on successive, small selections of an artifact. In addition, if small pieces of the artifact remain, sometimes it's easiest to choose the Lasso Selection tool (or press D), draw around the remaining pieces, and then press the Delete key.

8 Release the mouse button, and then click the Transport Play button. The cough will be gone, and Audition will have "healed" (reconstructed) the audio behind the cough. (The healing process uses audio on either side of the deleted audio, and through a complex process of copying and crossfading, fills in the gap caused by removing the artifact.)

9 Choose File > Close All in preparation for the next exercise.

Results with the Spot Healing Brush tool will vary depending on the audio you are working with. Still, it can be incredibly effective and is always worth trying with coughs and other spot audio problems in the background.

Manual sound removal

Sometimes you don't need sophisticated audio restoration but simply need to remove something like finger squeaks on a guitar string, breathing while a person plays an instrument, and similar artifacts. For these types of simple repairs, you can use the Marquee or Lasso tool to define the artifact you want removed, and then delete it or reduce its level.

It takes experience to recognize what's an artifact and what's part of the sound, as well as whether to drag the Spot Healing Brush tool across the sound or to use the Lasso Selection or Marquee Selection tool. With sufficient practice, however, this type of restoration is extremely effective. This exercise shows you how to remove finger noise from a classical guitar piece, again played by Nestor Ausqui.

1 Choose File > Open, navigate to the Lesson05 folder, and open the file Guitar.wav.

2 Click the Transport Play button. Note that there are finger noises from around 18.5 seconds to 19 seconds.

3 If the Spectral Frequency Display is not already visible, press Shift+D, and then zoom in on the finger noises.

4 Select the Lasso Selection tool ⌀ or press D, and then draw a line around the finger noises.

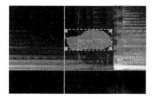

5 Press Backspace (Windows) or Delete (macOS) to remove the finger noises.

6 Note that there's still an artifact at 18.6 seconds. Select the Spot Healing Brush tool, and use the same technique described in the previous exercise to remove this one little artifact. Remember to use a circular cursor that's only as wide as the artifact. Now all the finger noises are gone.

7 Keep Audition open in preparation for the next exercise, but close the file without saving.

> **Tip:** You can drag the divider between the waveform display and the Spectral Frequency display to expand the view of one or the other.

> **Note:** Remember to use artistic judgment in the quest for perfection. Sometimes it's the little noises and artifacts that make a performance sound "real" and human. You may find it's often better to reduce the level with the HUD's volume control than to remove an artifact completely.

The Spot Healing brush

You can use the Spectral Frequency Display to remove clicks. Although this is a manual process that is more time-consuming than using the Automatic Click Remover effect, the removal process will be more accurate and have less impact on the audio quality.

1 Choose File>Open, navigate to the Lesson05 folder, and open the file Crackles.wav.

2 Because you had the Spectral Frequency Display open in the previous lesson, Audition should open with the Spectral Frequency Display visible. If not, choose View > Show Spectral Frequency Display (or press Shift+D).

3 Zoom in until you can see the clicks toward the file's beginning as thin, solid vertical lines.

4 Press B to choose the Spot Healing Brush tool, and set its pixel size to the same width as a click.

5 Hold down the Shift key, and then click at the top of the click (noise) and drag down. This selects the noise in both channels.

6 Release the mouse button; the click will be gone and the audio behind it will be healed. Repeat steps 5 and 6 for each click you want to remove.

7 Return the playhead to the beginning of the file if necessary, and then click the Transport Play button. The file sounds as if the clicks had never been there.

8 Keep Audition open in preparation for the next exercise, but close the file without saving.

Automated sound removal

Audition's restoration tools aren't just for fixing problems: You can also use them in creative ways and for sound design. In this exercise, you'll use the Sound Remover function to remove the kick drum from a drum loop.

1 Choose File > Open, navigate to the Lesson05 folder, and open the file Electro.wav.

2 Click the Transport Play button and note where the kick drum sounds occur. There's a prominent, fairly isolated one at around 1.9 seconds.

3 As with the previous exercises, zoom in until the kick is big enough that it's easy to define.

4 Select the Marquee Selection tool, or press E. Select the kick drum hit.

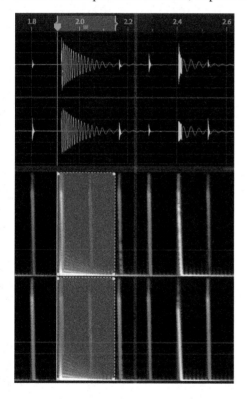

5 Choose Effects > Noise Reduction/Restoration > Sound Remover (process). If the (Default) Sound Remover preset is not already selected, choose it from the Presets menu.

Tip: If necessary, you can enhance the removal process by selecting Enhanced Suppression and increasing the suppression strength.

6 Click Learn Sound Model (the Visual Edit Preview opens). This captures the kick drum sound you selected in step 4 to use as a reference, so that any sound in the file with these characteristics will be removed. Before proceeding, because the file doesn't contain speech, deselect Enhance For Speech in the Sound Remover dialog box.

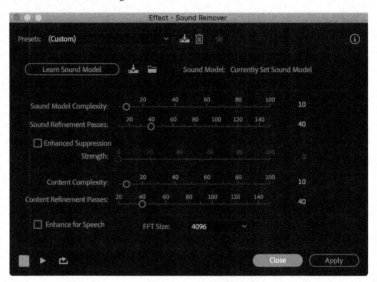

7 To ensure the Sound Remover effect will be applied to the entire waveform, choose Edit > Select > Select All, or press Ctrl+A (Windows) or Command+A (macOS), or click on the waveform to clear the selection completely (which means the effect will be applied to the whole file).

8 Play the file, and note that the kick drum is almost removed completely.

9 Click Apply to remove all the kick drums from the file. The Visual Edit Preview pane closes.

Review questions

1　Which is more effective, automatic or manual click removal?

2　What is a noise print?

3　Is noise reduction good only for removing hiss?

4　What does healing do?

5　Name two ways other than restoration where these tools can be useful.

Review answers

1　Automatic click removal is faster, but manual click removal can be more effective.

2　A noise print is like a fingerprint that represents the specific sonic character of a section of noise. Subtracting this from the audio file removes the noise.

3　Noise reduction can minimize or even remove any constant background sound, as long as there's an isolated section where you can capture a noise print.

4　Healing replaces audio removed by the Spot Healing Brush tool with crossfaded, "good" audio from either side of the artifact.

5　You can use them in highly creative ways, like removing specific drum hits from drum loops or performing sound design.

6 MASTERING

Lesson overview

In this lesson, you'll learn how to do the following:

- Use effects to improve the sound of a mixed, stereo piece of music

- Apply EQ to reduce "mud," emphasize the kick drum, and articulate cymbals

- Apply dynamics to give music more apparent level, which can also help overcome background noise in cars and other environments

- Create ambience for music that has a dry, sterile sound

- Alter stereo imaging to create a wider stereo effect

- Make small edits to emphasize particular parts of a piece of music

- Use diagnostic tools to monitor level and phase

 This lesson will take about 45 minutes to complete. Please log in to your account on peachpit.com to download the lesson files for this chapter, or go to the "Getting Started" section at the beginning of this book and follow the instructions under "Accessing the Lesson Files and Web Edition." Store the files on your computer in a convenient location.

Your Account page is also where you'll find any updates to the chapters or to the lesson files. Look on the Lesson & Update Files tab to access the most current content.

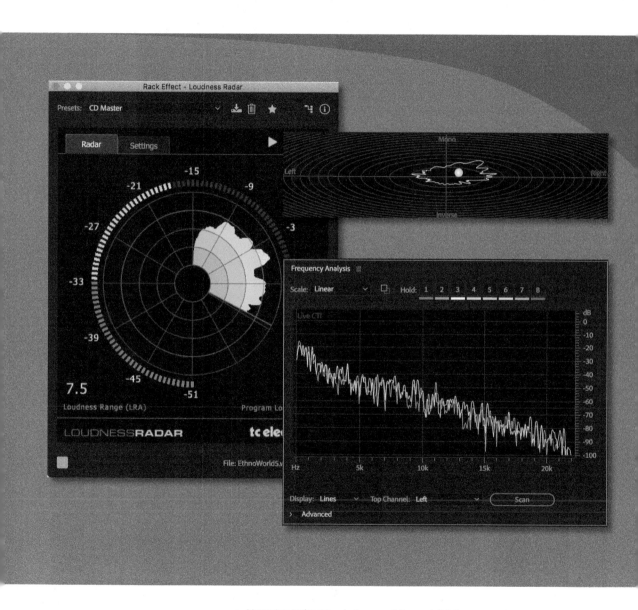

Mastering is the stage between mixing and distribution. By tasteful application of EQ, dynamics, waveform editing, widening, and other techniques, you can shape a piece of music into a refined audio experience that's ready for distribution or posting online.

Mastering basics

Note: If you have not already downloaded the project files for this lesson to your computer from your Account page, make sure to do so now. See "Getting Started" at the beginning of the book.

Mastering is the process that occurs after mixing but before distribution or publishing. It's when you add any final edits or enhancements (equalization, dynamics, fade-in or fade-out, and so on) to a stereo- or surround-mixed file, as well as run any diagnostics to make sure the file meets particular audio specifications.

With album projects (whether a CD or collection of music posted online), mastering also involves determining the correct order of the songs in the album (*sequencing* the songs) and matching their levels and timbres for a cohesive listening experience.

With film and television soundtracks, mastering involves matching levels to the deliverable standard and ensuring the mix will work on a variety of monitoring systems, from high-end cinema sound systems to tinny speakers on a laptop.

As the final link in the music production chain, mastering can make or break a project. As a result, people often hand off projects to veteran mastering engineers, not just for their technical expertise, but also to enlist a fresh, objective set of ears.

If your goal with mastering is simply to make a good mix better, however, Audition provides the tools required for professional-level mastering. The more you work with mastering, the more your skills will improve. But it can't be emphasized enough that the most important mastering tool is a good set of ears that can analyze where a piece of music is deficient, coupled with the technical expertise of knowing what processing will compensate for those deficiencies.

In addition, remember that ideally the purpose of mastering is not to salvage a recording, but to enhance an already superb mix. If there's a problem with the mix, remix first; don't count on mastering to solve the problem.

In Chapter 4, "Effects," you learned how to do basic mastering with the Mastering effects suite in the Special menu. This chapter takes a more "component" approach by using individual effects. You'll explore them in the order in which you would typically apply these effects (equalization, dynamics, ambience, stereo imaging, and waveform touchup). Note, however, that sometimes touching up the waveform occurs first if there are known problems that need to be fixed, such as using the Amplify effect to raise part of a track's level if it's too quiet.

Equalization

Usually, the first step of mastering involves adjusting equalization to create a pleasing tonal balance.

Note: The Mastering And Analysis workspace places emphasis on the analysis and metering panels. If you are working on a smaller screen, you may want to resize the Waveform Editor panel to navigate it more easily.

1 With Audition open to the Waveform Editor, choose Window > Workspace > Mastering And Analysis.

2 Choose File > Open, navigate to the Lesson06 folder, and open the file KeepTheFunk.wav.

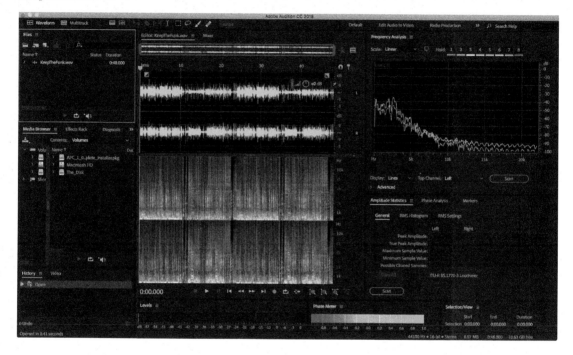

3 In the Effects Rack, click insert 1's right arrow and choose Filter And EQ > Parametric Equalizer.

4 If necessary, choose the Default preset from the Presets menu, and then select the 30 dB Range option toward the lower right.

5 Loop the file by pressing Ctrl+L (Windows) or Command+L (macOS) or by clicking the Transport Loop Playback button so the file keeps playing while you make the following adjustments. Click the Transport Play button and listen. The music sounds a little muddy in the low frequencies and lacks crispness in the highs.

Note: If you want to click the Waveform Editor's loop button, you may need to widen the Waveform Editor with its right splitter bar to reveal the button, or float the Transport panel by dragging its name while holding Ctrl (Windows) or Command (macOS).

6   One way to identify problem areas is to boost a parametric stage's Gain, sweep its Frequency range, and listen to whether any frequencies jump out as excessive. So, click the Band 2 control point on the filter's graph, drag it all the way up to +15 dB, and drag the box left and right. Note that the sound is "tubby" around 150 Hz.

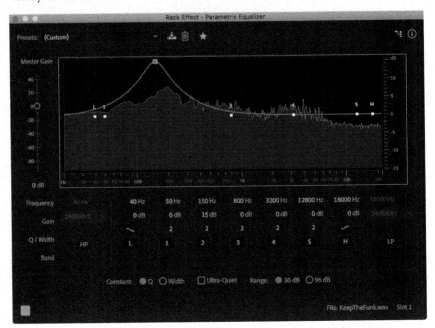

7   Drag the Band 2 control point down to around −5 dB at around 150 Hz. Note how this tightens up the low end. The difference is subtle (enable and disable the Band 2 button to hear the difference), but often, mastering is about the cumulative effect of multiple subtle changes.

8   The kick drum seems like it should be stronger and have more of a deep "thud" for this kind of music; use Band 1 to dial in the drum's frequency and add a narrow boost. Set Band 1's Q to 8, and drag the Band 1 box up to +15 dB. Sweep the Frequency back and forth between 20 and 100 Hz, and note that the kick really stands out around 45 Hz.

9   Bring the Band 1 level back down to around 5 or 6 dB so the kick isn't too prominent.

10 The hi-hat and cymbals seem kind of dull, but increasing the high-frequency response can improve that. Set Band 4's Q to 1.5, set Frequency to around 8000 kHz, and drag the Band 4 control point up to around +2 dB.

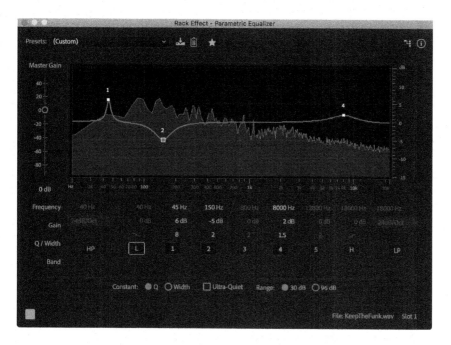

11 Toggle the Power button again for comparison. Note that in the figure, unused bands have been turned off for clarity. Close the Parametric Equalizer window, but keep this file open for the next lesson.

Dynamics

Dynamics processing can make a piece of music jump out of the speakers, giving it more punch and making low-level sounds louder. This can also help the music overcome background noises found in many different listening environments. To avoid listener fatigue, you don't want to add *too* much processing and kill the dynamics, but some processing can produce a nice, lively lift.

This exercise uses the Multiband Compressor to control dynamics. In addition to offering compression in four frequency bands, the Multiband Compressor also provides an overall output limiter.

The controls for each band are the same as those in the Single-Band Compressor. The major difference (apart from having a more colorful interface) is that the Multiband Compressor includes Crossover settings, which divide each of the four groups of settings into different frequency ranges.

Crossover: Low: 120 Hz   Mid: 2000 Hz   High: 10000 Hz

Note: Dynamics is usually the last processor in a mastering chain because it sets the maximum allowable level. Adding effects afterward could increase or decrease the overall level.

Note: The meters to the immediate right of each band's Threshold slider (whose position corresponds to the value in the numeric Threshold field) indicate the amount of compression. As more compression is applied, less red is visible in the meter.

1   In the Effects Rack, click insert 4's right arrow and choose Amplitude And Compression > Multiband Compressor. (The reason for choosing insert 4 is that you'll want to add some effects later between the EQ and dynamics.)

2   Choose the Pop Master preset from the Presets menu to give the music *much* more apparent loudness.

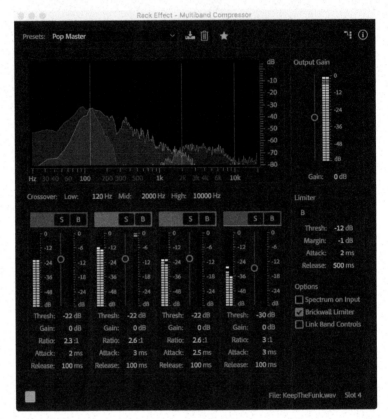

3   If you listen for a while, you'll hear that the dynamics have been reduced dramatically—too much, in fact. To restore some dynamics, set each band's Threshold parameter to −18.0 dB.

4   Drag the overall effect Limiter section's Threshold field down to −20 dB. The sound becomes overly limited, squashed, and uneven. Now drag up to 0. No limiting is being applied, and the sound lacks punch. Drag down to a good compromise setting between these two extremes, like −8.0 dB.

5   Toggle the Effects Rack's Power button to compare the sound with and without the EQ and Multiband Compressor. The processed sound is fuller, tighter, more distinct, and louder. Also, note that the Multiband Dynamics effect has emphasized the EQ changes made previously. Close the Multiband Compressor effect window but keep this file open for the next lesson.

Ambience

Although reverb is seldom added during mastering, the music seems a little lifeless. To give the illusion of the music being played in an acoustic space, you'll add some ambience.

1   In the Effects Rack, click insert 2's right arrow and choose Reverb > Studio Reverb.

2   If the music is still playing, you'll need to stop playback to choose a preset. Choose the Room Ambience 1 preset from the Presets menu. After choosing the preset, click the Transport Play button.

3   Set the Dry slider to 0 and the Wet slider to 40% so it's easy to hear the results of any edits.

4   Set Decay to 500 ms, Early Reflections to 20%, Width to 100, High Frequency Cut to 6000 Hz, Low Frequency Cut to 100 Hz, and both Damping and Diffusion to 100%.

5   Adjust the blend of Dry and Wet signals. Set Dry to 90% and Wet to 50%.

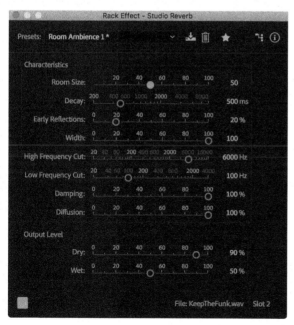

Tip: With albums that contain tracks recorded at different times or in different studios, sometimes adding a subtle overall ambience produces a more cohesive sound.

Note: The Studio Reverb trades off sound quality for real-time adjustment. For critical applications, one of the other reverbs is preferable, but for learning how reverb affects the sound, the Studio Reverb is a better choice due to its immediacy in changing settings.

Tip: Remember you can always click and type anywhere you see blue numbers, if you know exactly the number you want. Otherwise, drag on those numbers to update the setting gradually.

6   Toggle the Reverb's Power button; you won't hear much difference unless you listen very carefully, because this adds just a tiny bit of spice. The added ambience is most noticeable when the drums hit by themselves. To hear more ambience, increase the Wet slider value. Close the Studio Reverb effect window, but keep this file open for the next exercise.

Stereo imaging

Stereo imaging stretches the stereo image so the left channel moves more to the left, and the right channel moves more to the right. In this exercise, increasing the stereo image helps separate the two guitars in the opposite channels even more.

1   In the Effects Rack, click insert 3's right arrow and choose Special > Mastering. Only the Widener will be used.

2   To clear any previous adjustments, choose the Default preset from the Presets menu.

3   Set the Widener slider to 85%.

4   Toggle the Effects Rack's Power button to compare the sound with and without the various mastering processors; the results speak for themselves. Also, try turning the Power button on and off for the individual processors to hear each processor's overall contribution to the sound.

5   Often during the mastering process, one processor will change the effect of another, requiring a readjustment. In this case, the compression has perhaps overemphasized the brightness. Open the Parametric Equalizer interface, and turn off Band 4 to hear if you like the result better.

Close any open effect windows before starting the next exercise.

Push the drum hits; then apply the changes

You can make edits to the waveform before, during, or after adding effects. There are four drum hits at the end of the music. Boosting them just a bit gives them more emphasis. To do so, first change the time display.

1 Right-click the time display at the bottom-left corner of the Editor panel.

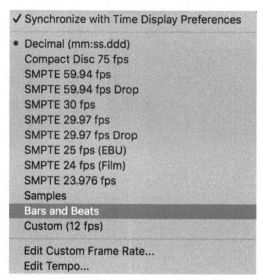

You can choose from a range of time display options. If you were working on a film soundtrack, you would normally choose a frame rate that matches the film project to make it easier to sync with the visuals. For now, choose Bars And Beats.

2 Starting at 24:3.08, there are four drum hits that could be a little louder. Select the four hits (zoom in if necessary) and add +3.9 dB of gain with the HUD (heads-up display).

3 Play the file to hear the result of boosting these four drum hits.

In addition to previewing effects by adding them to the Effects Rack, Audition allows you to see a preview of the waveform and spectral frequency displays at any time. The preview shows the results of any effects that have not yet been applied.

4 Click the Show Preview Editor button 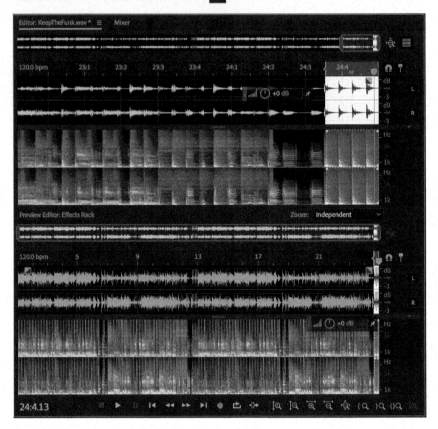.

The Editor panel now shows both the original and modified versions of the audio.

Some of the effects you applied earlier automatically enabled the Preview Editor, but you can toggle the display at any time. It takes a moment to draw the preview, so you will generally want to keep the preview display turned off.

Now you'll apply all the effects in the Effects Rack to make them a permanent part of the file, which will also redraw the waveform to show the changes caused by mastering.

5 Turn off the Preview Editor, and in the Effects Rack, make sure Entire File is chosen from the Process menu.

6 Click Apply in the Effects Rack. Audition applies the result of all the effects to the file and removes the effects from the Effects Rack.

Note: When you click Apply in the Effects Rack, all effects are reset to their default value. If you change your mind, choose Edit > Undo to restore the effects and the settings you adjusted.

Note: It can take years to become good at the art and science of mastering, especially if a file has problems that need to be fixed. Nonetheless, most mastering simply involves EQ, dynamics, and some other selected effects.

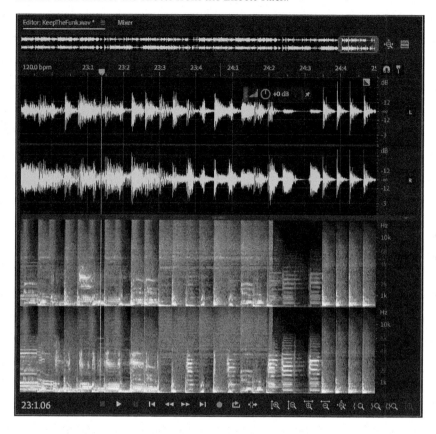

7 Choose File > Close All, and then click No To All when asked if you would like to save.

Mastering diagnostics

Although it's best to listen with your ears, not your eyes, diagnostic tools and metering can tell you much about an audio file's characteristics. Audition's diagnostic tools are quite advanced and intended more for professional broadcast and similar uses, but some are applicable even to basic projects.

Checking phase

Chapter 17, "Mixing and Output," covers the importance of having your monitor speakers in phase—in other words, if the same signal is applied to both speakers, both speaker cones move outward or inward in sync. If one cone moves in one direction and the other moves in the opposite direction when fed the same signal, the speakers are *out of phase.*

When the speakers are out of phase, one produces low pressure just as the other produces high pressure, and the result can be a dead spot in the room where very little audio can be heard.

Out-of-phase conditions can also occur in audio files. Audition can detect and fix this condition.

1 If you are not already in the Mastering And Analysis workspace, choose it now. Then choose Window > Workspace > Reset To Saved Layout to reset the workspace.

2 Choose File > Open, navigate to the Lesson06 folder, and open the file EthnoWorld5_phase.wav. (This file was created using the Best Service Ethno World 5 sound library.)

3 Click the Phase Analysis panel name (in the same frame as the Amplitude Statistics panel at the lower right) to display it, and then play the file.

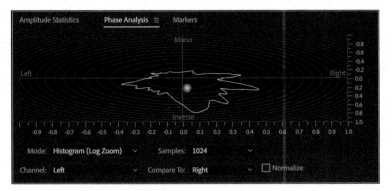

Observe the Phase Analysis panel as well as the Phase Meter to the right of the Levels meter. You may need to resize some of the panels to see the waveform, Phase Meter, and Phase Analysis panel simultaneously.

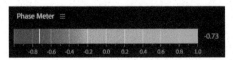

4 If the Phase Meter needle (the vertical white line) goes to the left of 0 or the Phase Analysis ball drops below the centerline and turns red, that means that one of the channels is out of phase with respect to the other. This is not desirable, because it produces a thin sound due to the cancellations occurring between the two channels.

5 Click the waveform and press Ctrl+A (Windows) or Command+A (macOS) to select all of it, or click the waveform to deselect all of it; either option will ensure your next change is applied to the whole file.

6 Press the Down Arrow key to select only the right channel. Then choose Effects > Invert to invert the right channel's phase.

7 Press the Up Arrow key so that both channels are selected, and start playback. Note that the Phase Meter needle now moves closer to the right, the Phase Analysis ball is now green and above the centerline, and the sound is much fuller.

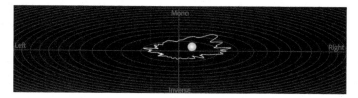

8 To compare the in-phase and out-of-phase sounds, choose Edit > Undo Invert. The sound is thinner, and the phase meters indicate the out-of-phase condition. Now choose Edit > Redo Invert; the channels are no longer out of phase, and the sound is fuller.

Amplitude statistics

Audition can analyze your file to provide statistics for amplitude, clipping, DC offset, and other characteristics.

1 If the entire waveform isn't already selected, press Ctrl+A (Windows) or Command+A (macOS) to select it.

2 Click the Amplitude Statistics panel name, and then click Scan Selection.

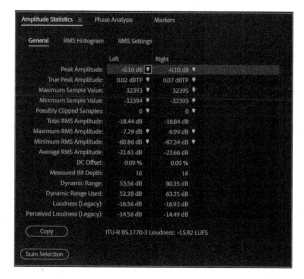

Note: Total RMS Amplitude is another useful statistic, because it represents a file's overall loudness. If two files have very different Total RMS Amplitude statistics, one will probably sound much louder than the other.

3 The Amplitude Statistics panel shows peak levels, whether some samples may be clipped, average (RMS—Root Mean Square) amplitude, DC offset, and other statistics. Here's one example of how these statistics can be useful: Note that there's a little DC offset in the left channel, which reduces the available amount of headroom. Choose Favorites > Repair DC Offset, and then click Scan Selection again. The left channel no longer has any DC offset.

4 Keep this file open for the next lesson.

Frequency analysis

The Frequency Analysis panel shows which frequencies are most prominent in an audio file or selection. You can freeze the frequency analysis graph at specific times during file playback for review and comparison.

Frequency analysis can help show if there are "rogue" peaks, excessive bass or treble, and the like.

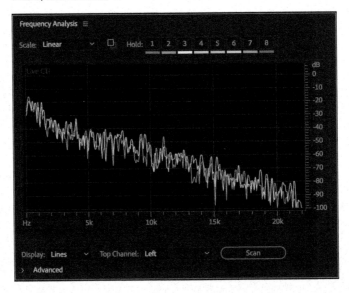

1 If necessary, resize the Frequency Analysis panel to see the entire graph.

2 Choose Logarithmic from the Scale menu, because this most closely approximates the way the human ear responds to frequencies.

3 Start playback, and you'll see the amplitude of various frequencies change as the file plays. To "freeze" (hold) the response at a specific part of the file, click one of the eight Hold buttons. Each held response will have a different color.

4 Choose File > Close All, and then select No To All when you are asked if you would like to save.

Loudness metering

Audition incorporates a version of TC Electronic's ITU Loudness Radar, a plug-in that indicates peak and average loudness levels, as well as whether the levels conform to specific broadcast regulations. The following describes in general how to use the ITU Loudness Radar plug-in.

1 Choose Window > Workspace > Reset to Saved Layout.

2 Choose File > Open, navigate to the Lesson06 folder, and open the file EthnoWorld5.wav.

3 Click the Effects Rack tab, click insert 2's right arrow, and choose Special > Loudness Radar Meter. In the Loudness Radar window, choose CD Master from the Presets menu, and then start playback.

Note: Explaining conformance to international broadcast regulations is beyond the scope of this book, but TC maintains the Loudness Authority website at www.tcelectronic.com/loudness, which offers a wealth of information on this topic.

Tip: The default radar rotation is 4 minutes. To change this, click the Settings tab, and then choose a different Radar Speed from the menu.

4 The outer dotted ring indicates the momentary loudness, like a standard level meter. As the "radar" follows the song over time, the concentric rings farther away from the center indicate louder signals. The Loudness Range (LRA) statistic describes the overall program material range, from softest to loudest; however, to exclude extreme levels from the overall result, the top 5% and lowest 10% of the total loudness range aren't included in the LRA measurement.

Note: For more information on the ITU Loudness Radar's statistics, see the "Loudness Authority" website (www.tcelectronic.com/loudness).

5   To see how changing dynamics alters the Radar display, click the Effects Rack tab, click insert 1's right arrow, and choose Amplitude And Compression > Hard Limiter.

6   Reset the ITU Loudness Radar by clicking the Resets Measurement button toward the window's upper right.

7   Start playback, and move the Hard Limiter's Input Boost control to around +6 dB. Note how most of the signal now hits the outer concentric band, and the Peak indicator lights up occasionally. Stop playback.

8   Select the audio file in the Files panel and press Backspace/Delete to close it. Click No when asked if you would like to save changes.

Review questions

1 At what stage of the production process does mastering occur?

2 Does mastering exclusively involve optimizing individual tracks?

3 What are the most essential processors used in mastering?

4 Is adding ambience recommended when mastering?

5 What is the main disadvantage of excessive dynamics compression?

Review answers

1 Mastering occurs after mixing but before distribution.

2 With album projects, mastering also sequences the songs in the correct order and aims for sonic consistency from track to track. For film and television mixing, it may include arranging multiple versions of a mix for international distribution.

3 Typically, EQ and dynamics processors are the main effects used in the mastering process.

4 No. Normally, ambience is added during the mixing process but can sometimes improve the sound when added while mastering.

5 The main disadvantage is a lack of dynamics, which can lead to listener fatigue because there are no significant variations between loud and soft passages.

7 SOUND DESIGN

Lesson overview

In this lesson, you'll learn how to do the following:

- Apply extreme processing to everyday sounds
- Create special effects
- Change the environments in which sounds occur
- Use pitch shifting and filtering to alter sounds
- Use the Doppler Shifter effect to add motion

 This lesson will take about 45 minutes to complete. Please log in to your account on peachpit.com to download the lesson files for this chapter, or go to the "Getting Started" section at the beginning of this book and follow the instructions under "Accessing the Lesson Files and Web Edition." Store the files on your computer in a convenient location.

Your Account page is also where you'll find any updates to the chapters or to the lesson files. Look on the Lesson & Update Files tab to access the most current content.

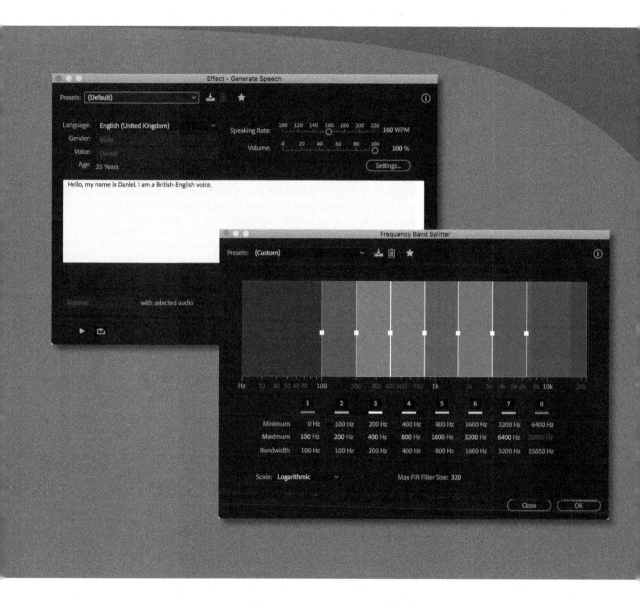

With an array of effects built into Audition, it's possible to modify common, everyday sounds into something completely different—like transforming a wall fan into a spaceship's engine room or a running faucet into crickets at night.

About sound design

● **Note:** If you have not already downloaded the project files for this lesson to your computer from your Account page, make sure to do so now. See "Getting Started" at the beginning of the book.

Sound design is the process of capturing, recording, and/or manipulating the audio elements used in movies, television, video games, museum installations, theater, post-production, and other art forms that require sound. Sound design can refer to music, but this chapter emphasizes sound effects and ambience. These types of sounds are common in sonic logos (such as the MGM lion roar) or the atmospheric sounds used in movie scenes to create a mood.

No one was swimming alongside or crushing actual submarines in *The Hunt for Red October* or *Das Boot*; it was up to the sound designers to create the atmosphere of high pressure in deep water and creaking metal.

Sound effects libraries are available from several companies, but sound designers often modify these or record their own sounds using a field recorder. For example, early in *Raiders of the Lost Ark*, a giant stone ball chases Indiana Jones. The rumble of the rolling boulder was created by recording a Honda Civic backing over gravel. Subsequent sound design work turned this into a huge, ominous sound. Similarly, sound designers modified an elephant cry to create the sound for TIE fighters diving to attack in *Star Wars*.

Although the results may not be quite as iconic, in this lesson, you'll learn how to turn two ordinary sounds into a variety of sound effects and ambience. The two files you'll be using—a wall fan and water running into a sink from a faucet—were recorded using a portable digital recorder.

Generate noise, speech, and tones

Audition provides excellent audio editing and processing tools, but it can also generate original audio files. The newly created audio can be simple tones, noise, or full speech, which can be useful when creating temporary voice-over or in the early stages of producing an audio mix for film or television.

Generate Noise

Audition can generate full spectrum noise, which covers the full range of frequencies. You can then use the noise as a mask for other low-level sounds or, perhaps, to fill out a soundtrack for a film.

You can create four noise types, each distinguished by having different emphasis on particular frequencies:

- **White Noise:** This has equal proportions of all frequencies. Because human hearing is more sensitive to high frequencies, white noise sounds hissy.

- **Grey Noise:** This is psychoacoustically designed to sound the way humans expect white noise to sound. The emphasis on different frequencies compensates for the varying sensitivity of human hearing. It's educational to try out this option in Audition just to see the graph indicating human perception.

- **Brown Noise:** This type of noise has more low-frequency content than White or Grey noise. Its sounds are thunder- and waterfall-like. The name comes from the Brownian motion curve used to calculate it.

- **Pink Noise:** The most natural sounding of the noises. By applying an equalizer effect to the sound, you can generate rainfall, waterfalls, wind, rushing river, and other natural sounds. Because pink noise is between brown and white noise, it is sometimes described as *tan noise*.

To begin, try generating some white noise.

1   Choose the Default workspace, and then choose Window > Workspace > Reset To Saved Layout.

2   Choose Effects > Generate > Noise.

3   New audio needs to be stored in a file, so the New Audio File dialog box opens. Choose a sample rate of 48000 Hz, Stereo channels, and a Bit Depth of 16 (the most common settings for film and television soundtracks). Provide a File Name, and click OK.

● **Note:** If you have an existing audio file open, newly generated noise will be inserted into the audio. If you make a selection, the noise will replace the selected duration.

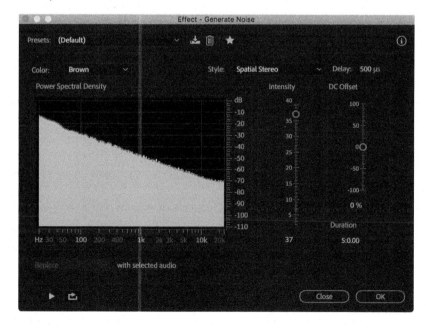

4   Sample the different options on the Color menu by choosing a color and clicking the Preview Play button ▶ .

5 Choose White from the Color menu.

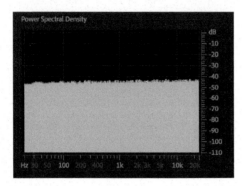

6 Set the duration to 5 seconds. You can click the duration number and simply enter a 5, then click away to let Audition add the zeros and punctuation.

Note that the Style menu allows you to choose Spatial Stereo, Independent Channels (for which each channel is calculated separately), Mono, and Inverse, for which the two channels created are identical but inverted, resulting in sound that, when listened to with headphones, seems to come from inside your head.

7 Click OK.

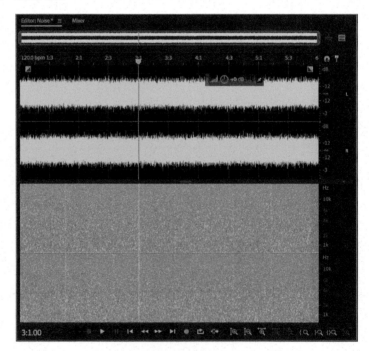

The result is particularly striking if you enable the Spectral Frequency Display. White noise covers the entire frequency spectrum with evenly distributed random noise.

Generate tones

Audition can generate a full range of tones with up to five frequency components that combine to produce potentially complex sounds.

1 Click the New File menu button in the Files panel, and choose New Audio File.

2 Choose a sample rate of 48000 Hz, Stereo channels, and 16 for Bit Depth. The name isn't important for this exercise, so now click OK.

3 Choose Effects > Generate > Tones.

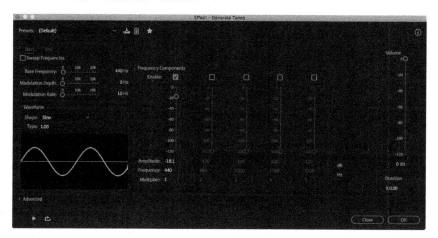

4 With Default chosen from the Presets menu, press the spacebar to play the sound.

The various components of the tone are calculated from the Base Frequency setting. By default, this is 440 Hz or standard Concert Pitch (for A above middle C). As you can see in the Frequency Components area, the first enabled frequency is 440 Hz, with an amplitude of –18.1 dB.

5 Choose the Major Chord preset.

Now most of the frequency components are enabled. Each Multiplier setting multiplies the Base Frequency for the frequency component, creating an overtone.

You can also select the Sweep Frequencies option to produce a sound that ranges between two frequencies.

6 For now, check that the Duration (at the lower right) is set to 5 seconds, and click OK.

7 Play the file to check the result.

8 Close the file, and choose No when asked if you would like to save.

Generate speech

Perhaps one of the most useful functions in Audition for filmmakers is the option to create speech based on text. This is helpful if you're waiting for a professionally recorded voice over, but need something to use temporarily to estimate timing and levels in a mix. This feature is also useful when creating audio assets to give an editor, because they can use the generated speech to time the edit.

1 Choose File > Close All, and choose No To All when asked if you would like to save.

2 Choose Effects > Generate > Speech.

3 The New Audio File dialog box opens. Choose a Sample Rate of 48000 Hz, Mono from the Channels menu, and 16 for Bit Depth. The name isn't important for this exercise so click OK.

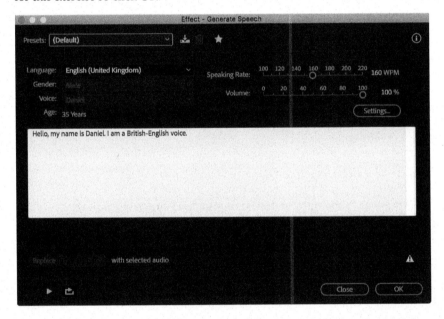

Audition uses the voice libraries available in your operating system, and they vary depending on whether you are working on a Windows or macOS system. Both operating systems give you the option to add voices. By default, macOS includes more voices than Windows.

4 The Presets menu allows you to choose among available voices. Choose a voice.

5 Add any text to the text entry box. If you have text already in a document, you can paste it here.

6 Click the Preview Play button ▶ at the bottom left of the Generate Speech dialog box.

7 Stop the playback, and try a new voice. Slow the speaking rate down to hear the difference.

8 Once you're happy with the speech, click OK.

9 Close the file, and choose No when asked if you would like to save.

Note: The Settings button takes you to the Speech settings in your operating system.

Creating rain sounds

With sound design, it helps to start with a sound in the same genre. To create rain, for instance, the running water audio file will most likely produce a better end result than the recording of the fan.

1 Choose File > Open, navigate to the Lesson07 folder, and open the file RunningWater.wav.

2 Make sure the Transport Loop Playback button is selected so the water sound plays continuously. Click the Transport Play button to preview the loop.

   You'll first change this sound to a light, spring rain.

3 Resize the Effects Rack panel to allow you to see more of the effect inserts.

4 Click Effects Rack insert 1's right arrow button, and choose Filter And EQ > Graphic Equalizer (10 Bands). Ensure that Range is 48 dB and Master Gain is 0.

5 Pull the sliders for all bands other than 4k and 8k all the way down to –24 dB.

6 Bring the 4k and 8k sliders down to –10 dB.

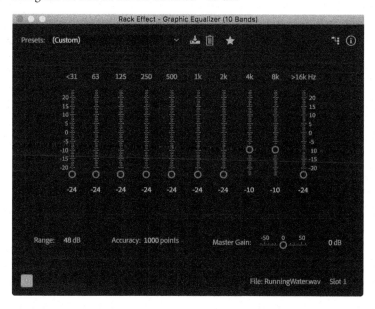

7   Toggle the effect's power state on and off a few times to compare how the EQ has changed the overall sound. With the EQ power on, you now have a light spring rain. You might find the effect more realistic if you bring the 8k slider down to −15 dB.

8   Suppose you were designing sound for a scene in which the character is inside a house while it's raining. In this case, there would be fewer high frequencies because of the house's walls and windows blocking the highs. Pull the 8k slider down all the way, and the rain sounds more like it's outside.

9   Next, the script calls for the character to leave the house and stand in the middle of the rain. To surround the character with rain, click insert 2's right arrow button and choose Delay And Echo > Delay.

10 The Default patch spreads out the sound, but it's too separated: Rain wouldn't fall only to the character's right and left, but all around. Change both Mix controls to 50%, so there's a convincing panorama of rain.

11 To sound more natural, it's important that the delay not create any kind of rhythm. Set the Left Channel Delay Time to around 420 ms and the Right Channel Delay Time to 500 ms. These delays are long enough that you won't perceive a rhythm.

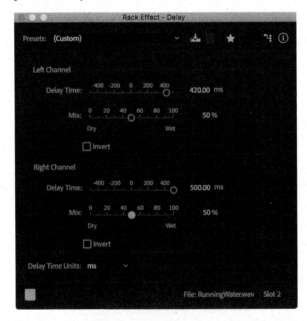

12 If the character then goes inside again, return to the Graphic Equalizer window by double-clicking its insert in the Effects Rack and increase the 8k slider to around −14 kHz. Keep this file open as you move on to the next exercise.

Creating a babbling brook

Changing the sound from rain to a babbling brook in the distance simply involves removing the delay and changing the EQ setting.

1 Click the Delay insert's arrow, and choose Remove Effect. A babbling brook has a more distinct sound than sheets of rain, so you don't need the additional "raindrops" created by the Delay.

2 Click the Graphic Equalizer's window to select it. Set the Range to 120 dB and make sure the Master Gain is 0 dB.

3 Set the Graphic Equalizer sliders. Move the <31, 63, 8k, and >16k sliders all to –60dB. Set the 125 and 250 sliders to 0. Move the 500 slider to –10 and the 1k slider to –20. Finally, slide 2k to –30, and lower 4k to –40.

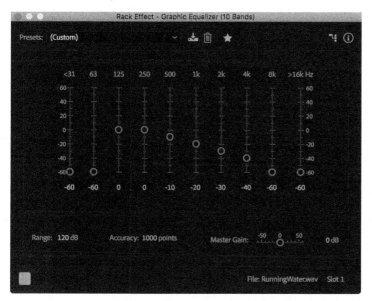

4 The babbling brook is now in the distance. As the character walks closer to the brook, increase the 2k slider to –20 and the 4k setting to –30. Now the brook sounds closer. Keep this file open as you move on to the next exercise.

Creating insects at night

You can even use running water to create the sound of nighttime insects and crickets. This exercise demonstrates how signal processing can turn one sound into something completely different.

1 Double-click in the Waveform Editor to select the entire waveform.

2 Choose Effects > Time and Pitch > Stretch and Pitch (process).

3 In the Stretch and Pitch window, choose the Default preset if it is not already chosen.

4 Move the Pitch Shift slider all the way to the left (−36 semitones), and then click Apply. It will take several seconds to process the effect.

▶ **Tip:** Extreme pitch shifting can add such anomalies as volume spikes or clicks at the file's beginning and end. If this happens, make an audio selection that excludes the first and last two seconds, and then choose Edit > Crop. Extreme shifting may also lower the volume, so you might want to increase the Effects Rack's Output value.

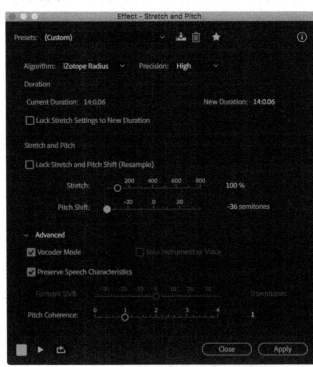

5 Click the Graphic Equalizer window to select it. With Range still at 120 dB, set the 4k slider to 10 dB and move the rest to −60 dB. Close the Graphic Equalizer window, and click the Transport Play button to hear the processed sound.

6 You can smooth out the sound and make the insects seem a little more distant by adding reverb. In the Effects Rack's insert 2, click the right arrow button and choose Reverb > Studio Reverb. Stop playback by clicking the Transport Stop button, so you can choose a reverb preset.

7 Open the Presets menu, and choose Great Hall.

8 Click the Transport Play button, and listen to your refined insects-at-night sound.

9 Close the Studio Reverb dialog box.

Creating an alien choir

For the last effect using the running water file, you'll create a totally abstract sound that's ethereal and quite evocative.

1 If the entire waveform isn't already selected, double-click in the Waveform Editor.

2 Choose Effects > Time and Pitch > Stretch and Pitch (process). The settings should be the same as they were previously, but if not, choose the Default preset.

3 If necessary, move the Pitch Shift slider all the way to the left (−36 semitones). Click Apply. Processing will take several seconds.

4 To remove distracting noises at the start and end, make an audio selection that excludes the first two seconds, and last two seconds, and then choose Edit > Crop.

5 The level will be very low, so bring it up. With the waveform still selected, choose Effects > Amplitude And Compression > Normalize (process).

6 Select Normalize To, and enter **50%**. Normalize All Channels Equally should also be selected. Click Apply.

7 Bypass the Graphic Equalizer. The Reverb should still have the Great Hall preset selected. Move the Decay, Width, Diffusion, and Wet sliders all the way to the right. Move the Dry slider all the way to the left. When you click the Transport Play button, you should now hear an ethereal, animated sound.

8 Now add some animation for the final touch. In an Effects Rack's insert after the Studio Reverb, click the insert's right arrow and choose Delay And Echo > Echo. Choose the preset Spooky.

9   In an Effects Rack's insert after the Echo, click the insert's right arrow and choose Modulation > Chorus. Choose the preset 10 Voices. You may need to turn down the Effects Rack's Output control to avoid clipping. Now extensive pitch stretching coupled with effects from the Studio Reverb, Echo, and Chorus has turned running water into an alien soundscape.

An example of the finished result of all these steps is included in the Lesson07 folder, with the filename RunningWater-finished_version.wav.

Creating sci-fi machine effects

Just as you used running water to generate water-based effects, the fan sound makes a good basis for machine and mechanical sounds. This exercise describes how to turn an ordinary wall fan sound into a variety of science-fiction, spaceship sound effects.

1   If you have any files open, choose File > Close All. Choose File > Open, navigate to the Lesson07 folder, and open the file Fan.wav. Click the Transport Play button to hear what the file sounds like.

2   Double-click inside the Waveform Editor to select the entire waveform.

3   Choose Effects > Time and Pitch > Stretch and Pitch (process).

4   Select the preset Default if it is not already selected.

5   Set the Pitch Shift slider to −24 semitones. Lowering the pitch makes the engine sound bigger, but lowering beyond −24 semitones makes the sound indistinct. Click Apply; processing will take a few seconds.

6   As in the previous exercises, for the smoothest sound, make an audio selection that excludes the first second and last second, and then choose Edit > Crop or press Ctrl+T (Windows) or Command+T (macOS).

7   In the Effects Rack, click insert 1's right arrow button and choose Special > Guitar Suite. From the Presets menu, choose Drum Suite. Click the Transport Play button, and note how the sound becomes more metallic and machine-like.

8   Click insert 2's right arrow button, and choose Filter And EQ > Parametric Equalizer. If the preset Default is not already selected, choose it from the Presets menu. Set the Range option to 96 dB.

9 Deselect bands 1 to 5, leaving only the L (low) and H (high) bands active.

10 Click the Q/Width buttons ![icon] for both the L and H bands to select the steepest slope (the button's center line is almost vertical).

11 If the file isn't already playing, click the Transport Play button. Pull the H control point all the way down and left to around 3 kHz.

12 Pull the L control point up to 20 and right to about 3000 Hz.

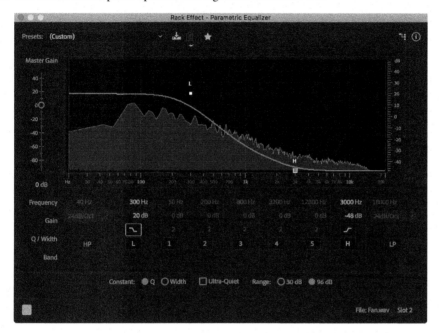

13 Add some character to the engine with a resonant peak that increases the level in a narrow band of frequencies. Click the Band 2 button to enable that parametric stage. Edit the Frequency to 500 Hz, Gain to 10 dB, and Q/Width to around 20. The Guitar Suite and Parametric EQ effects provide the main engine sound.

14 Suppose another scene is set in a different section of the spaceship, away from the main hum of the machine room but where characters can still hear the engine rumble. In the Effects Rack, click insert 3's right arrow button, and choose Reverb > Studio Reverb.

15 Click the Transport Stop button to change the Studio Reverb preset, and then choose Great Hall from the Presets menu.

16 Next, add lots of reverb but only to the low frequencies to emphasize the rumble: Set the Decay, Width, Diffusion, and Wet sliders all the way to the right. Set the High Frequency Cut slider to 200 Hz, the Low Frequency Cut slider full left, and the Dry slider full left. Click the Transport Play button.

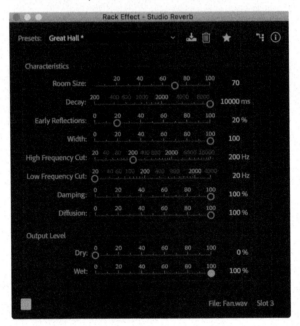

17 Bypass the Studio Reverb to return to the engine room sound, or enable it to move farther away to a different part of the ship. Leave this file open in preparation for the next lesson.

Creating an alien drone flyby

In addition to creating static sound effects, Audition includes a Doppler Shifter processor that imparts motion: from left to right, around in circles, tracing an arc, and so on. In this exercise, you'll take advantage of the Doppler Shifter processor to "animate" the sound of an alien drone.

1 If the waveform isn't already selected, double-click within the Waveform Editor to select the entire waveform.

2 Choose Effects > Time and Pitch > Stretch and Pitch (process).

3 Choose the preset Default from the Presets menu. Set the Stretch slider to 200%. Click Apply; processing will take a few seconds.

4   Either bypass the Parametric Equalizer effect, or click its insert's arrow and choose Remove Effect.

5   Either bypass the Studio Reverb effect, or click its insert's arrow and choose Remove Effect.

6   If the Guitar Suite window isn't open already, double-click its insert in the Effects Rack. Choose Lowest Fidelity from the Presets menu.

7   With the entire waveform still selected, choose Effects > Special > Doppler Shifter (process).

8   Choose the preset Whizzing By Left To Right from the Doppler Shifter's Presets drop-down menu, and then click Apply. Move the playhead to the beginning, and then click the Transport Play button to hear the drone fly by from left to right.

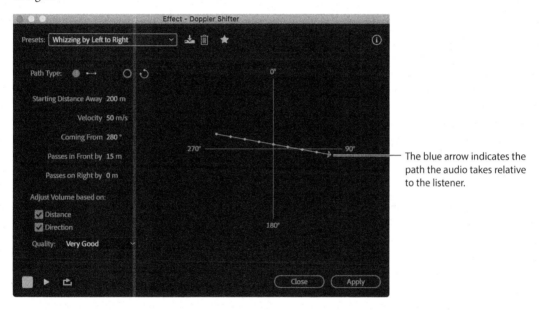

The blue arrow indicates the path the audio takes relative to the listener.

9   Because the sound is most effective if it fades up from nothing and fades out to nothing, in the Waveform Editor click the Fade In button in the upper-left corner, and drag it to the right about two seconds.

10 Similarly, click the Fade Out button in the Waveform Editor's upper right, and drag it left to about the 8-second mark.

11 To enhance the Doppler Shifter effect, click an Effects Rack insert's right arrow and choose Modulation > Flanger.

12 In the Flanger window, choose Heavy Flange from the Presets menu.

13 Click the Modulation Rate parameter, type **0.1**, and then press Enter (Return). Using the slider would make it almost impossible to choose this precise value.

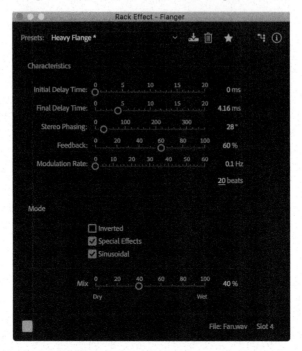

14 Click the Transport Play button, and the alien drone will sound even more realistic as it flies by from left to right.

15 Close Audition without saving anything to start fresh.

Extracting frequency bands

The Frequency Band Splitter can divide a file into different frequency bands and then extract each band to its own file. This has multiple uses with sound design, but also makes multiband processing possible. For example, you can split a guitar signal into three separate frequency bands, transfer them over to the Multitrack Editor, and then process each band individually.

1 Open Audition. Choose File > Open, navigate to the Lesson07 folder, and open the file DeepTechHouse.wav.

2 Either choose Edit > Frequency Band Splitter, or right-click within the waveform and choose Frequency Band Splitter from the menu.

3 Choose Default from the Presets menu, and then click buttons 2 to 8 to enable all eight bands.

4   Each band is represented by a color. Click the red bar, and drag left to 100. This sets the lowest band's range to cover 0 to 100 Hz (in this and subsequent steps, these frequencies don't need to be too precise, although you can always click and type the numbers for speed).

5   Similarly, drag the orange bar to 200 Hz, the yellow bar to 400 Hz, the bright green bar to 800 Hz, the dark green bar to 1600 Hz, the bright blue bar to 3200 Hz, and the dark blue bar to 6400 Hz. The top band automatically covers the range from the highest frequency of the previous band to the highest available frequency (22050 Hz).

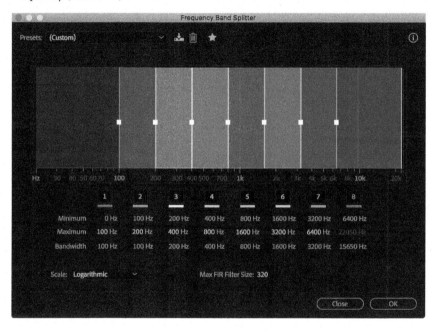

6   Click OK. It will take a few seconds for the splitter to extract each band to its own file. Each new file is added to the Files panel.

7 Click the Waveform Editor panel menu, and you'll see each frequency band. The name includes the frequency range. Select various bands to hear what the different frequency bands sound like.

8 Choose the original DeepTechHouse.wav file from the Editor panel menu to open it, and then choose Edit > Frequency Band Splitter.

9 Choose 5-Band Broadcast from the Presets menu. You don't have to extract all bands; click the Band 3 button to disable that band from extraction. The highest band cannot be disabled, and if you disable the second highest band, it merges with the highest band.

10 To add additional bands, click the highest number band button. Click the Band 5 button and a sixth band becomes available.

11 Close Audition without saving anything.

Review questions

1 What is sound design?

2 What effects can provide spatial placement within Audition?

3 What artifacts can extreme pitch shifting add?

4 Is the Guitar Suite useful only for guitar effects?

5 Do you need to use commercial sound libraries to create sound effects?

6 How might you use speech generated in Audition?

Review answers

1 Sound design is the process of capturing, recording, and/or manipulating the audio elements used in movies, television, video games, museum installations, theater, postproduction, and other art forms that require sound.

2 EQ, Reverb, Delay/Echo, and the Doppler Shifter can all contribute to placing a sound in the stereo or surround field.

3 Extreme pitch shifting may cause unpredictable amplitude spikes at the beginning and/or end of the file, as well as lower the file's overall level.

4 The Guitar Suite offers huge possibilities for sound design; this lesson has tapped only a bit of its potential. You can add richness to and texture to instruments, and even apply interesting vocal effects.

5 Not always. Because of Audition's rich selection of signal processors, ordinary sounds can be transformed into entirely different sounds.

6 You can use generated speech both as an original source for creative sound design and as a temporary media asset when timing an audio mix for film or television.

8 CREATING AND RECORDING FILES

Lesson overview

In this lesson, you'll learn how to do the following:

- Record into the Waveform Editor

- Record into the Multitrack Editor

- Drag files into the Multitrack Editor

- Import tracks from audio CDs into the Waveform Editor

 This lesson will take about 30 minutes to complete. Please log in to your account on peachpit.com to download the lesson files for this chapter, or go to the "Getting Started" section at the beginning of this book and follow the instructions under "Accessing the Lesson Files and Web Edition." Store the files on your computer in a convenient location.

Your Account page is also where you'll find any updates to the chapters or to the lesson files. Look on the Lesson & Update Files tab to access the most current content.

Not only can you record audio into the Waveform Editor or Multitrack Editor, you can also extract audio from standard Red Book Compact Discs or drag files from the desktop directly into either Audition Editor.

Recording into the Waveform Editor

Note: If you have not already downloaded the project files for this lesson to your computer from your Account page, make sure to do so now. See "Getting Started" at the beginning of the book.

Chapter 1 covered audio interfaces and how to map the interface's physical inputs and outputs to the virtual inputs and outputs in Audition. This chapter covers how to record and import audio into Audition, as well as how to extract audio from CDs. If necessary, review Chapter 1 to make sure you understand the principles behind interfacing. This chapter assumes you know how to map inputs and outputs.

In the first exercise, you'll record audio into the Waveform Editor. Before you begin recording, however, you need to set up the parameters of the audio file that you will capture. The settings you choose will be dictated by the way the audio file will be used:

Sample rate:

Note: You will need a standard audio CD and a CD drive to perform one of the exercises in this chapter.

- **44100 Hz** is the same rate used for CDs and is the most "universal" sample rate for audio.

- **48000 Hz** is the standard choice for video projects.

- **32000 Hz** is common in broadcast and satellite transmissions.

- **22050 Hz** was a popular choice for games and low-resolution digital audio. Sample rates lower than 22050 Hz are of very low fidelity and are generally used for speech, dictation, toys, and so on.

- **Sample rates above 48000 Hz** are becoming more common, as some studios record at 88200 or 96000 Hz to gain potentially improved sound quality or for high-fidelity archiving. However, most studies show that few people can consistently tell the difference between 44100 or 48000 Hz and higher sample rates. Higher sample rates also require more storage space; for example, a one-minute 96000 Hz file will require twice the space as the same file at 48000 Hz.

Bit depth:

The higher the bit depth, the more steps between silence and full volume for every sample that is recorded. The two settings combine to set the overall quality.

Like the sample rate, increasing the bit depth improves audio quality at the cost of processing time and storage space.

Note: The optimum input level should never go into the red on a level meter. Today's digital recording technology records so cleanly that it's safe to add sufficient headroom; it's not necessary to aim for the highest levels possible. Also, once a track is recorded in Audition, you can use the Amplify or Normalize effects to bring up the level as needed.

- **8-bits** is low resolution and is not used for professional audio. It's common for games and consumer devices.

- **16-bits** is the resolution for CDs and offers industry-standard audio quality.

- **24-bits** is preferred by most recording engineers because it provides more headroom and greater dynamic range, which makes setting levels less critical. Files that are 24-bit take up 50 percent more space than 16-bit files, but given the low cost of hard disk and other forms of storage, this is an acceptable trade-off.

- **32 (float)** results in the highest resolution, but aside from archiving, offers no significant advantage over 24-bit files. Many programs are not compatible with 32-bit float files, and they also take up even more space.

1 Connect a microphone, guitar, portable music player output, cell phone audio output, or other signal source into a compatible audio interface input or internal audio input on your computer.

2 Adjust the interface's Input level control for an appropriate signal level. The interface will have either a physical meter or dedicated control panel software that monitors the inputs and outputs, and displays signal strength. You can use the Levels panel in Audition to monitor the input level by choosing View > Metering > Meter Input Signal, or by pressing Alt+I (Windows) or Option+I (macOS).

3 Open Audition. Choose File > New > Audio File.

4 In the New Audio File dialog box, enter the File Name **RecordNarration**.

5 Audition defaults to a 48000 Hz sample rate, which is standard for video. For this exercise, however, choose 44100 Hz—the standard for CD audio—as the sample rate from the Sample Rate menu.

6 Choose the desired number of channels from the Channels menu. For a mic or electric guitar, choose Mono. For a portable music player or other stereo signal source, choose Stereo. The option 5.1 is for recording in surround sound.

7 Choose 24-bits from the Bit Depth menu and click OK to save your choices.

8 Assuming you're using an external audio interface, choose Edit > Preferences (Audition > Preferences) > Audio Hardware. Verify that the correct settings are selected for Device Class, I/O Buffer Size, and Sample Rate. For Windows users, also verify that the Device settings are correct. Click OK.

9 Choose the Default workspace. Then choose Window > Workspace > Reset To Saved Layout.

10 Click the red Transport Record button. Recording begins immediately. Speak into the mic or play whatever sound source connects to your interface. You'll see the waveform being drawn in the Waveform Editor in real time, and the meters will reflect the current input signal level.

11 Click the Transport Pause button. Notice that recording pauses, but the meters still show the incoming signal level.

12 To resume recording, click the Pause button or Record button.

13 Click the Stop button to stop recording. The waveform you recorded will be selected.

Tip: Being able to record over previously recorded material can speed up the recording of narration. If you make a mistake in a particular line, click at the beginning of the line and re-record it.

14 Click somewhere in the middle of the Waveform Editor (where you've already recorded something), and then click the Record button to record over the previously recorded material.

15 Record for a few seconds, and click Stop. The audio between where you started and stopped recording will be selected.

16 Leave Audition open and your signal source and interface set up, ready for the next exercise.

Recording into the Multitrack Editor

Tip: It's good practice to have a separate, high-speed drive with a dedicated folder for storing your projects. This separates streaming audio on the audio drive from program operations on your main drive. Also, backing up the audio drive backs up all of your projects.

Audition not only integrates the Waveform Editor and Multitrack Editor, but can transfer files easily between the two. This exercise shows you how to record into the Multitrack Editor, explains how to transfer your recording into the Waveform Editor for editing, and then describes how to return it to the Multitrack Editor.

1 Choose File > New > Multitrack Session.

The New Multitrack Session dialog box appears with fields for an editable Session Name and a Folder Location for storing the new session file, as well as a project Template menu. The dialog box also includes Sample Rate and Bit Depth menus identical to those in the New Audio File dialog box, and a Master menu that lets you choose whether the output is Mono, Stereo, or a surround format (if supported by your interface).

2 Enter the Session Name **MultitrackRecording**.

3 The default folder location for saving projects is your User Documents folder (Windows or macOS). For this exercise, click the Browse button and browse to the Lessons folder. Click Choose to accept the folder location.

Note: Sample Rate, Bit Depth, and the Master output are stored with the template, so once you've chosen a template, these options are dimmed. If you want to edit these settings, select None for Template.

4 Choose the 24 Track Music Session template.

5 Click OK. The Multitrack Editor opens.

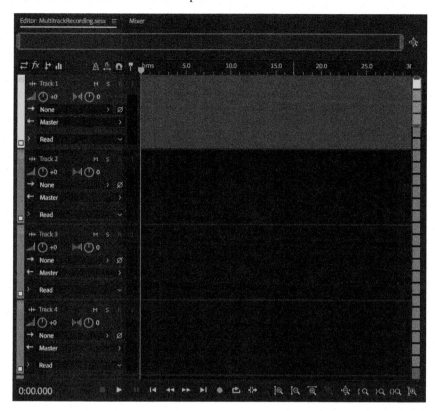

At the top left of the Multitrack Editor panel, there are four buttons for selecting the track header controls that will be displayed.

Inputs/
Outputs Sends

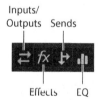

Effects   EQ

6 Click the Inputs/Outputs button, if it's not already selected. Each track has an Input menu identified by a right-pointing arrow at its left. The default is None. For Track 1, choose the interface input to which your signal source connects from the Input menu. A track can be stereo or mono.

7   As soon as you select an input, a track's R button  becomes available to Arm For Record (*arming* means the track is ready to record as soon as you click the Transport Record button). Click the R button (it turns red when armed) and talk into a mic or play your sound source; note that the track's meter indicates the incoming level.

8   Click the Transport Record button ⏺ to begin recording. Record your signal source for at least 15 to 20 seconds. As when recording in the Waveform Editor, you can pause and resume recording by clicking the Pause button. After you've finished recording, click the Transport Stop button.

Notice the label in the upper left corner of the recorded segment: **Track 1_001**.

9   Place the playhead around five seconds into the file.

10 Click the Transport Record button, and record for about five seconds or so, and then click Stop.

11 Click the track where you just recorded (between the 5- and 10-second mark). Notice that the newly recorded material is superimposed in front of the original recording in the same track. The new snippet is labeled **Track 1_002**. You can drag it left or right, or even drag it into another track, such as Track 2.

Switching editors

Audition makes it easy to transfer files back and forth between the Multitrack Editor and Waveform Editor. To open a Multitrack Editor audio file in the Waveform Editor, double-click the clip in the Multitrack Editor or right-click it and choose Edit Source File.

To transfer the file back into the Multitrack Editor at the position from which it came, click the Multitrack button or press 0. To transfer it elsewhere in the Session, or even to a different Session, right-click in the Waveform Editor and choose Insert Into Multitrack > [name of Multitrack Session]. The file will start at the Multitrack Editor's playhead position and be inserted into the first available track where no audio is recorded at the playhead position.

12 Click each of the newly recorded audio files in the Files panel, and press Backspace/Delete to them.

When the warning appears letting you know that you are removing audio files that are used in a multitrack session, choose Yes to remove them anyway.

Notice that the recordings remain in the multitrack session but they have turned gray—they are now *offline*, with no audio media files associated with them.

13 Select and delete the offline audio clips in the multitrack session, and click the R button to disarm recording on Track 1.

14 Click the Transport's Move Playhead To Previous button.

Checking remaining free space

Audition can update a readout of the amount of remaining space on your hard drive for recording, as well as the estimated remaining time in track-minutes. For instance, eight minutes of free time would allow you to record one eight-minute track, eight one-minute tracks, four two-minute tracks, and so on. This is very helpful, because you don't want to run out of recording time during an important session. Here's how to display this data.

1 Right-click the Status Bar strip at the very bottom of the Audition window.

2 Choose Free Space, Free Space (Time), or both.

3 The statistics appear in the Status Bar's lower right: for example, 89.95 GB free, and/or the amount free given in hours, minutes, seconds, and frames, such as 151:55:12.20.

44100 Hz • 24-bit • Mono   3.47 MB   0:27.538   10.95 GB free   24:41:09.51 free

Dragging into an Audition editor

In addition to recording files into Audition or dragging files in from the Media Browser (as described in Chapter 2), you can drag files from the desktop or any open computer folder into the Waveform Editor or a Multitrack Editor track. The file can be in any file format that Audition recognizes; in the Multitrack Editor, it will automatically be converted to the multitrack session settings. For example, if you created a project with 24-bit resolution, you can bring audio in as a 16-bit WAV file or even an MP3 file, and either one will convert automatically to the project's format.

With the Waveform Editor, you simply drag the file from the desktop into the editor. This exercise demonstrates how to drag a file into the Multitrack Editor.

1   If the Multitrack Editor is not open from the previous exercise, choose File > New > Multitrack Session to open it now. Leave the default folder location as is, and choose 24 Track Music Session from the Template menu.

2   Make sure the Lesson08 folder is on your desktop or a drive of your choice, and open the folder in Windows Explorer or the Finder to reveal its three files. If needed, resize the Audition window so you can see the tracks in the Multitrack Editor and the open Lesson08 folder at the same time.

Note: The clip start point can "snap" to particular settings, such as the exact beginning of a measure or a marker. For more on snapping, see Chapter 10.

3   Drag the file Caliente Bass.wav to the start of Track 1. When you drag in a file that you've opened before with Audition, you'll see the clip with its waveform being copied, because Audition previously stored the waveform in a companion graphic PKF (peak file). If the file hasn't been used before, such as this one, the waveform won't be visible, and Audition will display "Offline." Once you drop the file, Audition will generate the graphic file necessary to display the clip's waveform.

> Caliente Bass.pkf
> Caliente Bass.wav

Note: The line that separates the bottom of one track header and the top of another is a splitter bar. You can drag this line up or down to decrease or increase, respectively, the above track's height.

4   Drag the file Caliente Drums.wav into Track 2 and the file Caliente Guitar.wav into Track 3.

5   Click the Transport Play button to hear the tracks play simultaneously.

6   These tracks were recorded at a high volume, and they are overloading the output. Adjust each track's volume control to −12 dB (the Transport can either be playing or stopped).

Every track has its own Volume and Pan controls.

7 Click the Transport Stop button, then click Move Playhead To Previous until the playhead is at the beginning of the song.

8 Click Play. The sound is now undistorted, and none of the meters go into the red (clipping) zone.

Importing tracks as individual files from an audio CD

Because the tracks on audio CDs are in a specific file format, they cannot be dragged directly into Audition. However, you can access a function that extracts audio from CDs and places it into the Waveform Editor. You can then edit the audio or transfer it to the Multitrack Editor, as described previously.

You need a standard audio CD to complete this exercise.

1 Close all projects and files. You can extract audio from CDs in either the Waveform Editor or Multitrack Editor, whether or not a project is open.

2 Insert a standard audio CD into your computer's optical drive.

3 Choose File > Extract Audio From CD.

Note: To hear a track from the CD, click its Play button in the Track column. Click again to stop.

The Extract Audio From CD dialog box opens, listing the tracks on the drive. If the computer is connected to the Internet, Audition retrieves information from an online database to populate the Track, Title, and Duration fields.

If the CD you are extracting audio from is not fully registered in the database, a notice will advise you that no matching records were found (as in the figure). Each track will be numbered, and you can manually add information to the Artist, Album, and Genre fields, as well as click the CD track titles to add the correct names.

4   The Speed menu lets you choose the extraction speed. Leave it at the default (Maximum Speed); if errors occur during the extraction process, choose a slower speed.

5   All CD tracks are selected as the default. They are extracted sequentially, usually with each track as a separate file. You need to extract only one track for this exercise, so click the Toggle All button to deselect all tracks, and then select one track.

6   Click OK. The extraction process begins and places the audio in the Waveform Editor. Leave Audition open in preparation for the next exercise.

Importing tracks as a single file from an audio CD

It's also possible to extract any number of CD tracks to a single file. The procedure is similar to extracting individual files.

1   Follow steps **3** through **5** in the previous exercise.

2   Select the tracks you want to extract into a single file.

3   Select Extract To Single file, and then click OK.

All selected tracks appear as a single file in the Waveform Editor, complete with CD track range markers.

4   Close the file before proceeding to the next lesson.

Review questions

1 Can you monitor input levels with Audition's metering?

2 What is the most common sample rate for digital audio?

3 What is the preferred bit depth for professional audio?

4 How can you add audio to the Waveform Editor or Multitrack Editor without employing the process of recording?

Review answers

1 You can monitor input levels in both the Waveform view and the Multitrack view by choosing View > Metering > Meter Input Signal.

2 The most common sample rate is 44100 Hz, which is used for CDs and many other digital audio applications. For film and television, the most common sample rate is 48000 Hz.

3 Most engineers prefer to record with 24-bit resolution, although recording with 16-bit resolution is also common.

4 You can drag files to either editor, as well as extract audio from audio CD tracks and place them into the Waveform Editor.

9 MULTITRACK SESSIONS

Lesson overview

In this lesson, you'll learn how to do the following:

- Integrate the Waveform and Multitrack Editors so you can switch back and forth between the two

- Colorize tracks to more easily identify them

- Play back a specific part of music repeatedly (looped playback)

- Edit track level and position in the stereo field

- Apply EQ, effect, and sends areas in tracks

- Apply EQ to tracks using the Multitrack Editor's built-in Parametric Equalizer

- Apply effects to individual tracks

- Process multiple tracks with a single effect to save CPU power

- Set up side-chain effects so that one track can control the effect in another track

 This lesson will take about 70 minutes to complete. Please log in to your account on peachpit.com to download the lesson files for this chapter, or go to the "Getting Started" section at the beginning of this book and follow the instructions under "Accessing the Lesson Files and Web Edition." Store the files on your computer in a convenient location.

Your Account page is also where you'll find any updates to the chapters or to the lesson files. Look on the Lesson & Update Files tab to access the most current content.

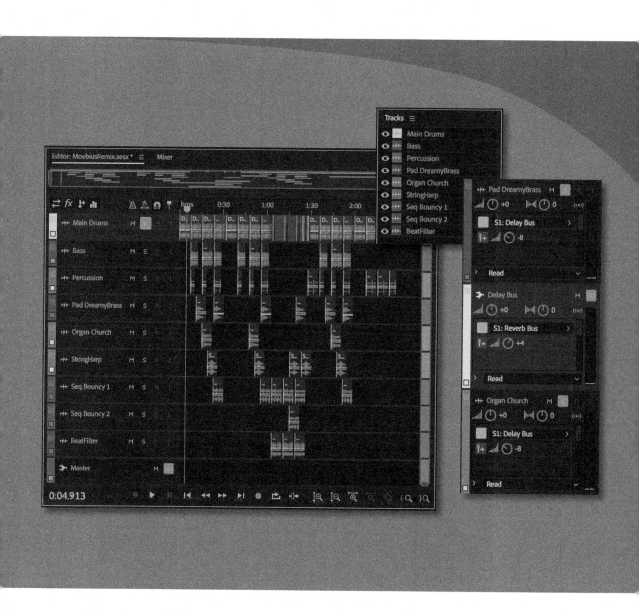

The Multitrack Editor is where you assemble clips, add
effects, change levels and panning, and create buses
for routing tracks to various effects.

About multitrack production

● **Note:** If you have not already downloaded the project files for this lesson to your computer from your Account page, make sure to do so now. See "Getting Started" at the beginning of the book.

Before beginning the lessons, it's important to understand a multitrack session's workflow so the lessons have a context.

In the Waveform Editor, a single clip is the only audio element. A multitrack production assembles multiple audio clips to create a musical composition. The audio resides in *tracks*, which you can think of as "containers" for clips. For example, one track could contain drum sounds, another bass, a third vocals, and so on. A track can contain a single long clip or multiple short clips that can be identical or different. A clip can even be positioned on top of another clip in a track (however, only the clip that is on top will play), or clips can overlap to create crossfades (described in Chapter 10, "Multitrack Session Editing").

The production process consists of four main stages:

- **Tracking.** This involves recording or importing audio into the multitrack session. For example, with a rock band, tracking could consist of recording drums, bass, guitar, and vocals. These might be recorded individually (each player records a track, typically while listening to a metronome for reference), in particular combinations (drums and bass recorded simultaneously, for instance), or as an ensemble (all instruments play live and are recorded as they play).

- **Overdubbing.** This is the process of recording additional tracks, such as a singer singing a harmony line to supplement the original vocal.

● **Note:** Some processes are available only in one editor or the other. If a menu option is dimmed in either editor, that option is not available.

- **Editing.** After recording the tracks, editing can polish them. For example, with a vocal track you could remove the audio between verses and choruses to reduce any residual noise or leakage from other instruments. You might even alter the arrangement, perhaps cutting a solo section to half its original length. When producing a film soundtrack, you might add spot audio effects, add Foley, and add background tracks.

- **Mixing.** After editing, the tracks are blended together into a final stereo or surround file. The mixing process primarily involves adjusting levels and adding effects. A multitrack session in Audition provides the tools to do most editing tasks during the mixing process, but if detailed edits are needed, session audio can be transferred to the Waveform Editor for further editing.

Create a multitrack session

When you're working with audio files in the Waveform Editor, the audio file itself is your project. You make adjustments to the audio and when you save, the original audio file is overwritten with the modified version.

When working on a multitrack session, the *session file* is your project. Changes you make will not replace the original audio files you have incorporated into a session. Instead, you'll make changes to virtual clips that link to your media files. In this sense, multitrack editing in Audition is similar to video editing in Premiere Pro. This makes it safe to experiment with changes in the multitrack editor, because you can always restore the original audio.

Because the multitrack session is stored as a file, which incorporates all of your creative work, it needs a name and a storage location.

Also, because the session is ultimately intended to be shared, it has a mastering setting, usually Stereo or 5.1. In many ways, the mastering settings of a multitrack session are the same as the settings for a newly created audio file. The difference is that the multitrack session is *conforming*, or converting, audio clips to ensure they match, every time a clip is added to a session.

Multitrack sessions allow you to apply effects to individual clips or whole tracks, or you can combine the output from multiple tracks in a single submix. In this way, the creative work you'll perform really is in the session, rather than the individual audio files that make up the session.

Multitrack session templates

Although you will often begin with a blank multitrack session, Audition comes with several pre-built session templates that include useful track names and track-based effects. These can save time when working with standard session types, and, of course, you can create your own template if you have a workflow you'll follow regularly.

Templates are made available by saving a multitrack session to a specific location on your system. This location differs, depending on your operating system (Windows or macOS).

Create a multitrack session template

A *template* is a snapshot of all the session settings at the time of saving the template, including effects that have been applied to tracks. Here's how to create one:

1   Choose File > New > Multitrack Session.

Leave the Session Name and Folder Location settings alone for now. They aren't important when creating a template.

2 Choose None from the Template menu, and then choose options from the Sample Rate, Bit Depth, and Mastering menus. Click OK.

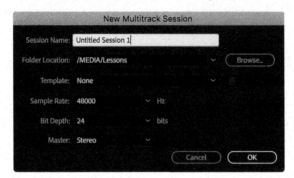

3 Arrange the multitrack session as desired, including the number of tracks, layout, processors in the tracks, levels, and so on. These settings will be incorporated into the template.

4 After everything is set to your liking, you're ready to make a template. Choose File > Save As.

5 Name the session with the desired template name (such as VO + Stereo Sound Track).

6 For the Location, click Browse. On Windows, navigate to Computer > C: Drive > Users > Public > Public Documents > Adobe > Audition > 11.0 > Session Templates, and then click Save. On macOS, browse to root drive > Users > Shared > Adobe > Audition > 11.0 > Session Templates, and then click OK.

Next time you open a new multitrack session, the template you created will be available in the menu of templates.

Note: You'll often see multiple versions of the same clip in the Multitrack Editor. However, there is only one physical clip, which is stored in RAM; the graphic clips in the Multitrack Editor just reference the physical clip. For example, if four copies of the same clip appear in a row, four separate clips don't play back sequentially. Instead, the clip stored in RAM plays four times, as instructed by the Multitrack Editor.

Multitrack and Waveform Editor integration

A unique Adobe Audition feature is that it offers different environments for waveform editing and multitrack production. In addition, these are not isolated from each other. Audio in the Multitrack Editor appears in the Waveform Editor's file selector, so any audio in the Multitrack Editor can be opened in the Waveform Editor for editing. This exercise illustrates how the Multitrack and Waveform Editors work together.

1 If you have any files or sessions open, choose File > Close All, and select No when asked if you would like to save changes.

2 Choose File > Open, navigate to the Lesson09 folder, and open the multitrack session named MoebiusRemix.sesx from the MoebiusRemix folder. Choose

the Default workspace, and reset the workspace by choosing Window > Workspace > Reset to Saved Layout.

3 Place the playhead at the beginning of the file if needed, and click the Transport Play button to play the song and become familiar with it.

Like the Waveform Editor, the Multitrack Editor plays linearly from start to finish. However, because the Multitrack Editor consists of multiple, parallel *tracks*, each of which can play back a clip, multiple clips can play back simultaneously.

Marker differences between the Waveform and Multitrack Editors

In the Multitrack Editor, the start and end of each clip is treated as a marker by the Transport's Move Playhead To Next, and Move Playhead To Previous buttons.

You can add cue markers at the top of the Multitrack or Waveform Editor panel ▓Marker 03▓ by placing the playhead where you would like a marker to be added, and choosing Edit > Marker > Add Cue Marker, or by pressing the M key.

Hold Ctrl+Alt (Windows), or Command+Option (macOS) and press the Left or Right Arrow key to move the playhead between cue markers only, ignoring the start and end of each clip in a multitrack session.

4 To check out the Waveform and Multitrack Editor integration, click the first clip in the Main Drums track (Drums_F#L) to select it.

Selected clips are highlighted in the Multitrack Editor.

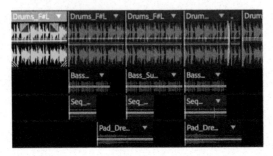

> **Tip:** You can rename any track in a multitrack session by clicking the name where it appears in the track header.

5 Click the Waveform Editor button at the top left corner to switch to the Waveform Editor, or press 9.

The clip you clicked on appears in the Waveform Editor, ready for editing.

> **Tip:** You could adjust the level of each clip in the Multitrack Editor or lower the level while mixing, but sometimes it's simpler just to modify the clip so all instances that "point" to this clip use the edited version.

6 Click the Waveform Editor panel menu. It shows all the clips in the multitrack session so that you can choose any of them for editing.

7 Choose the file Bass_Sub_F#H for editing. It sounds a bit too loud in the track, so you'll reduce the level by 1 dB.

8 Choose Effects > Amplitude and Compression > Amplify.

9 Reduce the levels of the right and left channels by typing in the value **–1 in the dB field,** and then click Apply.

> **Tip:** You can also double-click an audio clip in a multitrack session to open it in the Waveform Editor.

10 Click the Multitrack tab (or press **0**) to return to the multitrack session. All the Bass_Sub_F#H clip levels have been reduced by 1 dB.

11 Keep the session open for the next exercise.

Changing track colors

Assigning unique track colors makes it easier to identify specific tracks within a complete multitrack project, particularly if you standardize on particular colors (red for bass, yellow for voice, green for acoustic instruments, and so on). Track colors affect the color bar to the left of each track in the Multitrack Editor, the clip colors, and both the bottom of each channel in the Mixer and the fader controls in the Mixer. To change a track's colors:

1   Click the small square color swatch on the track's color bar.

The Track Color dialog box opens.

2   To choose one of the colors, click it and then click OK.

3   To modify a color, click it and then adjust the Hue parameter for the selected color.

4   Click OK.

5   Keep the session open for the next exercise.

Tip: To return the color palette to its set of default colors, click the reset button ![reset] just above and to the right of the Cancel button.

The Tracks panel

When working on more complex multitrack sessions, you may find it useful to selectively hide tracks. Doing so enables you to focus on specific clips, while still hearing the output from the tracks that are hidden.

Hiding tracks is easy to manage with the Tracks panel.

1   Choose Window > Tracks.

The Tracks panel shows every track in the current multitrack session. Notice that the names of tracks are displayed in the Multitrack Editor panel, the Tracks panel, and the Mixer panel (accessible by clicking the name of the Mixer panel, which is grouped with the Multitrack Editor).

2 To hide a track, click its Toggle Visibility button 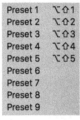 in the Tracks panel.

3 You can also automatically hide, or display, tracks based on the type of track, or the clips on them. Choose Track Visibility from the panel menu to check out the available options.

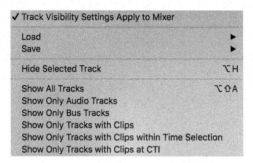

Notice also, you can choose Save or Load to create and access preset groups of tracks. The first five preset groups already have keyboard shortcuts assigned, so you can quickly toggle between these views once you have created them.

4 Leave all the tracks visible, and close the Tracks panel by choosing Close Panel from the panel menu.

Loop selections for playback

In several of these exercises, you'll be hearing what happens when several tracks play back their own clips simultaneously. As a result, you'll likely want to loop sections containing these clips for playback so that you don't have to wait through parts of the music that don't contain the clips you want to hear. Here's how to select a section of music for looped playback.

1 Select the Time Selection tool  from the main program toolbar, or press T.

2 Taking care not to select a clip, drag horizontally in the Multitrack Editor to select the portion of the music you want to loop. You can fine-tune this by dragging the edges of the selection or the white handles in the timeline that indicate the selection edges.

3 Make sure the Transport Loop Playback button is selected ▣ .

4 Click the Transport Play button. The selected area will loop and play continuously.

5 Click the Transport Stop button, and click the Transport Loop Playback button to deselect it.

6 Deselect the loop area by clicking anywhere in the Editor.

7 Return to the Move tool ▶ by selecting it from the main program toolbar, or press V.

Track controls

Each track has multiple controls arranged as two sections, which primarily affect playback. One section has a fixed set of controls, whereas the other section is an *area* whose controls change according to a particular selected function. To reveal these controls, complete the following steps.

1 Focusing on the track header controls, drag the divide between the Main Drums track and the Bass track downward. Keep dragging down until you can see all of the controls available on the Main Drums track header.

2 Hover over any track control header and scroll to resize all of the track simultaneously.

Main track controls

The main track controls are the most commonly adjusted parameters for mixing.

1. Return the playhead to the beginning of the session, and then click the Transport Play button to begin playback.

2. Click the Main Drums track's M (Mute) button 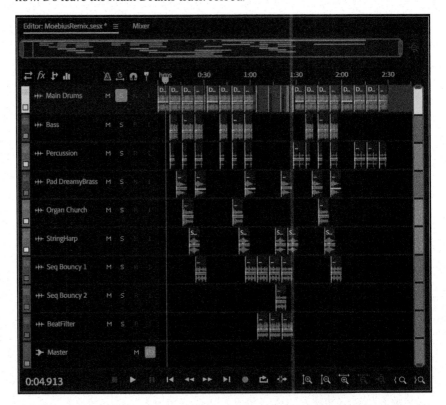 to silence it. Note that the Mute button turns bright blue-green 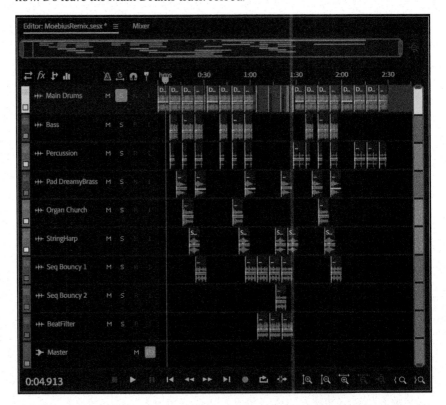 when the mute function is enabled.

3. Click the Mute button again to turn off muting.

4. Click the track's S button 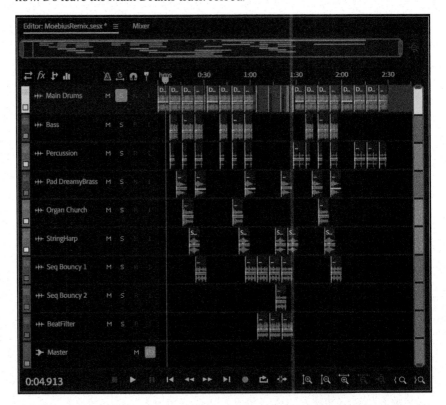 to solo the track; the button turns yellow 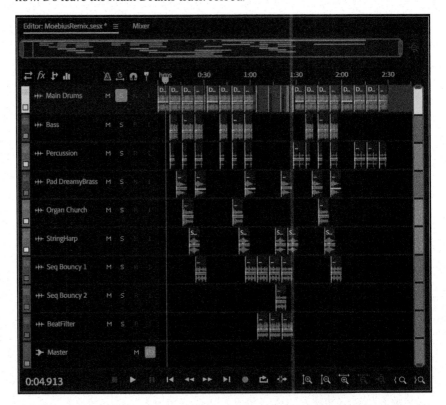. Only the Main Drums track will sound. The R button is for recording; don't click it now. Do leave the Main Drums track soloed.

Note: If both the Mute and Solo buttons are enabled, the Mute button has priority.

If you solo one or more tracks, the Solo button on the Master track lights up. Click that button to toggle Solo on and off for all tracks.

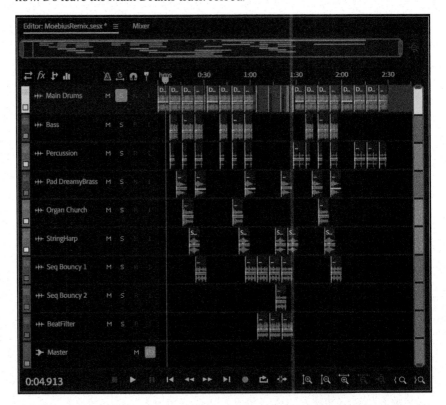

Note: Audition offers two solo modes: Exclusive (soloing one track mutes all other tracks) and Non-Exclusive (the default; you can solo multiple tracks simultaneously). To cancel soloing on any track, hold Ctrl (Windows) or Command (macOS) while clicking a Solo button. To choose one mode or the other as a default, choose Edit > Preferences > Multitrack (Windows) or Adobe Audition CC > Preferences > Multitrack (macOS), and then select the desired Track Solo preference.

You can move tracks to reorganize them in a way that makes sense to you. For example, you might prefer to have the Percussion track below the Main Drums track instead of the Bass track.

5 Drag the color handle for the Percussion track up, above the Bass track until a blue line appears between the Main Drums track and the Bass track. This line indicates where the dragged track will land.

 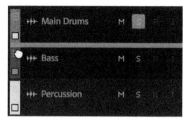

Drop the Percussion track below the Main Drums track.

6 With the Transport playing, find the Volume knob immediately below the left part of the Main Drums name, and then drag up/down or left/right to vary the playback volume. The track meters will go into the red if you turn this up too high. For now, leave the Volume at 0.

7 To change the track position in the stereo field, use the Pan or Stereo Balance knob to the right of the Volume knob. Drag left on the knob, and you'll hear the audio coming out of only the left speaker or headphone. Drag right, and the audio will play from only the right speaker or headphone.

8 Click the Sum to Mono button to the right of the Pan control. This collapses the stereo field to the center so the stereo file plays in mono. Click it again to return to stereo.

9 Return the Pan control to 0.

Track area

Extending a track's height, either by dragging the divider on the track header or hovering the mouse over a track header and scrolling, reveals an area below the main track controls. You can display one of four sets of controls in this area, as determined by the four buttons in the left section of the Multitrack Editor's toolbar:

Inputs and
outputs   Sends

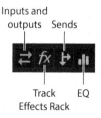

Track   EQ
Effects Rack

▶ **Tip:** If a track's signal goes into the red, the track meters' red lights will remain lit so you can see that the track exceeded the maximum level, even if you weren't looking at the exact moment it peaked. To reset the red lights and turn them off, click on the lights.

● **Note:** If dragging the Pan knob left places the audio in the right speaker, check the connections going to your speakers and audio interface.

▶ **Tip:** To return the Volume or Pan control to the default of 0 using a shortcut, hold Alt (Windows) or Option (macOS) and click the control you want to reset (not the number).

The EQ area

EQ is widely considered one of the most important effects for multitrack production, because it allows each track to carve out its own sonic space in the audio frequency spectrum. (See Chapter 17, "Mixing and Output," for an in-depth discussion of applying EQ during multitrack production.) Each track has the option to insert a Parametric Equalizer effect. Try that now.

1 Click the EQ button at the top of the track headers, and drag the divider at the bottom of the Main Drums track header down until you can see all of the controls.

The EQ area displays an EQ graph; it's currently a straight line, because no changes have been made.

2 Click the pencil button to the left of the EQ graph for the Main Drums track.

3 The Track EQ effect appears. This is functionally identical to the Parametric Equalizer effect covered in the "Filter and EQ effects" section in Chapter 4, "Effects."

Note: If you toggle on the Parametric Equalizer window's Power button before closing the window, the power will already be on in the EQ area.

4 Choose Acoustic Guitar from the Presets menu—just because it's named Acoustic Guitar doesn't mean it can't be used for drums!

5 Close the EQ window. Note that the EQ area now shows the EQ curve. Click the EQ area's Power button; the EQ frequency response curve turns blue to show that the EQ is active, and the Power button glows green. Leave the EQ enabled.

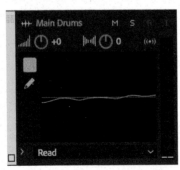

6   Click the Transport Play button. You'll hear that the EQ makes the drums sound a bit more defined. To hear the difference, click the EQ area's Power button off and then on again.

The Effects Rack area

Each track has its own Effects Rack so you can add signal processing to individual tracks; this Effects Rack is almost identical to the Waveform Editor Effects Rack covered in Chapter 4. This exercise demonstrates using the features that differ.

1   Click the Effects button (with the *fx* icon) in the Multitrack Editor panel, at the top of the track headers.

2   The track's Effects Rack area appears. Increase the height of the Main Drums track so you see 16 slots—just like the Effects Rack in the Waveform Editor. You can choose from the same effects, including VST (Windows or macOS) and AU (macOS-only) effects.

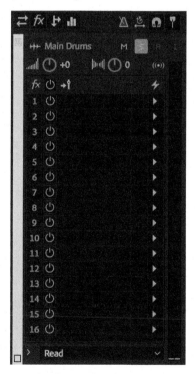

3   The main difference compared to the Waveform Editor Effects Rack is that you can change the position of the effects in the Multitrack Editor's signal flow. To hear how this works, in the Main Drums track, click insert 1's right arrow, and then choose Delay And Echo > Analog Delay.

4 Choose Canyon Echoes from the Presets menu, and then set Feedback to 70. Click the Transport Play button; you should hear lots of repeating echoes.

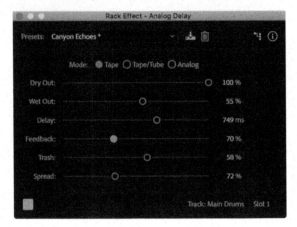

5 Three buttons are located in the strip immediately above the inserts. The leftmost button is a master effects on/off button, which is enabled automatically when you insert an effect. Click it to turn off the Analog Delay effect, and then click it again to turn the Analog Delay effect back on.

6 The next button to the right is the FX Pre-Fader/Post-Fader control, which selects whether the Effects Rack is before (the default) or after the track's Volume control. With the track playing, turn down the track's Volume control. Note that this turns down the echoes as well, because the effect is pre-fader; in other words, it's "upstream" of the fader.

7 Turn the track Volume control back to 0, and then click the FX Pre-Fader/Post-Fader button. It turns red and changes design [🔘] to indicate that the effect is now post-fader.

8 Let the track play for several seconds, and then turn down the track's Volume control. The echoes continue because you've turned down only the signal going to the Analog Delay, not the signal coming out of it.

9 Click the first insert's right arrow, and then choose Remove Effect so that the Analog Delay effect is no longer inserted.

10 Turn off the Main Drums track's Solo button so you can hear all tracks play simultaneously.

The Master Output bus

Before you look at the Sends area in the next section, you first need to understand the concept of a *bus*. Although buses in the Multitrack Editor look like tracks and have several elements in common, they serve a different purpose.

A bus does not contain audio clips but instead carries a specific mix of one or more tracks. Every multitrack session has at least one bus: the Master bus, which provides the Master Output. This can be mono, stereo, or 5.1 surround, as specified by the Master parameter when you create a new multitrack session.

All tracks feed into the Master bus by default on all sessions. Therefore, the Master bus's Volume control regulates the master volume of all tracks. This is essential because as you add more tracks to a composition, the output level increases. Eventually, it will likely start distorting, but you can use the Master bus Volume control to adjust the output level and prevent distortion.

1   Scroll down to the bottom of the Multitrack Editor, and locate the Master bus.

2   Extend the Master bus height sufficiently to see the Output meters. You may need to zoom in vertically using the scroll bar to the right of the Multitrack Editor to see the meters.

3   Click the Play button to start playback. Note that the Master bus Volume control is set to –4.5 dB: The project was saved this way so when you opened the file and started to play it, you wouldn't hear distortion. At no point does the Master bus Output meter go into the red.

4   Stop playback, and then return the playhead to the file's beginning.

5   Alt click (Option-click) the Master Volume control to return it to zero, and then click Play to start playback.

6   Note that the meter goes into the red starting around measure 5 when the Main Drums are joined by other tracks.

7   Click Stop to stop playback. Return the Master bus Volume control to –4.5 dB.

Audio moves through a multitrack session in a kind of chain, beginning with the original audio file, moving through clip Level adjustments and clip Effects, to track Level adjustments and track Effects, to buses (if they are used), to the Master bus.

You can modify the level at any stage in the chain but with differing results. Experience will help you judge where to make the adjustment you need.

Note: The Master bus is unique and omits some features that standard buses have (as described in the sidebar "About buses").

▶ **Tip:** To zoom a selected track to the maximum vertical height, click the Zoom Selected Track button (rightmost button in the Zoom panel toolbar) or press Shift+/. This command toggles between full vertical zoom and the previous amount of vertical zoom.

Note: Most engineers agree that you don't want to have to reduce a Master Volume control too much, and ideally, it should remain around 0 dB. If it becomes necessary to lower the Master Volume more than a few dB, reduce the Volume controls for individual tracks to reduce the Output level. Typical video projects have average levels of around –20 dB and peaks no greater than –14 dB to leave some headroom. Video for the web can be as loud as you like, but you'll still want to add some headroom.

About buses

In addition to the capabilities provided by a Master bus, buses have two other main functions: adding effects and creating monitor mixes.

Adding effects

You'll often want to add one or more effects to several tracks. A common example is reverb, which creates the illusion of those tracks playing in a common acoustical space, like a concert hall. Although you could add a reverb for each track, this has two main disadvantages:

- Each reverb requires CPU power. With older computers or highly complex projects, using more effects can slow down performance and possibly even reduce the total track count.

- It's more difficult to create the illusion of a single acoustic space if there are multiple acoustic spaces distributed among various tracks.

The third button at the top of each track header Effects Rack is Pre-Render Track ⚡ (this is also available in the Effects Rack panel). When you pre-render the effects, Audition processes them and creates a temporary file to play rather than the original audio combined with the effects. This saves CPU power and can be very useful in effect heavy sessions. The result is smoother playback, but if you modify the effects they'll need to render again, which may slow down your creative process more than you'd like.

Another solution is to send audio from each track that should have reverb to a bus and insert a *single* reverb in the bus's Effects Rack. This greatly reduces the amount of CPU load, and because there's only a single reverb, it sounds more like a single acoustic space. The amount of audio sent to the bus controls the amount of reverb; for example, if you want a vocalist to have lots of reverb, you would turn up the vocal track's Send control to the reverb.

Creating mixes (also called monitor mixes)

When musicians record a part, they often want to hear a specific mix in their headphones as they play. For example, the bass player will want to lock the rhythm to the drums and will likely want to hear louder drums compared to the other instruments. However, the vocalist, who is paying more attention to the melody, will likely want to hear more melodic instruments, such as piano and guitar.

To accommodate each musician, you would create two buses and send each bus's output to a separate headphone amp. The bus going to the vocalist would have more send from the piano and guitar, whereas the bus going to the bass player would have more send from the drums.

The Sends area

Each track has a Sends area. You can create buses in this area, as well as control bus levels and choose the send destinations.

1 Click the Sends button (the one between the Effects and EQ buttons) in the Multitrack Editor's main four-button toolbar. The track's Sends area appears.

2 Increase the Main Drums and Percussion track heights so you can see the Sends area's controls.

3 To add stereo reverb to both tracks, click the Main Drums' Sends area menu and choose Add Bus > Stereo. This creates a bus immediately below the Main Drums track.

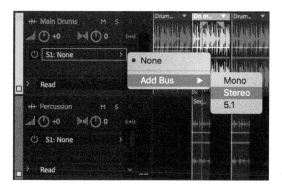

▶ **Tip:** You can also add a bus by right-clicking in a blank space in a track and then choosing Track > Add (Mono, Stereo, or 5.1) Bus Track. The bus appears immediately below the track where you right-clicked. Another way to create a bus is to choose Multitrack > Track > Add (Mono, Stereo, or 5.1) Bus Track. Note that when you create a bus, its output is assigned automatically to the Master bus as the default, like any other track.

4 Click in the Bus A name field, and type **Reverb Bus**. Note that after you enter this name, the bus name changes automatically in the Main Drums Sends area menu.

5 Click the Percussion Sends area menu. Because you created a reverb bus, it appears in the list of available send destinations. Choose Reverb Bus.

6 Now insert a reverb in the Reverb bus. Start by clicking the Effects button in the track toolbar.

● **Note:** When you're using effects with Wet/Dry controls as send effects, the tracks providing the sends are already providing dry audio to the Master bus. Therefore, the effects are set to full wet audio and no dry audio. The bus Volume control sets the overall amount of wet signal present in the Master bus.

7 An Effects Rack appears in the Reverb bus that works identically to the Effects Rack in individual tracks.

8 Click the right arrow in the Reverb bus's first insert, and then choose Reverb > Studio Reverb.

9 When the Studio Reverb window appears, choose Drum Plate (Large) from the Presets menu. Set the Dry slider to 0 and the Wet slider to 100%. Close the Studio Reverb window.

10 Return to the Sends area by clicking the Sends button in the toolbar.

11 Solo the Main Drums and Percussion tracks to make it easy to hear the effect of adding reverb. Audition knows to solo the Reverb bus automatically, because the Main Drums and Percussion tracks send signal to it.

12 Click the Transport Play button to begin playback.

▶ **Tip:** A track's Sends area also includes an FX Pre-Fader/Post-Fader button. This determines whether the signal going to the send Volume control is pre or post the track Volume control. The default is post-fader, because if you reduce the track level, you generally don't want to still hear the wet sound at the same level as when the track level was higher. If you do (perhaps for a special effect where a track goes from dry+wet to full wet), click the FX Pre-Fader/Post-Fader button so that the button is not red.

13 By default, sends do not have any level. Turn up the Main Drums send Volume control from −∞ to around −6 dB. You'll now hear reverb added to the Main Drums track.

14 Turn up the Percussion send Volume control to around +5 dB. When the Percussion clips play, you'll hear lots of reverb. The reason is that more audio is being sent to the Reverb bus compared to the Main Drums.

15 You can set the overall amount of wet (reverb) sound with the Reverb bus Volume control. Vary this control between −8 dB and +8 dB to hear how it affects the sound. Then Alt-click (Windows) or Option-click (macOS) this control to return it to 0.

16 You can also pan a bus in the stereo field. Vary the Reverb bus Pan control from L100 to R100, and you'll hear the reverb effect move from left to right, respectively. Alt-click (Windows) or Option-click (macOS) this control to return it to 0.

17 Turn off the Solo buttons for the Main Drums and Percussion tracks. In preparation for the next exercise, leave this session open with the various track and bus controls set as shown.

Sending buses to buses

Buses can also send audio to other buses, which multiplies your signal processing options even further. In this exercise, you'll send two tracks to a Delay bus, and that bus will feed the Reverb bus created in the previous exercise.

1 Right-click a blank space in the Pad DreamyBrass track, and choose Track > Add Stereo Bus Track to create a bus immediately below the Pad DreamyBrass track.

2 Click in the Bus B name field, and type **Delay Bus**.

3 If necessary, extend the heights of the Pad DreamyBrass, Delay Bus, and Organ Church tracks so you can see their Sends areas.

4 Click the Pad DreamyBrass Send menu and choose Delay Bus.

5 Click the Organ Church Send menu and choose Delay Bus.

6 Now, insert a Delay in the Delay bus. Start by clicking the Multitrack Editor's main toolbar's Effects button.

7 Click the right arrow in the Delay bus's first insert, and then choose Delay And Echo > Analog Delay.

8 When the Analog Delay window appears, choose Round-Robin Delay from the Presets menu. Set the Dry Out slider to 0, the Wet Out slider to 100%, and Spread to 200%; enter exactly **2000** ms for Delay, and set Trash to 0. Close the Analog Delay window.

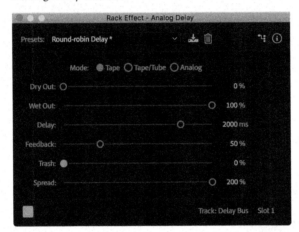

9 Return to the Sends area by clicking the Sends button in the toolbar.

10 Solo the Pad DreamyBrass and Organ Church tracks, and then set each of these track's send Volume controls to around –8 dB to add just a bit of delay.

11 Position the playhead at the start of measure 7, and then click the Transport Play button to begin playback and listen to the effect of the added delay.

12 Now that the delay effect is set up, stop playback and choose Reverb Bus from the Delay Bus Send menu. This sends the Delay bus output to the Reverb bus, and you'll hear delay going through the reverb.

Note: The Delay value of 2000 ms (in the "Sending buses to buses" section) is chosen so that the delay correlates to the tempo. For details on how to arrive at this number, review the "Analog delay" section in Chapter 4.

Tip: You can always change the time measurement system in the Editor panel by right-clicking the current time at the bottom left of the panel. To see Bars And Beats, choose this option from the menu.

13 Turn up the Delay bus Send control to around +4 dB, and playback. You'll now hear reverberated delay.

14 To contrast the delay sound with and without reverb, toggle the Delay bus Power button.

15 Choose File > Close All, and then select No To All in the dialog box that appears to close the project in preparation for the next exercise.

Channel mapping in the Multitrack Editor

The channel-mapping feature is available for all effects in the Waveform Editor and the Multitrack Editor, but it is most appropriate for multitrack productions. It allows for mapping any effect input to any effect input and any effect output to any effect output. This is primarily of interest for surround mixes, because you can place an effect output in a particular surround channel. However, this exercise shows that channel mapping can also be useful with stereo effects for altering the stereo image.

1 Choose File > Open Recent > MoebiusRemix.sesx.

2 Click the Solo button 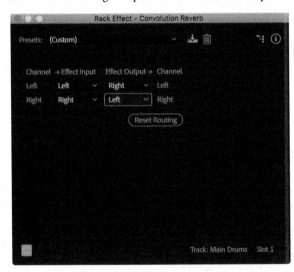 on the Main Drums track, and click the Effects button in the toolbar. Extend the Main Drums track enough to see the Effects Rack inserts.

3 Click insert 1's right arrow and choose Reverb > Convolution Reverb.

4 From the Impulse (not Presets) menu, choose Massive Cavern. Set Width to 300% and Mix to 70%.

5 Select and loop a portion of the Main Drums track, and then click the Transport Play button.

6 Click the Convolution Reverb effect's Channel Map Editor button ⬚ at the top-right corner.

7 When the Channel Map Editor opens, open the Effect Output menu for the Left channel, and choose Right.

Note: Because both outputs can't be assigned to the same audio channel in the Channel Map Editor, the Right Effect Output, which had been assigned to Right, is now assigned to (None). Therefore, you will hear the Right channel effect output in the Left audio channel, and no effect output in the Right audio channel.

8 Open the Effect Output menu for the Right channel and choose Left. The output channels are now reversed, which reverses the reverb output's stereo image. The image is wider, because some of the left input now appears in the right output, and some of the right input is now in the left output.

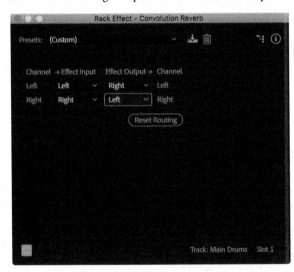

9 To hear the difference, click the Channel Map Editor's Reset Routing button. If you listen on headphones, you'll hear a definite collapsing (narrowing) of the stereo image; this will be more subtle on speakers. Choose File > Close All, and click No To All when asked if you would like to save any changes.

Applying the Channel Map Editor in the Multitrack Editor

The applications for the Channel Map Editor are obvious for 5.1 surround, because you can direct effect outputs to various audio channels: left, right, front, back, center, or even the sub-woofer.

With stereo, the Channel Map Editor is relevant only with effects that generate different audio for the left and right outputs, such as Reverb, Echo, and the various Modulation effects. The main uses in the Multitrack Editor are to create more interesting stereo images with individual tracks or when using the same effect in more than one place (for instance, the same effect in two buses, in one track and one bus, or in two tracks), because reversing the imaging on one of the effects can add more variety.

The Multitrack Editor Effects Rack

Now that you have explored quite a few effects workflows in both the Waveform and Multitrack editing environments, some clear differences should be apparent.

Although both Effects Racks work the same way, the Multitrack Editor Effects Rack has two additional buttons at the top to enable you to switch between viewing clip-based effects and track-based effects.

The difference in appearance in the Effects Rack when you're working on clip-based effects or track-based effects is quite subtle, so look out for those extra buttons at the top of the panel. Both types of effects work in the same way, and both combine to produce a final result.

Clip Effects   Track Effects

The Multitrack Editor is a more complex editing environment, and there is some repetition in the interface to allow you to access effects and settings in multiple locations. You'll find the effects you set for tracks in the Effects Rack will appear automatically in the track header Effects Racks, and in the Multitrack Mixer Effects Racks. They are truly multiple routes to the same settings.

Other than the pre- and post-fader option, and the pre-render option, the Effects Racks in both editing modes give access to the same controls. When you're working in the Waveform Editor, however, the changes you make are ultimately destructive, meaning they change the original audio file. Changes made in the Multitrack Editor are non-destructive, because they don't change your audio and can be adjusted at any time.

The Essential Sound panel

One obvious difference between the Waveform Editor and the Multitrack Editor is that the Essential Sound panel works exclusively on multitrack sessions.

The Essential Sound panel provides useful shortcuts to effects that are automatically added to the Effects Rack. Settings for the effects are adjusted in the Effects Rack by making adjustments in the Essential Sound panel.

The Essential Sound panel is particularly useful for film and television soundtrack mixing, as you'll discover in later lessons.

Review questions

1 What is the main difference between the Waveform Editor and the Multitrack Editor?

2 What's the advantage of sending tracks to a single effect through a bus instead of inserting the same effect on each track?

3 Is it possible to have buses send signals to other buses?

4 On what type of project is channel mapping most useful?

Review answers

1 The Waveform Editor can play back one file at a time, whereas the Multitrack Editor can play multiple files simultaneously.

2 Using a bus saves CPU power and is desirable when you want to apply the same effect (such as a specific acoustic space) to multiple tracks.

3 Yes, any bus can send audio to any other bus.

4 Channel mapping is most useful on surround productions, although channel mapping can also be used with stereo.

10

MULTITRACK SESSION EDITING

Lesson overview

In this lesson, you'll learn how to do the following:

- Use crossfading—both symmetrical and asymmetrical—to create remixes from individual clips

- Export a mix as a single file

- Merge multiple clips into a single clip that represents a single file

- Pan individual clips on a per-clip basis

- Edit a clip to fit a specific length of time, such as for a commercial

- Apply global clip stretching to fine-tune a piece of music's specific length

- Change volume on a per-clip basis

- Add effects to individual clips

- Set a new duration for a music clip

- Extend a clip via looping

 This lesson will take about an hour to complete. Please log in to your account on peachpit.com to download the lesson files for this chapter, or go to the "Getting Started" section at the beginning of this book and follow the instructions under "Accessing the Lesson Files and Web Edition." Store the files on your computer in a convenient location.

Your Account page is also where you'll find any updates to the chapters or to the lesson files. Look on the Lesson & Update Files tab to access the most current content.

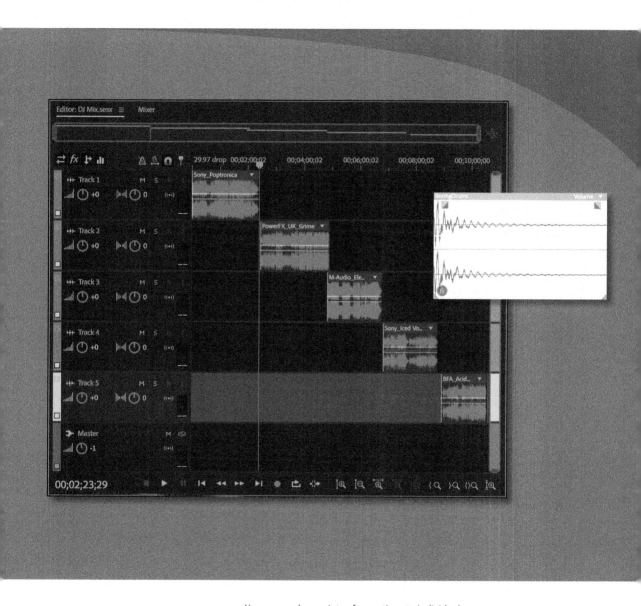

You can apply a variety of operations to individual clips, including combining them with crossfading to create a perfect DJ-style continuous mix of music, and then bounce the mix to a single file suitable for exporting, burning to CD, uploading to the web, and so on.

Create a mixtape

Note: If you have not already downloaded the project files for this lesson to your computer from your Account page, make sure to do so now. See "Getting Started" at the beginning of the book.

Note: The name for each piece of music in the multitrack session DJ Mix lesson starts with the name of the company that created the song and released the sound library; the song title is the name of the library.

Audition isn't only about serious audio work; it also provides a great way to create mixtapes. No one uses tapes anymore, and CDs are almost completely replaced by file-based music systems, so being able to export a mixtape to an MP3 file for a portable music player is very convenient.

The same techniques used for mixtapes are also applicable to creating DJ-style mixes and even some types of soundtracks, so this exercise isn't just about having fun. The emphasis is on crossfading between clips to provide for smooth transitions between the end of one clip and the start of another, especially when you're splicing clips and reassembling them. In this exercise, you'll use five clips to create a dance mix.

1   Choose File > Open, navigate to the Lesson10 folder, and open the multitrack session named DJ Mix.sesx located in the DJ Mix folder.

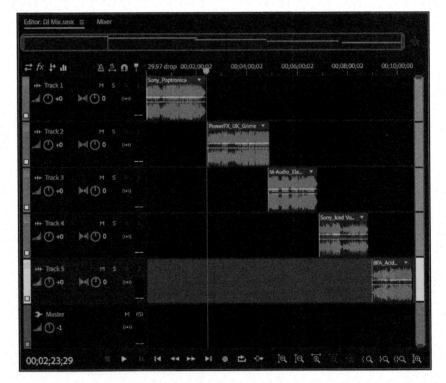

2 Right-click the timeline, and choose Time Display > Bars and Beats.

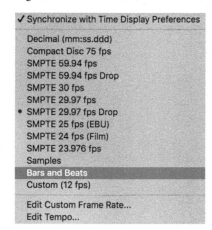

3 Right-click the timeline again, and choose Time Display > Edit Tempo. This is a shortcut to the Time Display preferences.

Make sure the Tempo is set to **120 beats/minute**, and click OK.

4 Make sure the Move tool  is selected. Click any clip to select it, open the Clip menu, and verify that Automatic Crossfades Enabled is selected. This setting means overlapping one clip with another will automatically create a crossfade in the overlapping sections.

5 Place the playhead at beginning of the session and click Play. Listen to the song "Poptronica," and as you listen, make a mental note of where you might like another song to start playing. Wherever you think it would be a good time to start the next track, insert a marker by pressing M. The theme returns at measure 57, and then repeats at measure 65 before fading out. So, measure 65 is a good candidate for another song to start.

6 Now listen to the song "UK Grime." The first eight measures are an introduction; the main part of the song doesn't start until measure 9.

When dragging clips in a multitrack sequence into new positions, you can move them freely, or have them snap to the ends of other clips, subdivisions of the Editor panel timeline, cue marks. There are several options when choosing what to snap to, and you'll likely change the setting when working with different clips and sessions.

> **Tip:** If snapping doesn't seem to be effective, zoom in further to increase the resolution and, therefore, the snapping sensitivity. It's *very* important in the crossfading exercise that clips snap precisely to the beat. If it doesn't, you'll hear what DJs refer to as a "train wreck" transition, because the clips will be out of sync with each other where they overlap. When you move a clip, zoom in to verify that the edge is aligned with a beat.

7 Choose Edit > Snapping > Snap to Ruler (Coarse). If snapping isn't already enabled, do so by clicking the Snap button to the left of the timeline until its icon is blue, or by pressing S on the keyboard.

Drag "UK Grime" into Track 1 so it overlaps "Poptronica". With snapping enabled, allow the clip to snap into position, starting at measure 65.

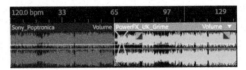

This timing is ideal, because "Poptronica" will fade out over eight measures, "UK Grime" will fade in over eight measures, and when "Poptronica" finishes fading out, the main part of "UK Grime" will start.

8 Position the playhead before measure 65, and click the Play button to hear the transition.

9 Try adding another transition. Listen to the end of "UK Grime;" it goes on for a long time, so you'll probably want to trim it. As the song starts getting repetitive at measure 122, you'll end the clip at measure 130 to allow for an eight-measure crossfade.

10 Hover over the right edge of the "UK Grime" clip so the cursor turns into a Trim tool (a red right bracket).

Drag left until the right edge of "UK Grime" snaps to measure 130. Note that you'll need to zoom in until every measure in the Timeline is labeled with a number for the snapping to be accurate.

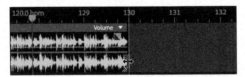

11 Move the playhead to the beginning of the song "Electro Patterns," on track 3 near measure 146, and then click Play to hear it.

12 Drag "Electro Patterns" into Track 1 so it overlaps "UK Grime" starting at measure 122. Play this transition.

13 Click the Fade In control square ◪ in the "Electro Patterns" file, and drag it straight up so the tool tip displays Fade In Linear Value: 100. This alters the crossfade so that the kick in "Electro Patterns" comes in sooner and sounds stronger.

14 Place the playhead before the transition, click Play, and then listen to the transition; it's much stronger.

15 Listen to the end of "Electro Patterns" and the beginning of "Iced." "Iced" doesn't really get going until after 16 measures, whereas the ending for "Electro Patterns" starts at measure 166. From a musical standpoint, the "Electro Patterns" measures that play after measure 166 are kind of heavy and bassy, whereas the first part of "Iced" is lighter. It's unclear what would make a good transition, so drag "Iced" into Track 1 starting at measure 166 so it overlaps "Electro Patterns," and you'll tweak it from there.

16 Now that "Electro Patterns" and "Iced" overlap, one clip appears in front of the other. This doesn't change the playback of the two clips but does mean you need to bring the clip you want to work on to the front.

To access the end of "Electro Patterns," right-click on the clip and choose Bring Clip To Front > M-Audio_ElectroPatterns.

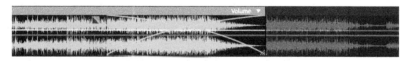

17 Hover over its right edge so the cursor turns into a Trim tool. Drag left to trim the clip, but leave enough audio to make a good transition area into the next clip; drag left to measure 174.

● **Note:** When you change the overlap for clips that fade together, the duration of the face updates automatically.

18 For the final transition, drag "Acid Jazz City" into Track 1 starting at measure 192 to create a *mashup* (two pieces of music playing at the same time for a fairly long amount of time). Return the playhead to the beginning, click Play, and enjoy your mix.

19 Keep this multitrack session open, so you can save your work as a single file in the next exercise.

Mixing or exporting a collection of clips as a single file

When creating a DJ mix or chopping up a clip to fit it to a specific length (as covered in the next exercise), you might want to save a collection of edited clips as a single file that incorporates all the edits you've made.

You have two options for doing this. The first option, which converts the clips into a single file that appears in the Waveform Editor, is ideal if you want to make some overall tweaks on the final, composite file.

1 Right-click an empty space in the track (in this case, Track 1) containing the clips you want to *bounce* (mix) together into a single, new clip.

2 Choose Mixdown Session To New File > Entire Session to create a new file in the Waveform Editor and automatically switch to the Waveform Editor. The new audio file also appears in the Files panel, with the same name as your multitrack session.

3 Click the Multitrack Editor button to return to the Multitrack Editor.

The second option exports the mix as a single file to your desktop or other designated folder without going through the Multitrack Editor. Exporting is covered in more detail in Chapter 17, "Mixing and Output," because in almost all cases you'll want to export a final mix to a mono, stereo, or surround file.

1 Right-click in an empty space in the track containing the clips you want to bounce (mix) together.

2 Choose Export Mixdown > Entire Session.

The Export Multitrack Mixdown dialog box opens in which you can specify several attributes of the mixed file, such as the folder location where the file will be stored, format, sample rate, bit resolution, and the like.

3 Select the desired attributes in the dialog box, and then click OK.

Merge clips into a single file

You can also convert selected clips into a single file within the Multitrack Editor. This is convenient with multitrack projects, because you can drag the collection of clips around within the project and edit them as a single entity.

1 To select all clips in a track, double-click in an empty space in the track.

2 To merge the clips, right-click any of the selected clips, and choose Merge Clips. The existing clips are removed and replaced with a single clip; Audition also creates an audio file of the new clip.

3 Choose File > Close All, and when the Save Changes dialog box appears, click No To All.

● **Note:** To edit a piece of music so that it's a particular length, you'll want to alternate the time display between Decimal (to see how edits to the music affect length) and Bars and Beats (for editing the music), so you can reference musical time.

● **Note:** If you select any clip when all clips are selected, view the Properties panel (Window > Properties) to see the Start Time, End Time, and Duration for the entire collection of clips.

● **Note:** If the original clips have any effects, volume/pan envelopes, fade envelopes, clip gain, or stretching, Audition will render these changes before merging the clips so that the single clip reflects any edits applied to individual clips.

Editing clip length

Music often needs to be cut to fit a specific amount of time—for example, a 30-second commercial. In this exercise, you'll use many of the clip-editing tools to trim down a 45-second music clip to make the background for a 30-second commercial. There is an automated way of achieving this result, using a feature called Remix (see below), however, manually selecting the sections of the audio you would like to keep gives you more control.

1 Choose File > Open, navigate to the Lesson10 folder, and open the multitrack session named 30SecondSpot.sesx located in the 30SecondSpot folder.

2 Right-click the time display at the bottom-left corner of the Editor panel, and choose Decimal (mm:ss.ddd); The music is about 45 seconds long. Right-click on the time display, and choose Bars and Beats for editing.

3 Right-click the time display, and choose Edit Tempo. Enter **125** in the Tempo field, and then click OK.

The first two measures and next two measures are similar except that a bass line in measure 4 leads well into the next section. So, you'll delete the first two measures.

4 Select the Time Selection tool ▯ or press T.

5 If necessary, click the Snap button 🔓 to enable snapping.

▶ **Tip:** You may find it easier to snap by first dragging a time selection close to the measure you want, then dragging the ends of the selection to snap them to the time measures displayed on the timeline.

6 Click at measure 3:1, and drag left to select the first two measures. Zoom in far enough to ensure accurate snapping.

7 Choose Edit > Ripple Delete > Time Selection In All Tracks.

Ripple Delete removes the selected section of a file; in addition, the section to the right of the selection moves left to where the selection started, thus closing the "hole" left by deletion.

8 The section of the music that starts at measure 7 is similar to the section that starts at measure 11. To eliminate measures 7–10, start by clicking at the beginning of measure 11:1, and drag left until measure 7:1.

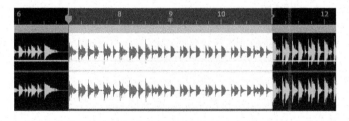

9 Choose Edit > Ripple Delete > Time Selection In All Tracks.

10 Keep this session open for the next exercise.

Editing individual clips in the Waveform Editor

For detailed or unusual edits, it's easy to flip a clip between the Waveform and Multitrack Editors.

1 The bass slide starting at 6:3 is good, but the slide ends too soon. Hover the cursor over the end of the first clip until the cursor turns into a red right bracket. Drag left to 6:4, which trims the last beat of the bass slide. Trimming the bass note to shorten it will make it easy to repeat the slide, which might sound more interesting than how it sounds now.

2 Select the Razor Selected Clips tool 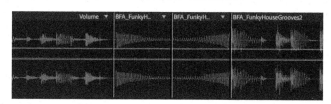 or press R.

3 Position the Razor tool so that there's a line at the beginning of the bass slide at 6:3, and then click to split the bass note from the rest of the clip.

4 Select the Move tool or press V.

5 Hold Alt (Windows) or Option (macOS) while you drag the bass slide clip you just split to the right so that the copied clip starts at measure 6:4.

6 Place the playhead around the beginning of measure 6, and then click Play to hear the result of the two bass parts playing in a row.

That's more interesting, but you can make it even more interesting by processing the second slide independently from the first slide.

A copied clip defaults to referencing the same original clip, so any change you make to either clip changes both clips. Let's create a separate file from the second clip instance.

7 To convert the second slide into a unique clip, right-click the second slide and choose Convert To Unique Copy. Although the unique copy takes up additional disk space, you can edit it without affecting any other related clips.

8 With the second slide clip selected, click the Waveform Editor button to edit it.

9 Choose Edit > Select > Select All or press Ctrl+A (Windows) or Command+A (macOS).

10 Choose Effects > Reverse to play the bass slide backward, so it slides up instead of down.

11 Click the Multitrack Editor button to return to the multitrack session. The reversed section will default to being selected, so click anywhere in Track 1 other than the selected section to deselect it.

> **Tip:** Be sure to begin holding Alt (Windows) or Option (macOS) before you drag a clip in the Multitrack Editor to create a copy of the clip. This doesn't create a new audio file—the same original audio file will now play twice.

12 Position the playhead around the beginning of measure 6, and then click Play to hear how the two slides sound when played together. Keep the session open for the next exercise.

Panning individual clips

Although Chapter 11, "Automation," covers clip automation in detail, now is an appropriate time to introduce the subject by altering the stereo position of the two bass clips. Automation allows you to adjust some settings over time. In this exercise, you'll use *panning*, which is the process of altering a sound's position in the stereo field (left, right, center, or anywhere in between).

1 Choose View > Show Clip Pan Envelopes, if it isn't already selected.

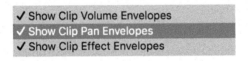

> **Note:** Control points are displayed only on clips that are selected.

2 For each bass slide clip (forward and backward), click the right and left ends of the horizontal blue Pan line (just inside the clip edges) to add control points at the Pan line ends. You'll find the Pan line parallel to and beneath the horizontal yellow line. Note that the clip must be selected to edit the Pan line, and you may also need to click again to select the Pan line itself. Once the Pan line is selected, you can click using the Move tool to add control points.

3 Drag the first bass slide's left control point all the way down to the lower-left corner. Then drag the right control point all the way up to the upper-right corner. Drag the second bass slide's left control point all the way up to the upper-left corner, and then drag the right control point all the way down to the lower-right corner.

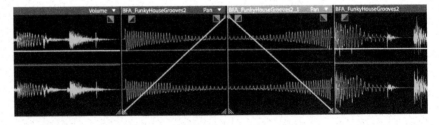

4 Position the playhead near the beginning of measure 6, and then click Play to hear how the two slides move in the stereo field.

Combining ripple delete edits and crossfading

The file is now about 34 seconds long, so it still needs one more ripple delete edit. However, any editing at this point could delete part of the audio you want to keep. This exercise shows you how to use crossfading to compensate for deletions caused by the effects of a ripple delete edit.

1 Change the time display to Decimal to verify that the file still needs to be a little shorter. Change the time display back to Bars and Beats for editing.

2 Position the playhead at measure 7, and click Play. The music gets a little quieter at measure 9, but then there's an interesting harmonic note at 10:3. So, using the Time Selection tool, select 8:3 to 10:3 and do a ripple delete as in step 7 at the beginning of the "Editing for length" section.

Although a ripple delete removes audio, you can use crossfading to alter the clip length and reintroduce some of the audio that was deleted—without adding to the total length.

3 Position the playhead just before the previous transition at 7:1, and then click Play.

The transition sounds okay, but originally there was a nice little drum fill in the two beats before 10:3. Now the fill is gone because it was in the section that was subjected to the ripple delete. You can reintroduce the drum fill by crossfading.

4 To restore the drum fill, you need to extend the beginning of the clip that starts at 8:3. Hover the cursor over the clip's left edge until the cursor turns into a red left bracket, and then click and drag left to 8:1. Now the section with the drum fill has been crossfaded with the end of the preceding clip.

● **Note:** When you trim a clip using the trim handles, you have not permanently altered the original audio file. Instead, you have changed the way Audition plays back the clip in RAM. You can always re-trim the clip to revert to the original length or re-trim the clip to a different length.

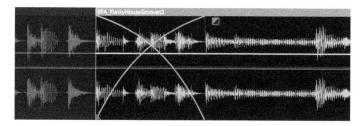

Using global clip stretching to make fine length adjustments

Global clip stretching can stretch all clips proportionately to fine-tune their total, combined length. Although extreme amounts of stretching can sound unnatural, relatively small changes alter the sound quality imperceptibly, if at all.

1 Change the time display to Decimal; the music is just a little over 30 seconds—very close to the goal. So, use global clip stretching to reduce the length slightly. Begin by selecting all clips; either double-click in an empty space in the track, or press Ctrl+A (Windows) or Command+A (macOS).

2   Click the Global Clip Stretching button 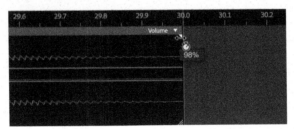 at the top left of the Multitrack Editor panel (to the immediate left of the Snap function's magnet icon) to enable global clip stretching.

3   Zoom in so you can see the difference clearly between where the music ends and the 30-second mark. Click the white stretch triangle toward the upper right of the clip, just below the name heading, and drag left until the end of the audio snaps to exactly 30 seconds.

All clips have been stretched proportionately so that the audio track is now 30 seconds long.

4   Position the playhead at the beginning of the file, and then click Play to listen to the entire 30-second music bed.

5   Collect your check from the ad agency.

6   Go to File > Close All, and choose No To All when asked if you would like to save.

Clip edits: Split, Trim, Volume

Digital audio editing allows for sound-warping options that would be difficult or even impossible to implement in any other way. Several of these involve isolating specific sections of a clip and processing them individually; the Split function is ideal for doing this. However, this exercise also employs other editing techniques to alter a clip.

1   Navigate to the Lesson10 folder, and open the multitrack session named StutterEdits.sesx from the StutterEdits folder.

2   Place the playhead at the beginning of the file, and click the Play button to hear the BoringDrums clip.

3   Right-click on the time display, and choose Bars and Beats.

4 Right-click the timeline and choose Time Display > Edit Tempo. Enter **100** in the Tempo field, and then click OK.

5 Choose Edit > Snapping > Snap to Ruler (Fine). Because you'll be zooming in quite a bit during this lesson, Fine snapping will allow for snapping to finer resolutions, like eighth notes.

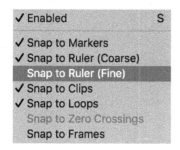

▶ **Tip:** It makes no difference whether you access the time measurement or tempo settings by right-clicking on the Timeline or the time display. You will find you prefer one route to those settings as you become more familiar with Audition.

6 Enable Loop Playback, and then play the audio from beginning to end.

7 Having two 16th note kick-drum hits at the end would make a better lead-in back to the beginning, so isolate a kick drum by zooming in until you can see both 1:3.00 and 1:3.04 in the timeline.

8 Click at 1:3.00 and drag right to 1:3.04 to isolate the audio containing the kick. Because you enabled Fine snapping, the selection should snap to these times on the timeline.

9 Choose Clip > Split.

10 Go to the end of the original clip, at 3:1:00, and use the Trim tool (hover over the end of the clip to display the tool and then drag) to bring the end from 3:1.00 to 2:4.08.

11 To make a copy of the short clip with the kick, hover over the isolated kick hit's name heading, and then Alt-drag (Windows) or Option-drag (macOS) right until the kick clip's left edge snaps to the end of the original clip, which is now at 2:4:08.

> **Tip:** If you are using the Move tool, you don't need to Alt-drag or Option-drag the name of a clip, any part of the clip will do. When using the Time Selection tool, clicking anywhere other than the name will make a selection.

12 Alt-drag (Windows) or Option-drag (macOS) the name heading of the same kick hit right until the newly copied kick clip's left edge snaps to the end of the previously copied kick hit. There should now be two kick hits between 2:4.08 and 3:1.00.

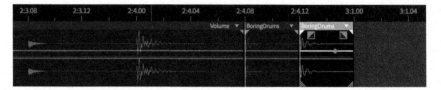

13 Click the background of a track, outside of any selected area so it won't loop, and then click Play. You'll now hear the clip with the double kick lead-in at the end.

14 Add some dynamics by making the first copied kick hit a little softer. If the clip's yellow volume envelope isn't visible, choose View > Show Clip Volume Envelopes. Drag the first copied clip's yellow volume line down to around –9 dB. Click Play to hear how the two kicks have become more dynamic.

Stutter edits

Stutter edits, which are commonly used in a variety of pop music, including dance music and hip-hop, slice and dice clips into pieces and then reassemble them in a different order. This lesson shows you how to stutter edit a hi-hat hit.

1 Similarly to the way you isolated the kick by splitting the clip, zoom in with the Time Selection tool still selected, drag from 1:4:08 to 1:4:10, and then right-click the clip and choose Split to isolate the hi-hat.

2 Trim the portion of the clip to the right of the hi-hat so that it starts at 2:1.00 instead of 1:4.10.

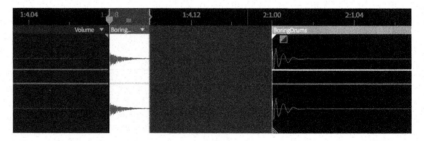

3   Alt-drag (Windows) or Option-drag (macOS) the isolated hi-hat three times so
     there are four hi-hat hits between 1:4.08 and 2:1.00 (starting at 1:4.10, 1:4.12,
     and 1:4.14).

     Click the empty background of a track, or press G to clear the selection.

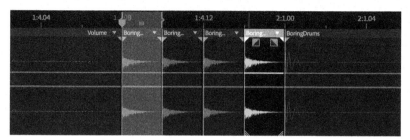

4   For a crazy stereo effect, make sure the clip pan envelopes are visible (choose
     View > Show Clip Pan Envelopes if necessary) and drag the blue pan line of
     the first of the four hi-hat hits, all the way up to L100. Drag the pan line of the
     second hi-hat hit up to around L32. Drag the pan line of the third hi-hat hit
     down to around R32. Drag the pan line of the fourth hi-hat hit down to R100.
     Click Play to hear how this affects the loop.

Note: A clip must
be selected to edit
its volume or pan
envelopes.

Adding effects to individual clips

Although adding effects to an entire track is convenient for making sweeping real-
time changes, it's also possible to apply one or more effects to an individual clip. In
this exercise, you'll put a big reverb on the snare that hits at 1:4.00.

1   To begin, isolate the snare: Drag from 1:4.00 to 1:4.08, and then choose Clip >
     Split, or press Ctrl+K (Windows) or Command+K (macOS).

2   Click the Effects Rack panel name if needed, and then click the Clip Effects button
     at the top of the panel. With the isolated snare clip still selected, click the Clip
     Effects' insert 1 slot's right arrow, and choose Reverb > Studio Reverb. You will see
     a little FX symbol in the lower-left corner of any clip with an effect assigned.

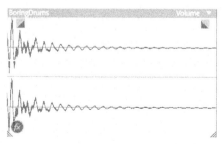

3   In the Studio Reverb window, choose Drum Plate (Large) from the Presets menu,
     and change the Wet slider to 50. Now when the drum loop plays, the snare will
     have reverb on just that single snare hit. Close the Studio Reverb settings.

4   To apply reverb to all the snare hits, because you like the reverb so much, simply copy the snare hit three times; Alt-drag (Windows) or Option-drag (macOS) from the clip name within the same track so that the start of this clip snaps to 1:2.00, 2:2.00, and 2:4.00. Because the snare hit is "on top" of the clip below in the same track, it will play back instead of what's in the clip underneath.

5   Try different options: For example, if you want to hear what the loop sounds like without the reverb effect on the first and third snare hits, right-click the first snare hit (the one that starts at 1:2.00) and choose Send Clip To Back. Next, right-click the third snare hit (starting at 2:2.00), and choose Send Clip To Back. Leave this as is for now, but if you want the snares to come back, you just need to right-click the clip covering the snare and choose Send Clip To Back.

Remember that with layered clips, the top layer has priority over the one underneath. It's possible to play a clip on top and the clip underneath it simultaneously by choosing Edit > Preferences > Multitrack Clips (Windows) or Adobe Audition CC > Preferences > Multitrack Clips (macOS), and selecting "Play Overlapped Portions Of Clips."

▶ **Tip:** If there were other clips in a track you didn't want to bounce, you could select only the clips you want and choose Bounce To New Track > Selected Clips Only.

6   Bounce all these clips to a new track so that all these changes are consolidated into a single file but you still have the original available if you want to make additional edits. Right-click anywhere in the selected track, and choose Bounce To New Track > Selected Track.

A new file appears in the track below that incorporates all your edits.

7   Keep the multitrack session open in preparation for the next exercise.

● **Note:** The Volume control for the track being bounced and the Master Output bus Volume control will affect the level of the bounced track. For example, if either control is set to –3 dB, the bounced track will be 3 dB lower in volume than the original track with the edits.

Extend a clip via looping

Any clip can be turned into a loop and extended for as many iterations as desired. Give it a try.

1   To convert the bounced clip created in the previous lesson to a loop, first verify that the clip start and end points line up with measure or beat boundaries. If a clip is slightly short or long, any errors will accumulate as you create more iterations of the loop.

2   Right-click anywhere in the clip (except for a fade control square, or the horizontal lines to control Volume or Pan), and choose Loop. A small loop icon appears in the clip's lower left.

3 Position the cursor over the clip's right edge. It turns into the Trim tool (red right bracket) but also shows a loop symbol. Drag right to extend the clip to the desired length. A vertical dashed line indicates the end of one iteration and the beginning of another.

Tip: To extend a clip earlier than its start, you can drag the clip's left edge to the left.

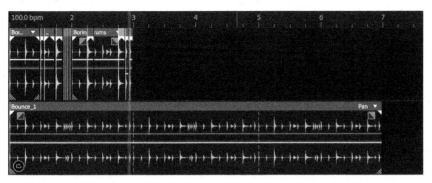

4 Choose File > Close All, and click No To All when asked if you would like to save.

Remix

Although you can manually edit clip length, selectively repeating or removing sections of audio to seamlessly play over a new duration, Audition also allows you to automatically adjust clip playback duration using a feature called Remix.

Remix can achieve remarkable results, although a degree of trial and error may be required for some content.

1 Navigate to the Lesson10 folder, and open the multitrack session named Remix. sesx from the DJ Mix folder.

2 Right-click the time display and choose Decimal (mm:ss.ddd). You'll use regular timing to choose a new duration.

3 Right-click the UK Grime clip in the multitrack session, and choose Remix > Enable Remix.

When Remix is enabled, small white zig-zag lines appear in the top-left and -right corners of the clip.

Tip: You can also enable Remix by selecting a clip and expanding the Remix settings in the Properties panel. There are also advanced options to precisely control the way Remix adjustments are applied.

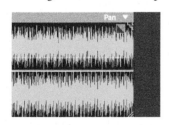

4   Position the cursor over the Remix icon on the top-right corner of the clip, and drag left until the end of the clip snaps to 2:00.

Jagged lines across the clip indicate regions that have been removed or repeated automatically by the Remix, and a Remix icon appears in the bottom-left corner.

5   Position the playhead at the start of the clip and play to hear the result.

6   Choose File > Close All, and click No To All when asked if you would like to save.

Remix is particularly useful for video projects where you want to use a piece of music that doesn't match the target duration of your delivered media.

It massively expands the range of useful library and royalty-free music you can use, without the complex selection and editing process required to achieve the same result manually.

Review questions

1 When you're crossfading clips to create a DJ mix, aside from their having a common tempo, what else is extremely important?

2 What is a ripple delete?

3 How do you apply an effect to something like a single drum hit within a clip?

4 What's the solution if snapping doesn't seem to work?

5 How can all clips be stretched proportionately to shorten or lengthen a piece of music?

Review answers

1 Make sure clips snap precisely to the beat. Otherwise, the clips can be out of sync with each other during the crossfaded section.

2 A ripple delete removes a selected section of a file; in addition, the section to the right of the selection moves left to where the selection started, which closes the "hole" left by the deletion.

3 Isolate the hit by splitting it into a separate clip, and then insert an effect for only that clip.

4 Zoom in further for a higher resolution; you might also need to enable Fine snapping.

5 Select all clips, turn on Global Clip Stretching, and drag the right edge of the last clip to the desired length.

11 AUTOMATION

Lesson overview

In this lesson, you'll learn how to:

- Automate volume, pan, and effect changes within clips by using automation envelopes

- Use keyframes to edit automation envelopes with a high degree of precision

- Use spline curves to smooth automation envelopes

- Show/hide clip envelopes

- Automate Mixer fader and Pan control moves

- Create and edit envelopes in the Multitrack Editor automation lanes

- Protect envelopes from accidental overwriting

 This lesson will take about 60 minutes to complete. Please log in to your account on peachpit.com to download the lesson files for this chapter, or go to the "Getting Started" section at the beginning of this book and follow the instructions under "Accessing the Lesson Files and Web Edition." Store the files on your computer in a convenient location.

Your Account page is also where you'll find any updates to the chapters or to the lesson files. Look on the Lesson & Update Files tab to access the most current content.

Audition can retain parameter changes you make in a multitrack session and store those changes as part of the session file—whether those changes are performed in real time as control movements or created/edited in non-real time. These automation processes can apply to individual clips or complete tracks.

About automation

Note: If you have not already downloaded the project files for this lesson to your computer from your Account page, make sure to do so now. See "Getting Started" at the beginning of the book.

Automation records the control changes you make while mixing, including track parameters and effects. Before automation existed, if during mixdown you forgot to mute one channel at the right time or alter a mixer channel's volume when needed, you usually needed to start the mix from scratch all over again. With automation, not only can you record your mixing "moves," you can edit them. For example, if a mix is perfect except that you didn't mute a track in time, with automation you can simply add the mute where needed.

Audition offers two types of automation in the Multitrack Editor: clip automation and track automation. Although you can use effects to adjust level and pan over time in the Waveform Editor, these adjustments will need to be written into the file at some point, and in this sense the Waveform Editor does not support automation.

Automation can be recorded during recording or during playback; it is not necessary to put a track into record mode to record automation moves. These moves are recorded as *envelopes*, which are lines—superimposed on a clip or track—that graphically indicate the value of the parameter being automated over time. There are multiple ways to create and edit envelopes, as you'll see in this chapter.

Clip automation

Every clip includes two default envelopes: one for controlling volume and the other for pan. You can manipulate these envelopes to create automation within a clip. Later in this chapter, you'll learn how to automate clip effect envelopes as well.

Tip: If you create a keyframe accidentally or want to remove a keyframe, click it to select it and press Backspace (Windows) or Delete (macOS), or right-click it and choose Delete Selected Keyframes.

Tip: If multiple keyframes are selected, deleting one keyframe will delete all selected keyframes. You can also remove a keyframe by dragging it completely off the clip.

1 Navigate to the Lesson11 folder, and open the multitrack session named AutomationClip.sesx. Right-click the time display and choose Bars And Beats.

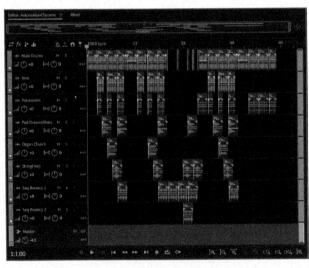

2 You'll add a volume fade-in to the first clip in the Main Drums track. For easy viewing of the envelope, extend the track height and zoom in so the first clip fills much of the window.

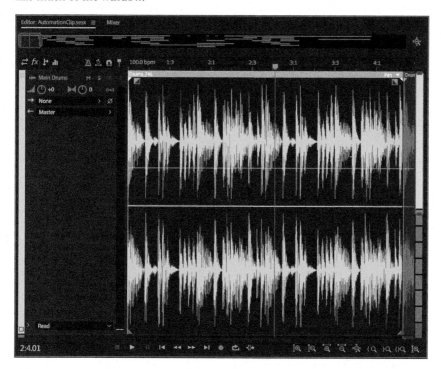

3 Note the yellow Volume envelope (currently a straight line) in the clip's upper half and the blue Pan envelope that marks the clip's middle. Drag the Volume envelope down. The tool tip shows how much the gain is being reduced; this acts like a volume control, because you're changing volume for the entire clip.

Because the goal is to create a fade-in, drag back up so the tool tip shows a level of +0.0 dB.

4 Once the envelope is selected, you can add control points called *keyframes* to change the line's shape. Click the Volume envelope once around 3:1. This places a keyframe on the envelope. Click the envelope again around 1:3 to create a second keyframe.

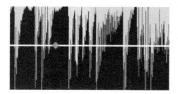

5 Drag the keyframe at 1:3 down and to the left so it's at the clip beginning and shows a volume of around −14.0 dB.

▶ **Tip:** Hover the cursor over a keyframe to see a tool tip with the keyframe's parameter value.

▶ **Tip:** Once you start dragging a keyframe, you can drag beyond the beginning or the end of a clip to set the level. When you release the drag the keyframe will be at the very end of the clip.

6   Start playback from the beginning of the song, and you'll hear the drums fade in.

Tip: If you hold Shift while dragging an existing keyframe, the movement will lock to vertical or horizontal, allowing you to move the keyframe in time or level, but not both.

7   Suppose you want the music to fade in a little faster but not reach full volume until 3:1. Drag the line between the first and second keyframes to around −3.6 dB at 1:4. Click Play, and you'll hear that the fade-in is a little faster at first and then fades in at a slower rate.

8   Click the blue Pan envelope to select it, then click again around 2:4 to add a keyframe. Click again around 4:2 to add another keyframe. This will be where the panning returns to center.

Tip: Remember, you can hold Ctrl (Windows) or Command (macOS) and scroll while the pointer is over the Editor panel to zoom in and out in time.

9   Drag the Pan keyframe you added at around 2:4 all the way down so the tool tip shows R100.0.

10 Toward the beginning of the Pan envelope, drag all the way up and to the left until the tool tip shows L100.0.

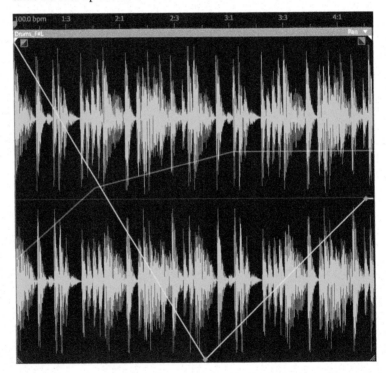

11 Click Play, and you'll hear the sound pan.

12 Try making the pan a little more complex: Click the Pan envelope around 3:3 to place a new keyframe, and drag this keyframe all the way up. Click Play, and you'll hear the sound move from left to right, back to left, and then end up in the center.

13 The panning transitions seem a little abrupt because the lines change angles sharply at each keyframe. To change these angles into smooth curves, right-click anywhere on the envelope line and choose Spline Curves. Now the envelope becomes similar to a rubber band, which allows you to drag to create any kind of curved shape you want.

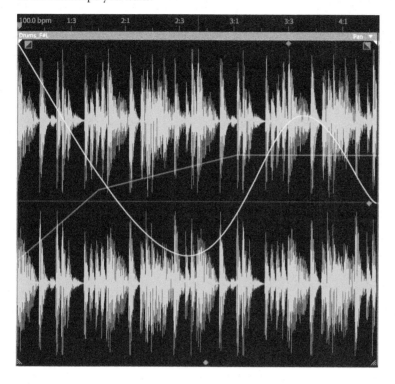

14 Keep this session open for the next exercise.

Move parts of an envelope or an entire envelope

You've already learned that you can drag a single keyframe to move it around. You can also select multiple keyframes and move them around as a group. For example, suppose you like the shape of the fade-In you created for the drums but want to raise the level of the entire envelope so that it makes for a slightly louder introduction before more clips start playing. Here's how to do it:

1 Click the Volume envelope in the first Main Drums clip to select it for editing.

2 Right-click the envelope or any Volume envelope keyframe, and choose Select All Keyframes to select all the keyframes on that clip.

▷ **Tip:** If a Volume or Pan envelope is already selected, you'll add a keyframe every time you click it (unless you click an existing keyframe). To select the envelope without adding a keyframe, right-click it.

▷ **Tip:** To select a string of keyframes, click the leftmost one, and then Shift-click the rightmost one. Those keyframes and all keyframes in between are selected. You can also select several keyframes by Ctrl-clicking (Windows) or Command-clicking (macOS).

3 Drag any keyframe up so the tool tip shows approximately +4 dB more than its original value. All the other keyframes on the clip move simultaneously.

4 You can also select particular keyframes and have them move together as a group. Click the clip outside of the Volume envelope (click the clip, not outside of the clip) to deselect all keyframes.

5 Click the leftmost keyframe (the one at the beginning of the clip) to select it, and then Ctrl-click (Windows) or Command-click (macOS) the second keyframe from the left.

6 Drag the first selected keyframe up until the second selected keyframe reaches the top of the clip but don't release the control. The line defined by the two keyframes will move, maintaining their relative levels. Non-selected keyframes to the right will remain "anchored."

7 Keep moving the first keyframe up, and keep holding the control. Note that the second keyframe remains "stuck" at the top; however, it "remembers" its original position. Drag the first keyframe back down again to where it started (around −7.5 dB), and the second keyframe will return to its original position.

8 Now try this without holding the control all the way through. Drag the first keyframe up to the top of the clip, and release.

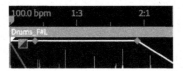

Now the envelope is flat, at the top of the clip.

9 Drag the first keyframe down to its original position. The second keyframe maintains its new relative level, and the fade up is gone.

10 Undo twice by pressing Ctrl+Z (Windows) or Command+Z (macOS) twice to restore the original position of the keyframes.

11 Keep this session open for the next exercise.

Keyframe hold

The Hold Keyframe option keeps an envelope at the current value set by the keyframe until the next keyframe, at which point the envelope jumps instantly to the next value. Here's how to use this effect to create abrupt panning changes.

1 The second track in this multitrack session is called Bass. Locate the first clip in that track, called Bas_Sub_F#H. Zoom in so you can easily see the clip and its automation envelopes.

2 Click the Pan envelope to select it, and click it again just before the note that starts after 6:4 to create a keyframe.

3 Click the Pan envelope just before the note that starts after 5:4 to create another keyframe, and drag it all the way down.

4 Click the Pan envelope toward the left of the envelope to add a keyframe, and then drag the keyframe to the upper-left corner.

5 Hover the cursor over the leftmost keyframe until you see the tool tip, which means you're hovering directly over the keyframe. Right-click, and choose Hold Keyframe.

6 Similarly, hover over the next keyframe to the right, right-click it, and choose Hold Keyframe. The envelope now makes sharp, right-angle turns as the envelope jumps to the next value.

> **Tip:** If Global Clip Stretching is turned on, small white triangles are displayed in the top corners of clips and you may not be able to position keyframes in the corners. Turn off Global Clip Stretching by clicking the Toggle Global Clip Stretching button ⚏ at the top of the track headers.

Note: A Hold Keyframe has a square shape, while a standard keyframe has a diamond shape.

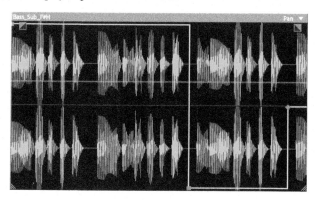

7 Leave this session open for the next exercise.

Clip effects automation

In addition to volume and pan, you can automate the parameters of effects that have been applied to clips (see Chapter 10 for more information about clip effects).

1 Rather than working with the clip you just used to learn about Volume and Pan envelopes, you'll use a different clip to learn about clip effects automation. Locate the clip in the Main Drums track that begins just after 7:3, and select it.

2 In the Effects Rack, click the Clip Effects button. You'll add a wah effect using EQ.

3 In the first Effect Rack insert, click the right arrow, and choose Filter And EQ > Parametric Equalizer. Make sure Default is chosen from the Presets menu.

Tip: You will need to set the Parametric Equalizer effect range to 96 dB to be able to see level adjustments beyond 15 dB in the graph.

4   Turn off all bands except band 2. Set its gain to around 20 dB and Q to around 12, and close the Parametric Equalizer effect window.

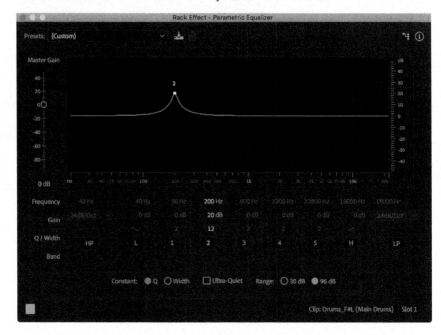

At the top-right corner of the clip, the word "Volume" appears, with a small triangle beside it. The triangle is a menu that allows you to access any effect settings, including the Parametric Equalizer effect you just added.

5   Click the triangle, and choose Parametric Equalizer > EQ Band 2 Center Frequency. This adds an automation envelope along the bottom edge of the clip to allow adjustment of this setting. A small fx icon also appears at the bottom-left corner of the clip.

Because the Parametric Equalizer Band 2 Center Frequency is set low already, the new automation envelope appears close to the bottom of the clip.

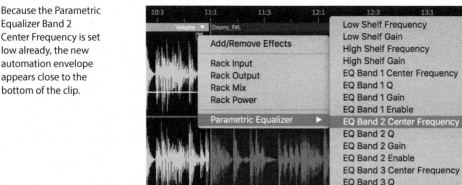

6 Click at each end of the envelope to add a keyframe.

7 Drag the left keyframe to the lower left until the tool tip indicates a frequency of around 130 Hz. You may need to extend the track height to obtain the necessary resolution.

8 Drag the right keyframe to the upper right until the tool tip indicates a frequency of around 4000 Hz.

Note: When you select an automation envelope in a clip, the upper right of the clip header displays the name of the parameter it controls.

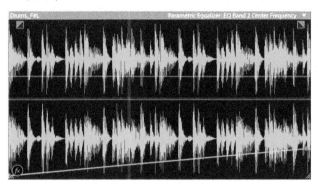

9 Place the playhead before the clip starts, and then click Play. You'll hear a filtering effect that goes from low to high over the course of the clip. You may want to click the track's Solo button so you can focus in on hearing the effect. To see the parameter change in real time, keep the effect's window open.

10 Choose File > Close All, and click No To All when asked if you would like to save.

Show/hide clip envelopes

If you have lots of envelopes displayed in a clip, the view can become cluttered. However, you can show and hide a particular envelope type for all clips by choosing the envelope type from the View menu. This changes the view for all clips in the session, not just selected clips.

✓ Show Clip Volume Envelopes
✓ Show Clip Pan Envelopes
✓ Show Clip Effect Envelopes

Track automation

Track automation has some similarities to clip automation but is more flexible and applies to an entire track. You can work with track automation from either the Multitrack Editor or Mixer view.

For individual tracks, you can automate:

- Volume

- Mute

- Pan

- Track EQ (including all Parametric Equalizer parameters—frequency, gain, Q, and so on)

- Rack Input level

- Rack Output level

- Rack Mix (crossfades between the dry sound and the sound processed by the Effects Rack)

- Rack Power

- Most plug-in parameters, including VST and AU-format plug-ins. (For example, you could automate delay so that the delay feedback increases over a certain number of measures and then decreases.)

Clip versus track automation

Given that you can automate volume changes with clip automation or track automation, sometimes you need to decide which to choose. The most important consideration is that you can create complex volume, pan, or effect changes within a clip, but also subject these changes to overall level changes using track automation. For example, you could apply clip automation to boost individual sections of dialog in a soundtrack, and then use track automation to give the impression of the speaker coming closer or moving away from the microphone.

An important major difference is that clip automation is part of the clip, so if you move the clip, the automation moves with it. If you move a clip that's being automated by track automation, the automation will remain stationary. However, you can select multiple automation keyframes and move the envelope so it matches up with the clip you moved. In this case, it's a good idea to put a keyframe where the clip starts or ends *before* you move the clip, so you have a reference point for timing when you move the envelope.

You can create track automation not only by drawing and modifying envelopes, but also by moving onscreen controls. With clip automation, you can only redraw the existing clip envelopes.

What makes clip and track automation so useful goes beyond simply being able to capture mixing moves like levels and panning, because automation can add nuanced expressiveness to electronically oriented music by automating signal processing plug-ins. Also, note that you can edit automation data, so you can tweak one parameter to perfection, and then another, and so on.

There are three main ways to work with track automation:

- Move onscreen controls in real time during playback, and record the changes to controls as keyframes on envelopes.

- Create an envelope, and then manually add keyframes to create an envelope shape.

- Combine the two—add the envelope keyframes during playback by adjusting controls, and then manually add, move, or delete them to make precise adjustments.

Automating fader mixes

In addition to automating using keyframes, you can also take a more "hands-on" approach by automating mixing moves you make with the Mixer faders.

1 Open Audition, navigate to the Lesson11 folder, and open the multitrack session named AutomationTrack.sesx. The Default Workspace is recommended; reset to the workspace if needed.

With most of the steps in this exercise, you'll want to start the file from the beginning after stopping playback.

2 To start file playback from the beginning whenever you stop, position the playhead at the beginning of the file, and then right-click the Transport Play button and choose Return Playhead To Start Position On Stop.

3 Click the Mixer panel name at the top of the frame containing the Editor panel.

In the Default workspace, the Mixer panel shares the same frame as the Editor panel. Like any other panel, it can also always be found in the Window menu.

When you first view the Mixer, it can be a little overwhelming. However, notice that every control is repeated multiple times; each track in the current multitrack session has a set of controls. Learn the controls for one track, and you will know them for all tracks. For more information on working with the Mixer, see Chapter 14, "The Multitrack Mixer."

4 Associated track names appear at the bottom of the Mixer controls. Look for the Main Drums track controls (on the left). Open the Track Automation Mode menu just above the Main Drums track's fader, and choose Write.

Note: Because the Mixer panel and Editor panel are grouped by default, you won't be able to see the session tracks now. If you have positioned the playhead at the start of the session, you can start and stop playback in the Mixer panel using the spacebar, knowing you'll hear and adjust the audio from the beginning.

▶ **Tip:** If you have enough space on-screen, you can move the Mixer panel to a new frame and display both panels at the same time for direct access without switching between them.

The text turns red—adjustments you make will be recorded.

5 Start with the fader for Track 1 (Main Drums) at around –18 dB, because you'll fade the level up.

Start playback from the file beginning. As the file plays, bring up the fader to around 0. Let the file play for several seconds, and then fade the drums out all the way.

6 Stop playback. Note that the Main Drums Track Automation Mode menu option changes automatically from Write to Touch. As you'll see, this makes it convenient to fine-tune your fader moves.

Track automation modes

The Mixer panel allows you to make subtle adjustments to track level, pan, and track effects. These combine with clip level and clip effects to produce the final output. Changes made in the Mixer panel don't affect clips, only tracks.

There are four industry-standard modes that change the way the fader controls and pan controls interact with existing keyframes and add new ones.

If the Track Automation Mode menu is set to Off, automation adjustments are ignored and the controls will stay where they are, setting a consistent level or pan for the track.

- **Read:** This is the default mode. The controls move based on the track automation envelope setting, which in turn changes the level, pan, or effect settings.

- **Write:** In Write mode the controls ignore any existing keyframes and create new ones as soon as you start playback. Existing keyframes are overwritten, and the level, pan, or effect settings will continue to be applied as long as playback continues.

- **Latch:** In Latch mode, any existing automation remains as is until you "touch" (click) a control and move it. Then new keyframes are added, overwriting any existing keyframes as you make adjustments. When you release control, settings will continue to be applied as long as playback continues.

- **Touch:** In Touch mode, any existing automation remains as is until you "touch" (click) a control and move it. Then new keyframes are added for as long as you hold the control. When you release control, it returns to following any existing keyframes.

7   Start playback, and the fader re-creates the fader moves you made. After the fader fades out, stop playback.

8   Suppose you decide that fading out all the way wasn't a great idea, and once the level starts fading out, you want the drums to fade back in again. You can always write new automation, but it's easier just to "punch in" with the new automation move by using Touch mode. Start playback, grab the fader partway through the fadeout, and then fade back up to 0. Let the file play for a few seconds, and then release the mouse and stop playback. The adjustment is applied, to the automation envelope.

9   You can also automate panning. With the Track Automation Mode menu set to either Touch or Write, start playback and move the Pan control. Panning back and forth rhythmically will provide plenty of data to work with. When you've done at least several measures of panning moves, stop playback.

▶ **Tip:** You cannot automate the power state of individual effects in a track's Effects Rack, but you can automate the track Effects Rack's master power state. Turning this off when not in use saves CPU power, improving playback performance.

● **Note:** You can also automate Send level, pan, and power state. You cannot automate the Send Pre-Fader/Post-Fader button.

10 Now automate an effect. Make sure the fx section of the Mixer is expanded, by clicking its disclosure triangle on the far left, if necessary. (The triangle is stylized, and looks more like a v than a triangle.)

The fx sections of track controls in the Mixer are a duplicate of the track effects rack in the Editor panel, and the Effects Rack panel.

11 Open the Percussion channel's Track Automation Mode menu, and choose Write.

12 In the Percussion track's fx area, double-click the Echo insert to bring up its interface so you can modify its controls. Locate the 1.4k slider in the Successive Echo Equalization area; that's the one you'll be altering.

13 Start playback from the file beginning, and move the 1.4k fader up to around 5 dB.

14 The echo sound will start feeding back after a few seconds. Before it gets too out of control, pull the fader down to around –5 dB to reduce the amount of echo feedback. Stop playback.

15 Start playback, and you'll see the 1.4k slider re-create your mixing moves. When the mixing moves end, stop playback, and close the Echo effect window.

16 When you're finished making automation moves, change the Track Automation Mode menus for the Main Drums and Percussion channels to Read. This will prevent accidental erasures or edits. (Off ignores any automation data.)

17 Keep this session open in preparation for the next exercise.

Editing envelopes

Although you can edit automation by using the Touch, Latch, and Write modes to make real-time edits, these automation moves also create envelopes that you can access and edit in the Multitrack Editor, similarly to the way you edit clip envelopes.

1 Click the Editor panel name to leave the Mixer.

2 Expand the Main Drums track height until you see the Track Automation Mode menu (which should show Read).

3 Click the disclosure triangle to the left of the automation menu to view the automation envelope lanes.

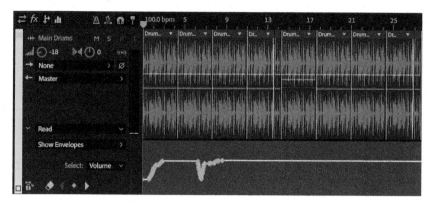

▶ **Tip:** If you want to edit automation on a single parameter, it's usually best to display only that envelope. However, sometimes two parameters are interrelated, and you'll want to edit one envelope while referencing changes in another envelope. In these situations, being able to show multiple envelopes is ideal.

4 If you use lots of envelopes, displaying them all simultaneously will clutter up a lane. As a result, Audition lets you specify which envelopes you want to see in the automation lane. Because you recorded both Volume and Pan automation, open the Show Envelopes menu, and choose those.

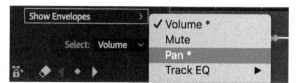

When multiple envelopes are displayed, all those keyframes can sometimes be confusing. Therefore, Audition lets you choose which envelope to edit. When you choose the envelope you want to edit from the Select menu, only that envelope will be highlighted, and the other envelopes will be dimmed. (You can still see the other envelopes you've chosen to show, but you can't edit them.)

Keyframes in track envelopes work exactly as they do in clip envelopes. For example, suppose your panning envelope doesn't look smooth enough but more like an on-off switch. You can fix this with spline curves.

5 Apply Spline Curves to the Volume envelope by right-clicking the envelope and choosing Spline Curves from the context menu, as you did with Clip Automation. Straight lines between keyframes will be replaced by curved lines.

You can also delete selected keyframes to "thin out" the curve, either by clicking them and pressing Backspace or Delete, or by right-clicking a keyframe (or a selected number of keyframes) and choosing Delete Selected Keyframes.

Creating envelopes in the automation lane

In addition to editing existing envelopes, you can also create and edit track envelopes, as you did with clip envelopes. In this exercise, you'll create a precise, hard-limiting change to make the drums beefier when they first start playing, and then dial back on the beefiness when the bass starts. Stay in the Editor panel for this exercise:

1   In the first Effect Rack insert for the Main Drums track, click the right arrow, and choose Amplitude And Compression > Hard Limiter. Make sure Default is chosen from the Presets menu, and close the effect settings.

2   Open the Main Drums track's Show Envelopes menu, and choose Hard Limiter > Input Boost. As soon as you choose a new envelope, it's automatically selected for editing and highlighted in the automation lane (you don't have to use the Select menu). For now, the envelope will be set to whatever its current value is in the effect. The default Input Boost for the Hard Limiter is 0.0 dB (no boost).

3   Because you don't want any boost when the bass starts playing (at measure 4:2), click the Input Boost envelope at 4:2. This places an envelope keyframe at 0.0 dB.

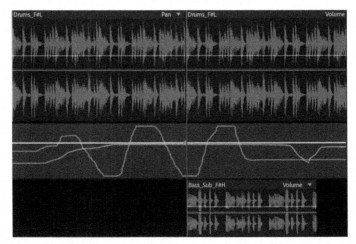

4   Drag the envelope to the left of the new keyframe up to around 20 dB, and position it just before the keyframe at measure 4:2.

5   Start playback from the beginning, and listen to how this processing affects the sound.

6   Keep this session open for the next exercise.

Precision keyframe editing

In some cases, you might want to do precise keyframe editing. Selecting and deleting can become tedious, so Audition includes four keyframe editing tools.

1 Use the Select menu to choose the Pan envelope, which should have multiple keyframes after the earlier exercise.

2 Click the Next Keyframe button, and the playhead will move to the right from its current position to the next keyframe.

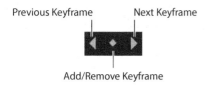

Previous Keyframe   Next Keyframe

Add/Remove Keyframe

3 Click the Add/Remove Keyframe button (the diamond icon to the immediate left of the Next Keyframe button) to delete the keyframe. If the playhead is not on a keyframe, clicking this button adds a keyframe.

4 The Previous Keyframe button (left-arrow icon) to the immediate left of the Add/Remove Keyframe button steps through keyframes from right to left. Click this button a few times to see how the playhead moves.

5 Click the Clear All Keyframes button to the immediate left of the Previous Keyframe button ◈ to delete all keyframes for the selected Pan envelope.

6 Keep this session open for the next exercise.

Protecting automation envelopes

When you're performing lots of complex automation, you want to avoid accidentally writing new automation where it's not intended or overwriting existing automation. (It can happen!) You can protect an envelope from these kinds of mistakes with a write-protect feature.

1 With Hard Limiter: Input Boost chosen from the Select menu, click the Protection button 🔒. The envelope turns into a dotted line to show it's protected, even though it's selected.

2 In the Main Drums track, with the Hard Limiter: Input Boost envelope still selected, choose Write from the Track Automation Mode menu.

The track header Track Automation Mode menu in the Editor panel is the same as the one in the Mixer panel—changing one updates the other.

3 In the Effects Rack panel, click the Track Effects button and double-click the Hard Limiter insert to open its user interface window.

4 Make sure the playhead is at the beginning of the file, and then start playback.

5 Move the Hard Limiter's Input Boost control back and forth. Stop playback. No change has been made to the envelope.

6 Turn off the Protection button, start playback, and then vary the Hard Limiter Input Boost control again.

7 Stop playback. Now the Hard Limiter Input Boost envelope has been overwritten.

8 Choose File > Close All, and click No To All when asked if you would like to save.

Review questions

1 Is there any parameter you can automate in tracks that you can't automate in clips?

2 What is a keyframe?

3 What is an automation lane?

4 What is the difference between Touch and Latch mode for writing automation?

5 How does Audition prevent accidental editing of the wrong envelope?

Review answers

1 Clips cannot automate mutes.

2 A keyframe is a point on an automation envelope that represents a particular parameter value.

3 A lane is part of the Multitrack Editor where you can create and edit envelopes for a track. Every track has a corresponding lane.

4 After releasing a control in Touch mode, from that point on the automation returns to any previously written automation. After releasing a control in Latch mode, the automation envelope retains the last control value prior to releasing it.

5 Only the selected envelope can be edited, even though other envelopes are visible. You can also select the Protection button to prevent overwriting automation moves when recording automation.

12 VIDEO SOUNDTRACKS

Lesson overview

In this lesson, you'll learn how to do the following:

- Load a video preview file into Audition

- Synchronize ADR (dubbed) dialogue with original dialogue

- Evaluate which type of dialogue synchronization provides the best audio quality

- Edit Adobe Premiere Pro CC audio files in Audition

- Open Premiere Pro project files in Audition

- Export a multitrack project's tracks to Premiere Pro

- Link a multitrack project to Premiere Pro so that edits in the Audition project are reflected in Premiere Pro

 This lesson will take about 60 minutes to complete. Please log in to your account on peachpit.com to download the lesson files for this chapter, or go to the "Getting Started" section at the beginning of this book and follow the instructions under "Accessing the Lesson Files and Web Edition." Store the files on your computer in a convenient location.

Your Account page is also where you'll find any updates to the chapters or to the lesson files. Look on the Lesson & Update Files tab to access the most current content.

Audition and Premiere Pro can work together using
Adobe Dynamic Link and shared audio effects, so that
clips from Premiere Pro can be edited in Audition,
and multitrack projects can be transferred back to
Premiere Pro and updated in the sequence.

Multitrack session video

Although in Audition it's not possible to edit video clips or combine video clips in multitrack sessions, you can include one video clip or one dynamically linked Premiere Pro video sequence. The Video panel will display the video in high quality, allowing you to create precisely timed soundtracks.

Supported formats and codecs include: AVI (Windows only), DV, MOV, MPEG-1, MPEG-4, 3GPP and 3GPP2, FLV, R3D, SWF, and WMV,

You can add one video track to a multitrack session. When you add a clip with video to a multitrack session that has no video track, a track is added automatically.

You can click the disclosure triangle next to file name in the Files panel to access individual audio channels from compound media files, such as video clips that are combined with audio.

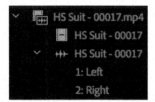

You can drag individual audio elements into a multitrack session or double-click them to apply changes in the Waveform Editor.

Audition integration with Adobe Premiere Pro CC

Adobe Premiere Pro CC integrates with Adobe Audition CC in several ways, such as:

- You can edit Premiere Pro sequences and audio files in Audition.

- You can export each Audition Multitrack Session track to a Premiere Pro sequence.

- You can link an Audition multitrack session to its mixdown file. From Premiere Pro you can choose to edit the original multitrack session or open the mixdown file in the Audition Waveform Editor.

- You can open a Premiere Pro project file directly in Audition and select a sequence to import. Changes made in Audition do *not* modify the original Premiere Pro project file. Rather, a new multitrack session is created based on the Premiere Pro project file.

These features make it easy to send a variety of materials from Premiere Pro, ranging from individual clips to a selected work area, into Audition for restoration, mastering, or processing ("sweetening"). With individual clips, saving any edits made in Audition will automatically update the clips in Premiere Pro. Similarly, you can edit clips from Adobe After Effects CC.

The level of integration between Audition and Premiere Pro can smooth your workflow dramatically when you're combining audio and video projects. Although covering all aspects of this integration is beyond the scope of this book, many tutorials, blog posts, and additional information are available on the Adobe website.

Installing Adobe Premiere Pro CC

The following exercises require that Adobe Premiere Pro CC be installed on the same computer as Audition. If Premiere Pro is not already installed, please do the following.

1 If you have a Creative Cloud membership that includes Premiere Pro, open the Creative Cloud desktop app and click to install it. If not, go to *www.adobe.com*, and download a trial version of Premiere Pro. It's fully functional for 30 days.

2 Follow the installation instructions.

3 Launch Premiere Pro, and it will scan any existing audio plug-ins. Premiere Pro may quit when it reaches plug-ins that are not compatible. If so, launch Premiere Pro again, and it will skip the plug-in that caused it to quit. You may need to repeat this process several times if you have lots of installed plug-ins that are not compatible.

4 After Premiere Pro displays the main Welcome screen, it's ready to use in the following exercises. Keep Premiere Pro open for the next exercise.

Editing Premiere Pro audio files in Audition

This exercise demonstrates how to edit a Premiere Pro clip in Audition and have that clip within a Premiere Pro project reflect these edits.

Premiere Pro sequences are similar to Audition multitrack sessions, in that they allow you to combine multiple clips to create a final composite result.

1 Start Premiere Pro, click Open Project in the Start screen, and navigate to the Lesson12 folder. Open the Edit In Audition folder, select Edit In Audition. prproj, and then click Open (or double-click the Edit In Audition.prproj file).

2 Click the Play button ▶ at the bottom of the Program Monitor panel, and listen to the soundtrack. The track providing the background music is too long. We need only about 32 seconds, and a better musical choice would be the section of the soundtrack file that starts at around 41 seconds.

The Timeline panel below the Program Monitor shows Sequence 01 in the top-left corner.

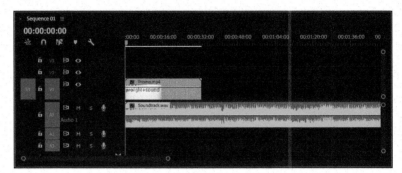

In the Timeline panel, the sequence contains two items: a video clip called Promo, on the Video 1 track, and an audio clip called Soundtrack, on the Audio 1 track.

3   Right-click the Soundtrack.wav clip, and choose Edit Clip In Adobe Audition.

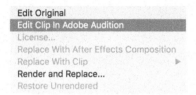

Several things happen in quick succession:

*   The audio file you right-clicked is duplicated in Premiere Pro—a new audio file appears in the Project panel (which is similar to the Files panel in Audition), called Soundtrack Audio Extracted.wav. This is a new, separate audio file from the original.

*   The original clip in the Premiere Pro sequence is replaced with the new copy.

*   Audition opens.

*   The new copy of the audio file is opened in Audition, ready for you to work on it.

4   In Audition, right-click the time display and choose Decimal (mm:ss.ddd). Drag to the left from 0:41.500 (where we want the sound track to begin) to the beginning to select the first part of the track.

5   Press Backspace (Windows) or Delete (macOS) to remove the selected part of the waveform.

6   Click at 0:32.715, and drag right to select everything to the end. Then press Backspace/Delete to remove the selected part of the waveform.

7   Create a fade-out that starts at 30 seconds, and then choose File > Save.

8 Return to Premiere Pro. Start playback, and you'll hear that the edits you made in Audition are reflected in Premiere Pro.

Notice that the audio clip in Premiere Pro shows diagonal lines where there is no longer any audio. You shortened the original audio file, but this did not change the clip in the sequence in Premiere Pro. This won't cause any playback issues in Premiere Pro; it's just good to know why that additional visual indicator appears.

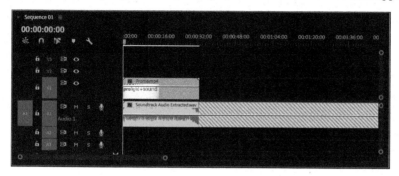

9 In Audition, choose File > Close All, and click Yes if asked if you would like to save changes. Keep Premiere Pro open for the next exercise.

Destructive and non-destructive workflows

The Audition Waveform Editor and Premiere Pro have fundamentally different approaches when it comes to media management.

In many ways, Premiere Pro treats media just as the Audition Multitrack Editor does: Both make changes to clips, rather than audio files, and so no changes are ever made to the original audio files.

The Audition Waveform Editor follows the more traditional audio approach, writing changes directly into the audio file when you save.

This introduces a conflict when you are sending files from Premiere Pro to Audition to work on them, most commonly to clean up noisy audio or add compression: Should the original media files be left untouched (the traditional non-linear editing non-destructive approach), or should the original media files be modified when adjustments are made (the traditional audio editing destructive approach)?

To solve this dilemma, Premiere Pro creates a duplicate file when you send a clip from Premiere Pro to Audition. Your subsequent changes are then saved to the duplicate, not the original, protecting the original media.

Premiere Pro always plays the latest version of any file, which is why you can simply save the file you are working on in Audition to have the file update automatically in Premiere Pro.

Sending a Premiere Pro sequence to Audition

Premiere Pro can also send whole sequences to Audition, bringing existing audio level and pan adjustments and effects right into the Audition Multitrack Editor.

Give it a try:

1 In Premiere Pro, make sure the Timeline panel is active, with a blue outline, by clicking anywhere in the panel.

2 Choose Edit > Edit In Adobe Audition > Sequence. The Edit In Adobe Audition dialog box appears.

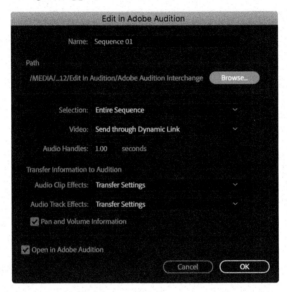

When you click OK, Premiere Pro will create a new, separate, multitrack session with copies of all of the audio clips included in the Premiere Pro sequence (in this example, it's just one clip). The multitrack session will open automatically in Audition.

Noteworthy options in this dialog box include:

- **Path:** The location to place the newly created files.

- **Selection:** You can choose the whole sequence or a section ranging between In and Out marks.

- **Video:** Export no video, export a DV Video Preview file (a flattened single video file; useful when transporting the new files to a different system), or use Dynamic Link to send the video "live" from the Premiere Pro timeline to Audition. This last option is the default, and it means any changes made to the visuals in Premiere Pro will update dynamically in Audition (only visual changes update, not the audio).

- **Audio Handles:** By default, Premiere Pro exports only the parts of the audio files that are used in the sequence, plus 1 second of additional audio at the start and at the end of the clip. For example, if you used 3 seconds of a 10 minute clip, only 5 seconds would be copied. The additional 1 second at either end is called a *handle*, and you can change how much additional content is included with this setting.

  You can also choose to include clip and track audio effects, as well as Pan and Volume adjustments. These will all be reflected in the newly created Audition multitrack session.

3 Leave the settings at their default values and click OK.

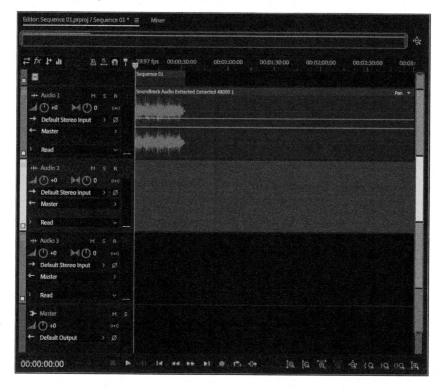

Connected but separate

It's important to be clear about the distinction between the original Premiere Pro sequence and the newly created multitrack session.

Although the new session is based on the Premiere Pro project file, there is no direct connection between them. If you enabled the option to send video via Dynamic Link, then changes made to the visuals *do* update in Audition but no changes to audio clips in Premiere Pro will update in Audition.

Audition opens with the newly created multitrack session ready to edit. The Video panel shows the contents of the Premiere Pro timeline, via the video clip that has been added to the multitrack session.

4   In Audition, choose File > Close All, and click No To All if asked if you would like to save.

5   Quit Premiere Pro, and click No if asked if you would like to save.

Opening Adobe Premiere Pro project files in Audition

In addition to sending clips and sequences from Premiere Pro to Audition, you can open Premiere Pro projects directly in Audition, and select a sequence to open as a multitrack session.

The result is similar to sending a sequence from Premiere Pro, without needing to have Premiere Pro installed.

There are a couple of differences when accessing Premiere Pro sequences this way:

• If Premiere Pro is not installed, you can't view the video via Dynamic Link.

• The original source media is used, rather than copies of the media.

Give it a try:

1   In Audition, choose File > Open.

2   Browse to the Lesson12 folder, and then to the Edit In Audition subfolder. Select the Premiere Pro project file Edit In Audition.prproj.

3   Click Open.

There is only one sequence in this Premiere Pro project file, and it is imported and opened in the Multitrack Editor panel, ready to work on. If there were more sequences, you would have the option to choose which you want to open.

4   Choose File > Close All, and click No To All if asked if you would like to save.

Exporting a multitrack project's tracks to Adobe Premiere Pro CC

You can export each track of an Audition multitrack project into its own audio track within Premiere Pro.

1 Open Premiere Pro. Click Open Project in the Start screen, navigate to the Lesson12 folder, and open the folder Export Multitrack. Select ExportMultitrack.prproj, and then click Open.

2 Open Audition (if it's not already running). Choose File > Open, navigate to the Lesson12 folder, and if necessary, open the folder Export Multitrack. Select MultitrackSoundtrack.sesx, and then click Open.

3 In Audition, choose Multitrack > Export To Adobe Premiere Pro. The Export to Adobe Premiere Pro dialog box appears.

Retain the existing default File Name. For Location, if necessary, browse to the Export Multitrack folder in Lesson12 and open it; then click Save. For Sample Rate, leave the setting at 44100 Hz.

In the Options area, select:

• Export Each Track As Stem

• Open In Adobe Premiere Pro

Now click Export. Premiere Pro appears, with the Copy Adobe Audition Tracks dialog box displayed.

Note: If you prefer to have the tracks start at track Audio 1, choose Audio 1 from the Copy To Active Sequence menu.

Note: Once tracks are in Premiere Pro, you can add fades, change levels, trim clips, and more.

4 Use this dialog box to choose where the new audio will be added to the current sequence. The default option of New Audio Track is fine, so click OK.

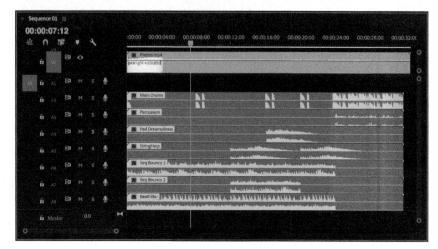

All the Audition tracks now appear as separate tracks within Premiere Pro, starting with the track named Audio 2. Notice that the gaps in the tracks are incorporated into continuous audio files as silence.

5 In Premiere Pro, start playback. Note that the levels are a bit hot and the Output meter is going into the red. Click the Audio Track Mixer panel name (it's at the top left of the interface, in the same panel group as the Source Monitor; if you can't find it, you'll locate it in the Window menu).

There are two audio mixers in Premiere Pro, and this one functions in a very similar way to the Mixer in Audition. Set all the track faders to –6.0, and Start playback again.

This time the master level remains undistorted.

6 Close Premiere Pro and Audition without saving anything so that neither is open at the start of the next exercise.

Linking a multitrack project to Adobe Premiere Pro

When importing an exported multitrack session mixdown audio file into a Premiere Pro project, additional metadata (data about data) can be included with the file, including a project link. This project link allows you to open the audio file's original multitrack session in Audition to make changes.

When you are happy with your adjustments, you can export a new multitrack session mixdown audio file from Audition for use in the Premiere Pro project.

If the new mixdown audio file replaces the previous version (with the same filename and location), it will also automatically replace the audio in the Premiere Pro project sequence.

Being able to open the original multitrack session in Audition, directly from Premiere Pro is a real time-saver, as it means you don't need to search for the original content manually. You need the multitrack session to be in the same location as it was when the mixdown output file was created.

1 Open Audition. Choose File > Open, navigate to the Lesson12 folder, and open the folder Linking. Select MultitrackSoundtrack.sesx, and then click Open.

2 Choose Edit > Preferences > Markers & Metadata (Windows) or Adobe Audition CC > Preferences > Markers & Metadata (macOS). Make sure that Embed Edit Original Link Data In Multitrack Mixdowns is selected, as well as Include Markers And Metadata In Recordings And Multitrack Mixdowns. Click OK.

3 Choose File > Export > Multitrack Mixdown > Entire Session. In the Export Multitrack Mixdown dialog box, keep the default for File Name. Make sure that Include Markers And Other Metadata is selected. For Location, browse to the Linking folder in Lesson12 and click Save.

4 Click OK to dismiss the Export Multitrack Mixdown dialog box, and then choose File > Close All.

5 Open Premiere Pro. Click Open Project in the Start screen, navigate to the Lesson12 folder, and open the folder Linking. Select Linking.prproj, and then click Open.

6 In Premiere Pro, choose File > Import. Navigate to the Linking folder in Lesson12, and then select the MultitrackSoundtrack_Mixdown.wav file you just created. Click Import. An icon representing the file appears in the Project panel.

There are two viewing modes in the Premiere Pro Project panel: List View and Icon View.

7 Drag this icon into the Timeline panel, at the very beginning of the A1 Audio track in Sequence 01.

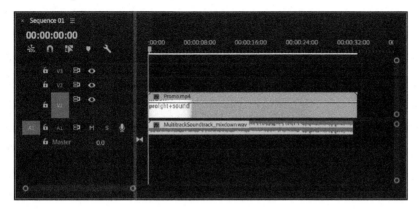

8 Start playback in Premiere Pro, and listen to the mix.

9 To edit this audio mix, right-click the MultitrackSoundtrack_Mixdown clip in the Premiere Pro, sequence and choose Edit Original. In the Audition dialog box that opens select Open The Audition Multitrack Session That Created The File, and then click OK.

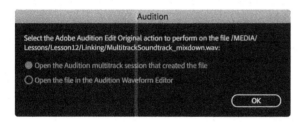

10 Add a fade-out starting at 29 seconds to the last Main Drums and Percussion clips; this will fade out the sound track, because they're the only clips playing at the end.

11 After adding the fades, choose File > Export > Multitrack Mixdown > Entire Session. Specify the same name and location as the original file; the defaults are likely to be correct. Click OK, and when asked if you want to overwrite the existing file, click Yes.

12 Play the project in Adobe Premiere Pro; the sound track will contain the fades you added.

13 Close Premiere Pro, and click No if you are asked if you would like to save changes.

14 In Audition, choose File > Close All, and click No To All if asked if you would like to save.

Premiere Pro always automatically plays the latest version of any file. Because you chose to overwrite the mixdown file, you effectively updated it, replacing the original audio.

Note: After making edits in Audition and exporting them to Premiere Pro, you cannot make additional edits and re-export without closing the project and then opening it again using the Edit Original command described in step 9.

Automatic Speech Alignment

Automatic Speech Alignment is very important when you're processing dialogue in movies. Dialogue that's recorded on location is often subject to noise, an inability to get actors close enough to the microphone without the mic appearing in the picture, and other issues. As a result, the actors will come in after the shoot and dub new parts. This process is also called *looping* or *ADR (Automated Dialogue Replacement)*.

ADR is not easy to do. The actor typically listens to the original part on headphones in a recording studio (rather than on location) and tries to match the original speech as closely as possible. Sometimes actors do ADR even if it's not absolutely necessary, because they want to add a different emotional inflection than they originally used while shooting the scene.

Audition's Automatic Speech Alignment feature automates this process. You load the original reference dialogue (which can even be relatively noisy) into an Audition track, and then record the new dialogue into a second track. Audition then compares the new dialogue to the original and uses a combination of stretching and alignment processes to match the new dialogue to the reference track.

1   Navigate to the Lesson12 folder, and open the Multitrack Session named Vocal Alignment.sesx from the Vocal Alignment folder.

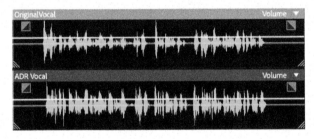

Note: The ADRVocal clip supplied with this project is deliberately way out of sync with the original dialogue so you can hear how Automatic Speech Alignment affects the sound quality of the dialogue when it has to do lots of correction.

2   Play the session to hear the session's two tracks, OriginalVocal and ADRVocal. ADRVocal is out of time with the original vocal track; you can use the ADRVocal track to experiment with the Automatic Speech Alignment feature, but it's instructive to record your own dialogue and try to match the OriginalVocal track.

3   Mute the ADRVocal track, and while listening to the OriginalVocal track on headphones, record a new vocal track where you'll try to match the OriginalVocal phrasing as closely as possible. If you decide to create your own ADR recording, the B-movie-type dialogue is:

"Helen said she thought she'd found Tesla's lab notes on wireless power transmission, and if she did, that would explain her disappearance. She would instantly be targeted as one of the most wanted people on this planet."

4 You now have two clips to align, using either the one supplied with the exercise or the one you created. If you recorded a vocal, trim the new clip to the same length as the OriginalVocal track. Select the Move tool 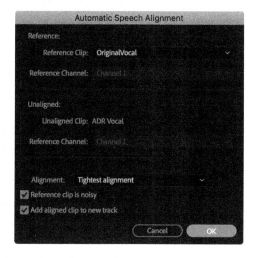, and draw a marquee to select both clips.

5 Right-click the OriginalVocal clip that will serve as the reference to which the other clip should be aligned, and choose Automatic Speech Alignment.

6 The Automatic Speech Alignment dialog box appears. For the Reference Clip, if needed, choose the clip to which you want the new dialogue aligned (in this project, OriginalVocal). There are three choices on the Alignment menu; you'll try all three, so start with Tightest Alignment. Select Reference Clip Is Noisy because in this case, it is; also select Add Aligned Clip To New Track to allow for easy comparison. Click OK.

7 A new track appears below the track containing the aligned clip. Solo the OriginalVocal and ADRVocal tracks (or OriginalVocal and the ADR track you recorded). Play them back together so you can hear the differences between the two clips.

8 Now solo the OriginalVocal track and the new, aligned track. You'll hear far fewer differences.

9 Click the OriginalVocal clip, and then Ctrl-click (Command-click) the ADRVocal track to select them both. Repeat steps 4 and 5, but this time choose Balanced Alignment And Stretching from the Alignment menu. Click OK.

10 Repeat step 8, soloing the original vocal and the new aligned track to compare the result.

Note: The Smoothest Stretching option usually provides the best audio quality, yet the alignment will still be very tight. Of course, the closer the ADR vocal is to the original, the less processing the Automatic Speech Alignment needs to do, and therefore, the higher the sound quality.

11 Repeat the process one more time, choosing Smoothest Stretching from the Alignment menu, and compare the result.

12 You now have three clips with the suffix "Aligned." Solo each one and listen carefully to hear how the three different processes affect the sound quality.

13 When you have finished reviewing the results, choose File > Close All, and click No To All if asked if you would like to save.

Review questions

1 Does Audition do video editing?

2 What is ADR or looping?

3 Why is it necessary to do Automatic Speech Alignment in the Multitrack Editor instead of the Waveform Editor?

4 Are you limited to a single speech alignment process?

Review answers

1 No. An imported video file is used as a preview, and Audition can add audio to the video.

2 ADR and looping are techniques that allow actors to replace low-quality dialogue in a movie with higher-quality dialogue, typically recorded in a studio instead of on location.

3 You must do Automatic Speech Alignment in the Multitrack Editor because you need to have two clips in the session: the original dialogue and the replacement dialogue you want to align to the original dialogue.

4 No; there are three different ways to do alignment that trade off tighter alignment for smoother vocal quality.

13 THE ESSENTIAL SOUND PANEL

Lesson overview

In this lesson, you'll learn how to do the following:

- Assign audio types in the Essential Sound panel
- Automatically set clip volume to industry-standard levels
- Quickly improve the clarity of vocals
- Apply audio ducking to reduce music levels when there is a vocal to be heard
- Improve the clarity of vocals

This lesson will take about 45 minutes to complete. Please log in to your account on peachpit.com to download the lesson files for this chapter, or go to the "Getting Started" section at the beginning of this book and follow the instructions under "Accessing the Lesson Files and Web Edition." Store the files on your computer in a convenient location.

Your Account page is also where you'll find any updates to the chapters or to the lesson files. Look on the Lesson & Update Files tab to access the most current content.

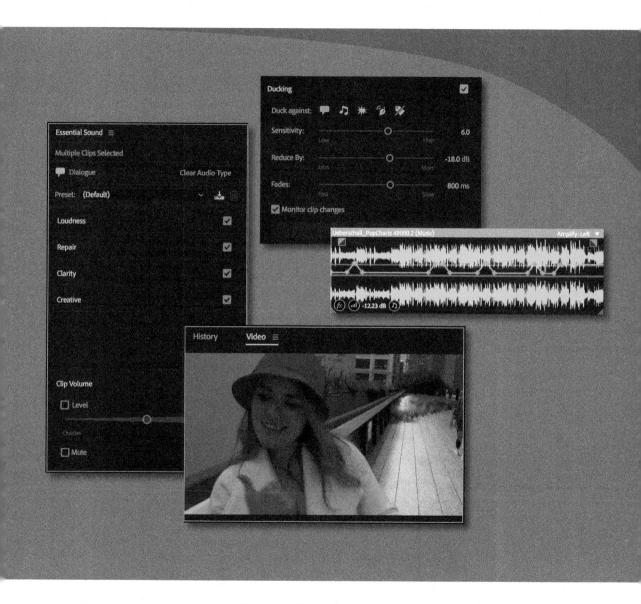

The Essential Sound panel provides a range of tools to quickly mix, adjust, and improve your audio. Clips are assigned a type, giving access to settings and effects suitable for that type. Adjustments applied using the Essential Sound panel are non-destructive.

Automating tasks

● **Note:** If you have not already downloaded the project files for this lesson to your computer from your Account page, make sure to do so now. See "Getting Started" at the beginning of the book.

Audition has an excellent range of analysis tools, adjustments, and effects for film and television soundtrack creation. So far, you have been using mainly manual controls to make precise adjustments, but Audition also offers several automated options that will get you close to an ideal result quickly. Once the automated settings are applied, you can make precise adjustments, just as you might adjust an effect preset.

Specifically, the Essential Sound panel includes a range of settings and effects to quickly adjust clips in multitrack sessions, and it's particularly well-suited to film and television soundtrack creation. Although the Essential Sound panel doesn't come close to the fine detail control available when working with other effects and tools, it's intended to provide quick and easy access to many of the adjustments you'll want to make on a regular basis when creating soundtracks.

Non-destructive workflows

Because the Essential Sound panel works exclusively in the Multitrack Editor, all changes are non-destructive. That means no changes will be made to your original audio files.

Many adjustments automatically add a clip-based (rather than track-based) effect to the selected clip, or clips.

As you adjust settings in the Essential Sound panel, the settings for the effect are dynamically adjusted too. This means you can adjust settings in the Essential Sound panel or in the effect's dialog box, and the result is the same. In this sense, it's helpful to think of the Essential Sound panel as a series of dynamic or "live" shortcuts to other useful areas of the Audition interface—in particular, the Properties panel and the Clip section of the Effects Rack.

Assigning audio types

To begin with using the Essential Sound panel, you will assign an audio type to one or more clips in a multitrack sequence. After you allocate the audio type, effects and controls relevant to that type of audio become available.

The four types of audio available are:

*   **Dialogue:** Any kind of vocals, including singing.

*   **Music:** Any continuous tonal audio; this type is particularly useful because it supports audio *ducking* (see below), which automatically lowers the volume of the audio in time with other audio clips (such as voice-over).

- **SFX:** Special effects, such as sword clashes, door slams, and Foley; sometimes these are called *spot effects*.

- **Ambience:** The kind of atmospheric sound the audience is not supposed to notice, such as air conditioning hum or the eerie hollow whisper of wind in a cave.

You can select as many clips as you like before choosing an audio type, and you can change the audio type at any time.

Automating a mix

To begin, you'll work with a simple voice-over soundtrack for a project created in Adobe Premiere Pro to try out some of the options in the Essential Sound panel for improving audio that's been assigned the Dialogue type. Although the Essential Sound panel has presets that incorporate an audio type selection, you're going to make selections and adjustments manually to better understand the processes.

The Essential Sound panel has several categories of adjustments for addressing different audio problems, each with a different set of options. The categories available vary depending on the audio type assigned to the selected clip.

The voice-over file is reasonably clean, without background noise, but its levels vary widely, which are distracting. In addition, the music track is too loud. You'll use the Loudness section of the Essential Sound panel to fix the voice levels and the overall music level, and then you'll use the options in the Ducking section to keep the background score from interfering with the voice-over.

The Loudness section contains only one real control: the Auto-Match button. Clicking this button applies an automatic Gain adjustment with a target Loudness of −23 LUFS (Loudness Units, Full Scale; see Chapter 4, "Effects," for more information about the Loudness scale). This level is an industry standard for broadcast dialogue audio.

Selecting the Ducking option for a selected clip adds an Amplify effect to it (visible in the Effects Rack), with automation applied that lowers the volume each time there is voice-over in another track. Audition provides several controls for refining your audio ducking:

Tip: You can reset any control to its default value in the Essential Sound panel by double-clicking it, so feel free to experiment.

- **Duck Against:** Select the types of clips you'd like to trigger ducking, including clips with no audio type assigned. To identify the audio type options here, hover over an icon.

- **Sensitivity:** The higher this is set, the louder the audio clip that triggers ducking will need to be before ducking is applied. Adjust this if ducking is being applied too often or too rarely.

- **Reduce By:** This important option sets the adjustment to the mix when ducking is applied. By default it's quite a dramatic −18 dB adjustment. This will definitely make a voice-over more audible but perhaps at the cost of hearing the music properly.

- **Fades:** When ducking is applied, the audio level doesn't jump, instead there's a fade up or down. You set the duration of the fade, which is 800 milliseconds by default. A millisecond is one thousandth of a second, so the default is 0.8 seconds.

- **Monitor Clip Changes:** When this option is selected, you can move clips to different relative positions in a session and the ducking will update automatically. When you deselect this option, the ducking will not update when you move clips but you can now manually adjust the control points for the effect on the clip.

The best way to understand how all these settings interrelate is to experiment with an actual multitrack session.

1 Choose the Default workspace, and reset the workspace.

2 Choose File > Open, navigate to the Lesson13 folder, and open NYC Project. prproj (not NYC Project With Hum.prproj).

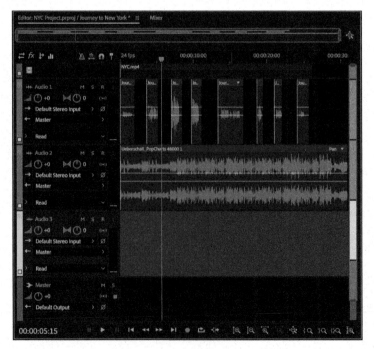

This is a simple Premiere Pro sequence with one video clip, a series of voice-over clips, and music track. Because this project only has one sequence, it's converted into a multitrack session without asking which sequence you would like to open.

The session file is independent of the original Premiere Pro project file, and appears automatically in the Files panel.

3 Play the session to familiarize yourself with it. The music is too loud, and the voice-over clips vary in volume wildly.

4 Solo the Audio 1 track, so you can hear the voice-over exclusively. Play the session to hear the varying voice-over levels more clearly. You'll fix that next.

5 Make sure the Move tool is selected, and drag across all the voice-over clips on the Audio 1 track. Be careful not to select the music clip.

6 In the Essential Sound panel, click the Dialogue button to assign that audio type to the voice-over clips.

Changing multiple clips

When you apply effects using the Effects Rack or the Effects menu, you're working on one clip at a time. The Essential Sound panel allows you to make changes to multiple clips in a single step.

Any clips that are selected when you're making changes in the Essential Sound panel will be modified at the same time. Because adjustments made in the Essential Sound panel result in effects that appear in the Effects Rack, it's a useful shortcut when working on multiple clips.

The Dialogue audio options appear in the Essential Sound panel. Notice there's a button to clear the currently assigned audio type, and at the bottom of the panel, there's an option to change the clip volume.

7 Click the Loudness section heading.

8 This section has just one option; to Auto-Match Loudness. Click the Auto-Match button now.

Every clip you selected now has an individual gain adjustment applied to bring it to a loudness of −23 LUFS.

Each clip you set as Dialogue now has a dialogue icon, and each clip you applied an automatic Loudness adjustment to has a Gain icon, and displays the amount of gain adjustment.

Although you used the Essential Sound panel to make the change, the result is actually an adjustment applied to each clip's properties.

9 Deselect by clicking the background (not a clip) in the Editor panel. Then right-click a clip and choose Clip Properties to open the Properties panel. Expand the Basic Settings to view the Clip Gain adjustment you just applied.

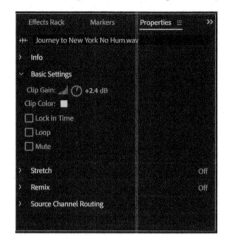

When using the Auto-Match option in the Essential Sound panel, each clip is adjusted by exactly the right amount to match –23 LUFS.

10 Deselect the Solo option for the Audio 1 track.

Applying audio ducking

This voice-over was recorded reasonably well, so you will come back to the other dialogue options later. For now, concentrate on setting the music level and adding some audio ducking, to lower the music level each time there is speech. You'll begin by setting the audio type.

1 Select the music clip on the Audio 2 track to select it (be careful not to double-click the clip, or it will open in the Waveform editor). In the Essential Sound panel, select the Music audio type.

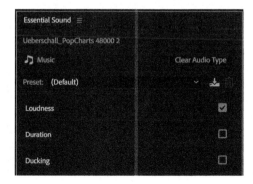

2　Start by setting the Loudness: Click the Loudness heading to expand the controls, and then click Auto-Match.

A gain adjustment is applied to the music clip, automatically set to achieve a Loudness level of −25 LUFS (a little quieter than the dialogue, which was automatically set to −23 LUFS).

3　Play the session to hear the improvements to the mix.

It's better, but it would be helpful if the music volume lowered during the sections of voice-over.

4　Still with the music clip selected, click the Ducking section of the Essential Sound panel to display the controls, and select the check box to enable the option. An Amplify effect is added to the clip, with automation that lowers the volume each time there is audio in the voice-over track.

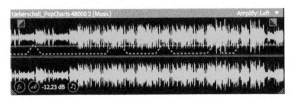

5　Play the session to listen to the result. This is a big improvement, but perhaps the ducking could be a little more subtle. Make sure the music clip is selected, and get ready to adjust the individual Ducking controls.

Notice the Amplify effect is chosen from the menu at the top-right corner of the clip.

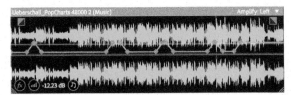

If Monitor Clip Changes is deselected, you can click the Generate Keyframes button to reset existing keyframes and apply new ones based on the current clip positions.

6　Leave the Sensitivity at 6.0, set the Reduce By amount to −7.0 dB, and set the Fades timing to 400 ms.

7　Play the session to compare the result. This is an improvement for sure, though you may be able to get more natural sounding ducking by working with the settings a little longer.

When applying audio ducking, the goal is usually for the listener not to notice the background music level is changing, and this is sometimes only possible by beginning with the automated adjustments, then fine tuning the control points after disabling the Monitor Clip Changes option.

8 Save the session. When you do, you may be invited to automatically move media files to the same folder as the multitrack session file you're saving.

It's important to manage media files, independently of managing clips in a session, as well as to be very clear about where they are and what you intend to do with them. In many ways, if you see this message, it could be an indication that you haven't organized your media sufficiently.

Ordinarily this might be useful, but because you are working on media associated with a Premiere Pro project, moving the files is likely to impact playback for that project—which would be a terrible idea! Click No.

9 Choose File > Close All, and click No To All if you are asked if you would like to save any files.

Saving open clips with session files

When saving a multitrack session, any clips that are already incorporated into the session will automatically be saved with it, and will appear in the Files panel when you open the session again in the future.

Clips that are open in the Files panel but *not* incorporated into the session will not be re-opened when you open the session in the future.

If you would like all clips that are displayed in the Files panel at the time you save a session (including the ones you haven't used in the session) to re-appear when you open the session in the future, there's a preference setting for that: Choose Edit > Preferences > Multitrack (Windows) or Adobe Audition CC > Preferences > Multitrack (macOS), and select the Reference All Open Audio And Video Files When Saving Sessions option. This is one of the most useful, and often overlooked, preferences in Audition CC, as it allows you to open and review media, and decide later if you would like to use it in a session.

Cleaning up audio

The Essential Sound panel also has some excellent tools for cleaning up audio. These tools are in the Repair section of the panel.

As with other adjustments in the Essential Sound panel, enabling a repair option will add an effect to the Effects Rack that you can manually edit later, finessing the result if you need to. Each option has an intensity slider, which allows you to adjust the overall strength of an effect whose character may itself be determined by settings of multiple controls:

- **Reduce Noise** adds an Adaptive Noise Reduction effect, which first identifies unwanted noise, then removes it. This is less effective than the full Noise Reduction (Process) effect that is available only in the Effects menu, but can be a good quick fix for longer audio clips.

- **Reduce Rumble** reduces low-frequency sounds and plosives, which is useful if, for instance, low-frequency wind noise or mechanical rumble was caught in the recording.

- **DeHum** reduces the low-frequency tone that is caused by electrical interference. This can occur when microphone cables lie parallel to power cables. In North and South America, as well as Japan, the power grid is 60 Hz alternating current, which can result in a 60 Hz interference hum in audio recordings. Pretty much the rest of the world uses a 50 Hz power supply, which can result in a 50 Hz interference hum.

- **DeEss** reduces amplitude at the frequencies you can expect to hear high tone sibilance, produced by such sounds as S's and F's. Depending on the voice of the speaker or the way the audio is recorded, these can be harsh and distracting. Selecting DeEss in the Essential Sound panel can soften the audio pleasingly.

Start with a simple example. You'll work with the same Premiere Pro sequence as in the previous exercise, but this time the original voice-over track is plagued by a loud electrical hum at 60 Hz.

1   Choose File > Open, navigate to the Lesson13 folder, and open NYC Project With Hum.prproj. Play the resulting session to get familiar with the media. The hum at 60 Hz is clearly audible.

2   Select the Solo option for the Audio 1 track. Select all the voice-over clips, and select the Dialogue audio type in the Essential Sound panel.

3   You'll adjust the Loudness in a moment. For now, select the Repair section in the Essential Sound panel to display the options. Play a section of the session now that the voice-over is soloed to get a clearer sense of the challenge.

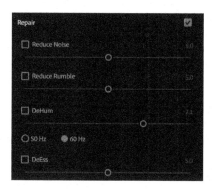

4 Select DeHum. It should be set to 60 Hz already by default. Make sure it has the default intensity of 7.1.

5 Play the voice session to hear the result. It's much improved, though there's a pop at the start of each clip.

6 Select the Loudness section of the Essential Sound panel, and click the Auto-Match button to set the voice-over Loudness to –23 LUFS.

7 Trimming the start of the clip won't remove the pops. They are there because it takes a moment for the DeHum to affect the clip. The solution is to add a short fade at the start of each clip. Do this now, dragging the Fade handle in and down to achieve a steep linear value of –50 for each clip.

The fades can be very short; be careful not to affect the speech.

Improving audio

In addition to cleaning up dialogue audio, the Essential Sound panel includes several options for making it even better. Of particular importance for dialogue is the Clarity section, which includes these options:

- **Dynamics:** Produces a similar result to compression or its opposite, expansion. The dynamic range of the audio (that is, the range of levels from completely silent to fully loud) is reduced or expanded, which can help to level out audio or to add more interesting variation.

- **EQ:** Applies a Graphic Equalizer (10 Bands) effect, which is listed in the Effects Rack. Double-click the listing to open the Graphic Equalizer window and adjust the frequency bands individually to improve the audio clips. Or, make a choice from the EQ Preset menu in the Essential Sound panel.

Note: Adjusting the Clarity and Creative options can produce quite subtle results, and it's important to have good quality monitors (loudspeakers) or headphones to clearly detect the results.

- **Enhance Speech:** Enhances slightly higher frequencies to add clarity to speech. The result is achieved by adding the Vocal Enhancer effect to the Effects Rack. The limited options in the Vocal Enhancer effect make it the kind of solution that either works perfectly for a particular audio source or does nothing significant. Sometimes the only way to know if an effect is going to work is to try it.

The Creative section of the Essential Sound panel contains the option to add Reverb. This can be useful for setting a dialogue track in a slightly different acoustical space to separate it from the other audio tracks in a mix.

In the following exercise, you'll add body to the voice over clips without overwhelming the clarity of the speech.

1 Make sure all the voice-over clips are selected, and click the Clarity section of the Essential Sound panel to display the options.

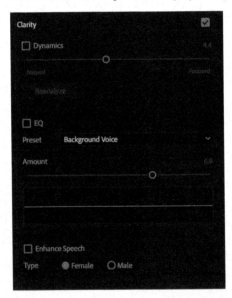

2 For this audio, select EQ (Equalization), and experiment with the various presets. After you have listened to a few options, choose the Vocal Presence preset, and set the Amount slider to 7.0.

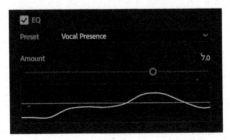

3 Disable the EQ option, and enable the Enhance Speech option, then set Female as the type.

4 In the Creative section of the Essential Sound panel, select Reverb and try a few presets. When you have listened to some options, and experimented with the Amount slider, choose the Warm Voice preset, and set the Amount to 4.0.

Other audio types

Most of the time, you're likely to use the Dialogue and Music audio types when using the efficient shortcuts provided by the Essential Sound panel. Still, there are two more audio types: SFX and Ambience.

SFX

Primarily intended for such spot effects as Foley, this audio type allows you to apply the same Loudness and Reverb options you chose for the dialogue earlier. It also offers a simple Pan adjustment. You could adjust the clip pan by moving the Pan envelope on a clip in the Editor panel, but by using the Essential Sound panel you can adjust Pan for multiple clips in a single step.

Ambience

Once again, the Ambience audio type gives you access to Loudness and Creative options, but also includes a Stereo Width option. Enabling this option adds a Stereo Expander effect to the Effects Rack (as a clip effect), which can increase the differences between audio in the Left and Right channels. This gives audio a wider or narrower feel, which can be effective for atmospheric, or *wild*, sound.

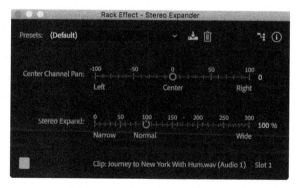

Essential Sound panel presets

After you select an audio type and select the options you want in the Essential Sound panel, you can create a new preset.

Though presets are linked to a particular audio type, it's not necessary to set the audio type to access them. They are all accessible in the Essential Sound panel as soon as you have selected one or more clips in a session.

Try creating a preset that sets the Loudness and DeHum options for a clip.

1 Select one or more of the dialogue clips you have adjusted. Make sure Auto-Match has been selected in the Loudness section and that DeHum is selected in the Repair section, with 60 Hz specified.

2 Click the Save Settings As A Preset button ![icon] at the top right of the Essential Sound panel.

3 Add the preset name **Loudness And 60 Hz DeHum**, and click OK.

The preset is added to the list in the Preset menu at the top of the Essential Sound panel.

4 Click the Clear Audio Type button to return to the Essential Sound panel audio type selection options.

5 Without choosing an audio type, choose the preset you just created in the Preset menu.

The audio type is applied, Loudness set, and DeHum added.

6 Choose File > Close All, and click No To All when asked if you would like to save changes.

Review questions

1 When making adjustments using the Essential Sound panel, how can you fine-tune the results?

2 What are the four audio types available in the Essential Sound panel?

3 What is power hum?

4 How can you add a preset to the Essential Sound panel?

5 What is audio ducking?

Review answers

1 All adjustments made in the Essential Sound panel result in an effect being applied. Locate the effect in the Effects Rack to make precise adjustments.

2 The four audio types are Dialogue, Music, SFX, and Ambience. Each type gives access to adjustments that are appropriate for the selected audio type.

3 Electricity power grids operate at 50 Hz or 60 Hz. When microphone cables lie parallel to, and in close proximity to power cables an interference hum is often induced along with the audio signal. This can be intrusive and loud relative to the audio you're recording, but it's easy to remove with the right effect.

4 After you choose the options you would like, click the Save Settings As A Preset button to add a new preset. You don't need to select an audio type before applying a preset; the audio type is automatically selected when you choose the preset.

5 Audio ducking lowers the level on one clip in response to level on another. The most common use is lowering the background music level for dialogue.

14 THE MULTITRACK MIXER

Lesson overview

In this lesson, you'll learn how to do the following:

- Switch between the Multitrack Editor and the Mixer views

- Adjust the Mixer fader heights to allow for greater resolution when setting levels

- Show or hide various sections of the Mixer

- Scroll through various Effects Rack inserts and sends within their respective areas

- Scroll to view different groups of channels if the Mixer window isn't wide enough to show them all

- Differentiate among channel types via color coding

- Rearrange the Mixer channel order

 This lesson will take about 30 minutes to complete. Please log in to your account on peachpit.com to download the lesson files for this chapter, or go to the "Getting Started" section at the beginning of this book and follow the instructions under "Accessing the Lesson Files and Web Edition." Store the files on your computer in a convenient location.

Your Account page is also where you'll find any updates to the chapters or to the lesson files. Look on the Lesson & Update Files tab to access the most current content.

The Mixer view is an alternate way to look at a multi-track project; it's optimized for mixing tracks together rather than working with individual clips.

Audio Mixer basics

Note: If you have not already downloaded the project files for this lesson to your computer from your Account page, make sure to do so now. See "Getting Started" at the beginning of the book.

In Audition, you can view multitrack projects in two different ways. So far, you've been working with the Multitrack Editor, which, as its name implies, is optimized for editing. However, the Mixer panel (which shares a panel group with the Multitrack Editor panel in the Classic and Default workspaces) provides another way to work with multitrack projects, and it is optimized for mixing.

The Multitrack Editor shows the clips within a series of tracks. The Mixer does not show clips at all but has a corresponding Mixer channel for each Multitrack Editor track. The reason for calling a Mixer channel a *channel* instead of a track is because hardware-based mixers use that term. In physical studios, there isn't necessarily a one-to-one correlation between tracks and channels; for instance, one recording track could feed more than one mixer channel.

The controls available in both the Editor and Mixer views are similar. The Multitrack Editor panel provides mixing functions and controls, but through dial controls not faders. In addition, several mixing functions (sends, EQ, effects, and ins/outs) share a common area, and you can see the settings for only one of these functions at a time. In the Mixer panel, on the other hand, all of these functions are arranged as rows and can be viewed simultaneously, plus it offers more mixing precision with fader-based controls.

Mixing typically occurs after the tracks in a session are recorded and edited, and you're ready to concentrate solely on blending all the tracks together to create a cohesive listening experience. Sometimes when you're editing, however, the most logical workflow is to temporarily switch over to the Mixer, then back to the Editor.

1   Navigate to the Lesson14 folder, and open the Multitrack Session named Mixer.sesx.

2 Choose the Classic workspace, and reset the workspace to the default layout by choosing Window > Workspace > Reset To Saved Layout.

The classic workspace emphasizes the Files and Editor panels.

3 Click the Mixer panel name, next to the Editor panel name.

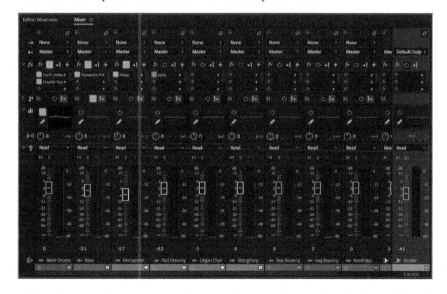

When you first look at the Mixer panel, you may feel a little overwhelmed. That's a lot of buttons! But look carefully at the design: There's a lot of repetition.

Every track in the current multitrack session is represented as a channel with a matching name in the Mixer panel, including the Master output track. Each channel's name appears below the channel controls. The controls for each channel are identical; learn them once, and you'll know them for every channel.

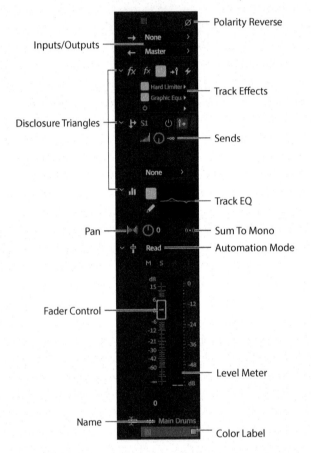

You'll also see a color label that matches the relevant track color in the Editor panel.

4 The Mixer uses faders instead of rotary controls to adjust level. If you resize the Mixer panel to make it taller, the faders will get longer, giving you more precision when making adjustments. Click the edge at the bottom of the Mixer panel, and drag down as far as possible to make the faders as long as possible.

▶ **Tip:** Undocking the Mixer panel is very convenient, because you can set it to a consistent size and you don't have to be concerned about resizing it. Undocking is also natural for two-monitor setups, because you can put the Mixer panel in its own dedicated monitor and the Multitrack Editor panel in the other monitor.

5 Drag the same bottom edge of the Mixer panel upward. Note that the faders get shorter. Continue dragging up; eventually the faders will collapse. Return the faders to the tallest size allowed by your screen while still being able to access the Transport controls.

Note: Long-throw hardware faders are desirable in hardware mixers because it's easier to do precise, high-resolution mixing moves. The same is true of virtual faders in software. When Audition's faders are extended to their greatest height, you can edit levels easily in 0.1 dB steps. In the Multitrack Editor, the most resolution you can achieve with the rotary Volume controls is 0.3 dB, and that requires a very precise touch.

6 Keep the session open, ready for the next exercise.

Mixer show and hide options

Most of the rows of controls in Mixer modules have a disclosure triangle; click the triangle to expand or collapse the row. You can customize how much space the Mixer takes up on the screen and automatically change the relative fader height by showing or hiding different parts of the Mixer.

1 When the fx area is collapsed, you can still see the fx area's master fx Power button, the FX Pre-Fader/Post-Fader button, and the Pre-Render Track button, which can be used to reduce CPU power when mixing complex projects (pre-rendering is described in Chapter 17, "Mixing and Output").

   If the fx area is not already displayed, click the disclosure triangle ![>] to expand its controls. Note that the faders become shorter because the fx area now takes up more space.

2 In all channels, you can now see three Effects Rack inserts. You can't resize this area to reveal more inserts, but the scroll bar to the right of the list lets you see every item. Drag the rectangle within the scroll bar up or down to see the other inserts.

3 With the Sends area closed, you can see the number of the currently selected send in the upper-left corner, the Power button, and the FX Pre-Fader/Post-Fader button. Click the Sends area disclosure triangle to expand it. Note that again the faders become shorter, because the Sends area now takes up more space.

Note: Two Mixer sections cannot be hidden: the I/O section at the top (Polarity Reverse button, Input Assign menu, and Output Assign menu) and the channel's Pan control and Sum To Mono button.

4   One send is shown at a time along with its Power button, FX Pre-Fader/Post-Fader, Send Volume, Stereo Balance controls, and menu for reassigning the send to a different send (or creating a new send bus or side-chain send).

Like the fx area, a scroll bar is available for choosing the current send. In the second channel from the left (labeled Bass), drag the rectangle within the scroll bar up or down to see the other sends. It takes precise control to scroll through the effects and sends, but it's functional and saves you clicking back into the Editor panel.

5   With the EQ area closed, no aspect of the EQ area is visible. Click the EQ area disclosure triangle to expand it. As with expanding the fx and Sends areas, the faders become even shorter to compensate for having less available space.

6   The EQ section works in the same way here as it does in the Multitrack Editor. The Power button can enable or bypass the EQ. Click the Show EQ Editor Window button to view the channel's Parametric Equalizer (you can also open it by double-clicking the EQ graph).

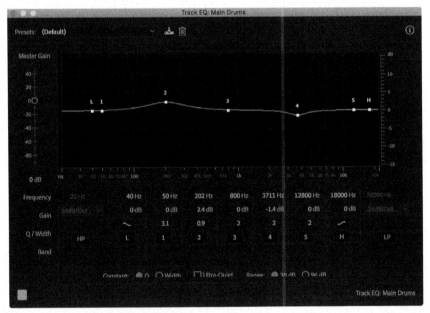

Close the Parametric EQ window, because you won't be making any adjustments for now.

7 Close the fader section by clicking its disclosure triangle.

The faders section collapses to show the Mute, Solo, Arm For Record, and Monitor Input buttons, with the track title and track label colors. Closing the fader section also reduces the fader to a Volume control that's identical to the one found in the Multitrack Editor panel.

Channel scrolling

With projects that have many channels, your monitor may not be wide enough to show them all. However, you can scroll though the various channels, as well as see which ones are buses, standard tracks, or the Master Track Output bus.

1 Drag the right edge of the Audition window left to narrow the Mixer. Make sure that you can't see all channels in the Mixer.

2 A navigator scroll bar appears along the bottom of the Mixer panel if the panel isn't wide enough to show all channels. Drag the scroll bar rectangle, all the way to the right. Now you can see the rightmost group of channels.

3 Restore the Audition window to full-screen size again, and drag the scroll bar rectangle all the way to the left in preparation for the next exercise.

Rearranging Mixer channel order

You're not limited to an existing left-to-right track order. For example, you may have recorded drums first in Multitrack Editor Track 1 and a percussion part in Multitrack Editor Track 3; these appear in Mixer channels 1 and 3, respectively. However, suppose you'd rather have the Percussion channel next to the Drums channel. You can move channels horizontally to anywhere within the Mixer.

1 Hover the pointer over the channel you want to move (in this case, the Percussion channel) until the pointer turns into a hand. There are several places in the channel where this happens, such as the color label.

2 Drag left until a vertical blue line appears to the right of the Main Drums channel. This is where the left side of the Percussion channel will be moved. (Note that if you drag right until you see a blue line, the right side of the channel will be moved there.)

3 Release the drag, and the Percussion channel will relocate to the right of the Main Drums channel.

Note: Channel fader controls have colors that match their track/channel label color. Different channel types (track, bus, master) have different icons next to the track/channel name.

Note: Changes made to the track/channel order in either the Editor panel or the Mixer panel update in both panels.

4 Click the Editor panel name to view the session tracks. Note that the track order has changed to reflect the channel change you made in the Mixer.

The controls in the Editor panel and Mixer panel really are the same. Changes to one will update the other. In fact, the track Effects Rack updates in the Effects Rack panel too—so there are three places you can add, change, and remove the same effects for all tracks.

Using hardware controllers

Although being able to mix onscreen is convenient, many engineers prefer the human touch of using physical faders. Audition supports various *control surfaces*, hardware devices that include faders and can control the onscreen faders. There are even control surface apps for tablets that will integrate with Audition via a shared Wi-Fi connection.

Many control surfaces can control the Mute and Solo buttons, panning, Transport, and arm tracks for recording.

Audition supports multiple protocols for the following control surfaces:

- Mackie MCU
- Mackie HUI
- Eucon/Avid
- Presonus Faderport
- ADS Tech Red Rover

Of these, the Mackie Control protocol is the most common, and several control surfaces from multiple manufacturers are compatible with this protocol. The newer Mackie HUI support expands the range of control surfaces supported.

Adding a control surface is easy; the following illustrates how to add a Mackie Control (or compatible) hardware controller. If you don't have a Mackie compatible hardware controller, you'll find the steps are similar for other controller types.

1 Choose Edit > Preferences > Control Surface (Windows) or Adobe Audition CC > Preferences > Control Surface (macOS).

2 Choose Add, and in the Device Class menu choose the control surface type (in this case, Mackie for Mackie Control). Then click Settings.

MIDI Issues

If your MIDI controller doesn't appear in at least the MIDI Input Device field, close Audition, reopen it, and then try again. If Audition still doesn't detect the controller, keep in mind that some controllers will appear if you restart the computer with the controller connected, whereas others work best if you restart the computer first, and then connect the controller (particularly with USB controllers).

Also, note that some controllers require installing driver software for them to work properly; and for some to emulate a Mackie controller, they may need to load a specific preset or be powered up with certain buttons held down. Refer to the controller's documentation for details.

3 In the dialog box that appears, click Add to add the control surface to the Control Surface pane of the Preferences dialog box.

4 In the next dialog box, choose a Device Type. For virtually all devices that offer Mackie compatibility, the standard Mackie Control is the correct choice. Next, choose the controller in the MIDI Input Device and MIDI Output Device fields, and then click OK. Click OK again to leave the Configuration window.

5 After returning to the Control Surface preferences, click Button Assignments to display assignments for the various assignable buttons available on the Control Surface you have selected.

Note that not all Mackie Control-compatible devices incorporate all buttons, and some may not incorporate any. The lower section shows available commands; drag a command next to the button to which you want the command assigned. Once you've made all your assignments, click OK, and then click OK again to exit the preferences.

6 When you have finished exploring these controls, choose File > Close All, and click No To All if asked if you would like to save any files.

Review questions

1 What are the main advantages of the Mixer panel compared to the Multitrack Editor panel?

2 What is the Mixer panel's main limitation?

3 How can you see all the Mixer channels if your monitor isn't wide enough?

4 How can you differentiate a bus from a track at a glance?

5 Is it possible to rearrange the left-to-right channel order to create a more logical workflow?

Review answers

1 The faders can have extremely high resolution, and if desired, you can see the fx, Sends, and EQ areas simultaneously.

2 You cannot edit clip properties in the Mixer panel.

3 A navigator scroll bar along the bottom of the Mixer panel lets you view different groups of channels.

4 Each channel type has a different icon at the bottom of the channel controls.

5 Yes, you can drag channels horizontally anywhere you want in the Mixer panel.

15 CREATING MUSIC WITH SOUND LIBRARIES

Lesson overview

In this lesson, you'll learn how to do the following:

- Create original music without needing to know how to play an instrument

- Preview clips in the Media Browser before bringing them into a multitrack session

- Modify clip lengths to add more variety to a composition

- Use files from a "music construction kit" to assemble music quickly

- Use pitch transposition and time-stretching to incorporate clips with a different native tempo or pitch than the current session

- Add effects processing to a track to complete the composition

 This lesson will take about 60 minutes to complete. Please log in to your account on peachpit.com to download the lesson files for this chapter, or go to the "Getting Started" section at the beginning of this book and follow the instructions under "Accessing the Lesson Files and Web Edition." Store the files on your computer in a convenient location.

Your Account page is also where you'll find any updates to the chapters or to the lesson files. Look on the Lesson & Update Files tab to access the most current content.

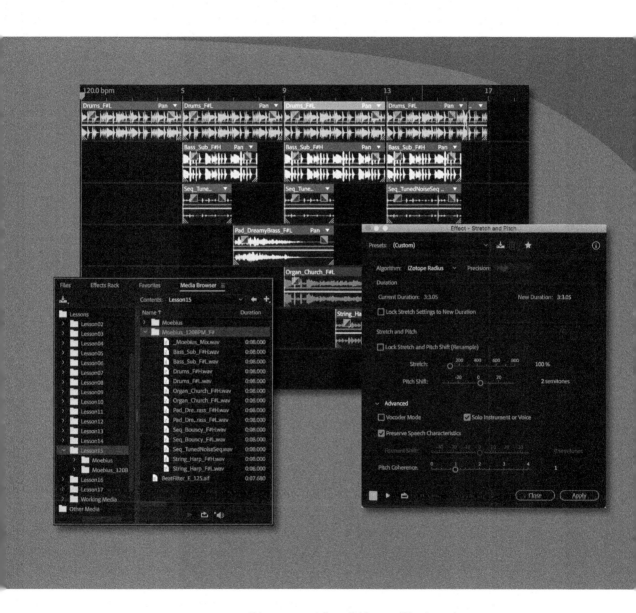

Using commercially available sound libraries and the Multitrack Editor, you can use Audition to create music for commercials and background audio for video, kiosks, and other applications—even if you don't know how to play a musical instrument.

About sound libraries

● **Note:** If you have not already downloaded the project files for this lesson to your computer from your Account page, make sure to do so now. See "Getting Started" at the beginning of the book.

Before computers, *needledrop music* often provided music for commercials, radio station breaks, and even some TV shows and movies. Needledrop music got its name because various companies produced sets of vinyl records with different types of music, sometimes classified by mood, and you would "drop the needle" on a suitable track for your background music. These records were usually expensive, and you needed to pay for a new license every time you wanted to use the music—even if the same song was used twice in a single project.

Today, many companies make sound libraries of musical fragments, loops, and sound effects available on CD-ROM, DVD-ROM, or more often via download. You can assemble these various sound clips to create professional-quality, custom music. Sound library licensing agreements vary; many are royalty-free, some just require the original artist to be credited. As in the days of vinyl, always read the fine print first to avoid potential legal problems later.

There are two main types of libraries:

- **Construction kits:** These typically include folders of compatible files. Files in each folder feature a consistent tempo and key, which makes mixing and matching files to create a custom arrangement easy.

- **General-purpose sound libraries:** These consist of collections of loops that share a common theme, such as dance music, jazz, rock, and so on. The key and tempo of the loops may vary.

The Lesson15 folder contains a construction kit called Moebius, which was created especially for this book. The kit contains 13 individual loops, as well as a loop called Moebius Mix that provides a representative mix of these loops. The construction kit loops are all at 120 bpm and in the key of F#. Although this lesson suggests assembling the various loops in a particular manner, music is all about creativity. Feel free to depart from the suggestions and create your own piece of music once you know how the process works.

Download Adobe sound effects

Adobe provides Audition users with thousands of royalty-free sound effects, music loops, and music beds that you can incorporate into creative projects.

Use of the files is subject to a license agreement that limits re-distribution (for example, you are not free to resell the files as a new sound library). You are free to modify, combine, and mix the files as part of a new creative work, making the

Adobe Audition Downloads a fantastic resource to help you get started creating new film soundtracks and music sessions.

You can access the files by choosing Help > Download Sound Effects And More, and then following the onscreen directions to download the content.

Preparing

To assemble a piece of music, you'll begin by creating a multitrack session to which you can add clips. You'll also want to first listen to the various available loops to become familiar with them.

1   Choose the Classic Workspace (as we don't need the Essential Sound panel), and reset the workspace by choosing Window > Workspace > Reset To Saved Layout. Click the Multitrack button at the top-left corner. Because Audition has no current multitrack session to open, the New Multitrack Session dialog box opens.

2   Enter **Moebius** for Session Name. Choose None for Template, and then for Sample Rate, Bit Depth, and Master, choose 44100 Hz, 16-bits, and Stereo, respectively. Click Browse to choose a location for the new session file (the Lesson15 folder is fine), and click OK.

When you create a new session file, Audition automatically places it inside a folder with the same name at the chosen location. This makes it easier to stay organized, as any new media you create will appear inside the new folder.

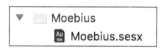

3   Choose Window > Media Browser (the Media Browser panel is not included by default in the Classic workspace). The Media Browser panel appears in the same panel group as the Files panel.

Tip: To fully reveal a long filename in the Media Browser, you may need to drag the divider between the Name and Duration headings to the right.

4   In the left side of the Media Browser panel, navigate to the Lesson15 folder and select it. In the right side, click the Moebius_120BPM_F# folder's disclosure triangle to expand it and show the files included in the Moebius construction kit. Click the Media Browser's Auto-Play button  to enable it.

5   Click files in the Moebius folder to hear them play. Click the file _MoebiusMix. wav to hear a representative mix of the various files playing together.

6   Choose View > Zoom Out Full (All Axes) to see an overview of the tracks as you build the composition in subsequent exercises.

7   Right-click the time display, or the timeline at the top of the Editor panel, and choose Time Display > Bars And Beats.

8   Right-click the time display again, and choose Edit Tempo. Set the Tempo to 120 beats/minute with a Time Signature of 4/4 and a Subdivisions setting of 16. Leave the Custom Frame Rate setting for now. Click OK.

9 If Snap is not already enabled, click the Snap button  at the top left of the Editor panel or press **S**.

Building a rhythm track

There are no rules about creating a piece of music, but it's common to start with a rhythm track consisting of drums and bass, and then to add other melodic elements. Feel free to customize the colors for each track by clicking each color label to make it easier to locate particular tracks at a glance.

1 From the Media Browser, drag the file Drums_F#L into Track 1 so its left edge is flush with the beginning of the session.

2 Hold down Alt (Windows) or Option (macOS) and drag the clip's name (Drums_F#L) right to copy the audio clip. Release the drag when the clip's start snaps to the beginning of measure 5, at the end of the first copy.

3 Repeat step 2 to create a copy so that the new clip copy starts at measure 9.

4 Create another copy so that the new clip copy starts at measure 13. There should now be four successive Drums_F#L clips in a row, lasting a total of 16 measures. The right edge of the last Drums_F#L clip will be at the start of measure 17.

5 Enable the Transport Loop button , return the playhead to the beginning of the session, and click Play. The music should play through to the end and then jump back to the beginning and repeat. Click Stop after trying this.

6 From the Media Browser, drag the file Bass_Sub_F#H into Track 2 so the clip's left edge starts at measure 5.

7 In the same way you copied the drum file, copy two more iterations of the Bass_Sub_F#H so that the second copy starts at measure 9 and the third copy starts at measure 13.

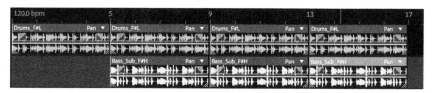

Note: Snap helps align the start of an audio clip to a rhythmic value. The resolution depends on the zoom level; for example, when zoomed full out, audio clips will snap to the nearest measure. Zoom in further, and they'll snap to the nearest beat.

Note: If you move the pointer after a clip has snapped to a rhythmic division, the clip may move off the rhythm. To make sure it has snapped properly, after dropping the clip, drag the clip by its name until it snaps into place.

Note: Adding more tracks increases the Output level. The quickest fix is to scroll down to the Master track and reduce the volume to prevent the Output meters from going into the red. Ideally, though, it's better to keep the Master level at 0 and adjust individual tracks to compensate for excessive Output levels.

8 Because a constant bass part can get monotonous, you can trim some of the file so it drops out and let the drums carry the beat. To do this, hover the pointer over the right edge of the bass clip that begins at measure 5 and ends at measure 9 (in the part of the waveform just below the name) until the pointer turns into a left-facing Trim tool, as signified by a red right bracket.

9 Drag left until the clip ends at the beginning of measure 8.

10 Drag the right edge of the third copy left so that it ends at measure 16.

11 Add some variety to the drum track as well by rearranging its pattern. Hover the right edge of the last drum clip until you see a red, right bracket (the right-facing Trim tool), drag to the left to trim the clip so that it ends at measure 16.

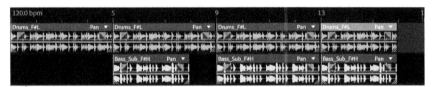

12 From the Media Browser, drag the file Drums_F#H into Track 1 so the clip's left edge starts at measure 16. Hover over the right edge of this drum clip until you see the red, right bracket, and then drag to the left so that this clip ends at the beginning of measure 17.

13 Return the playhead to the beginning, and click Play to listen to the drum and bass tracks.

14 The transition between the fourth and fifth drum clips seems a little abrupt. To smooth this, zoom in for a detailed view of the transition between the two clips at measure 16. Click the fourth drum clip (the one that ends at measure 16) to select it.

15 Hover over the right edge of the fourth drum clip to access the red, right-facing Trim tool, and then drag right so that the clip ends at measure 16, beat 2 (shown as 16:2 on the Editor timeline if you're zoomed in far enough). This will auto-crossfade the end of the fourth clip with the beginning of the fifth clip. Play that transition; it sounds much smoother.

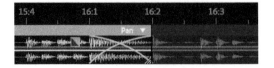

Adding more percussion

Before moving on to additional melodic elements, add a little light percussion to augment the rhythmic feel.

1   From the Media Browser, drag the file Seq_TunedNoiseSeq into Track 3 so its left edge snaps to the beginning of measure 5.

2   Hover over the right edge of this clip to access the red, right-facing Trim tool, then drag left so that the clip ends at the beginning of measure 7.

3   Hold down Alt-drag (Windows) or Option-drag (macOS) the clip by its name to the right to copy the audio clip. Release the drag when the clip starts at the beginning of measure 9.

4   Alt-drag (Windows) or Option-drag the clip by its name to the right to copy the audio clip again. Release the clip when it starts at the beginning of measure 13.

5   Hover over the right edge of this clip until the cursor turns into a right-facing Trim tool bracket, and then drag right so that the clip ends at the beginning of measure 16.

Note: The file Seq_TunedNoiseSeq.wav doesn't include a key because it's an unpitched percussion sound.

Tip: To remember which sounds are on which track, click in the track name field, and then type in a descriptive name.

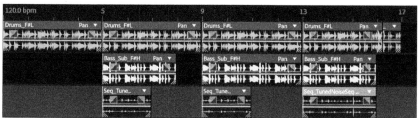

6   Return the playhead to the beginning of the session, and click Play to hear the music so far. After playing through the music once, click Stop.

Adding melodic elements

With drums, bass, and percussion covered, you'll now add some melodic elements. Because you're already familiar with the process of dragging from the Media Browser, aligning clips to rhythmic divisions via snapping, and shortening clips, this process should go quickly:

1   Drag the file Pad_DreamyBrass_F#L into Track 4 so it starts at measure 7.

2   Drag the file Pad_DreamyBrass_F#H into Track 4 so it starts at measure 13.

3   Drag the file Organ_Church_F#L into Track 5 so it starts at measure 9.

Tip: If you minimize the track heights and choose View > Zoom Out Full (All Axes), you'll see all the tracks and their associated clips.

4 Drag the file String_Harp_F#H into Track 6 so it starts at measure 11.

5 Drag the file Seq_Bouncy_F#L into the Master track so it starts at measure 13. A new track will be created and the clip will be placed in it.

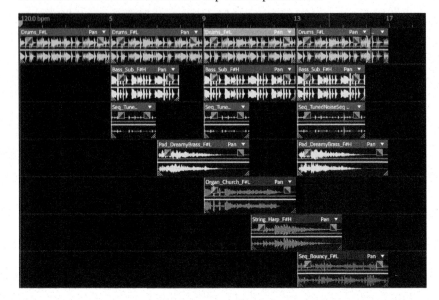

6 Return the playhead to the beginning, and click Play to hear what you've assembled so far.

Using loops with different pitch and tempo

The advantage of the construction kit approach is that files within the kit will have a common pitch and tempo. With a little fine-tuning, however, you can use files with different pitches and tempos—if they're not too different from the current session. Be warned, extreme adjustments can lead to an unnatural sound.

In this exercise, you'll use a file in the key of E instead of F# with a tempo of 125 bpm instead of 120 bpm. It even has a different file format: AIF instead of WAV.

1 If you need to create a new track for another loop, right-click within the Multitrack Editor and choose Track > Add Stereo Audio Track, or drag a new clip onto the Master track.

2 Drag the file BeatFilter_E_125.aif from the Lesson15 folder into Track 8 or any empty track. It should start at the beginning of the track.

3 Return the playhead to the beginning, and click Play. You'll hear that this new clip is out of time and out of tune with the rest of the music.

4 To match the clip tempo to the session tempo, toggle Global Clip Stretching on by clicking the button at the top left of the Editor panel ⬛. When Global Clip

Stretching is on, small white triangles appear at the end of every clip. Dragging a triangle stretches the clip, rather than trimming it.

5   Find the white Stretch triangle in the upper-right corner of the BeatFilter_E_125 clip (just underneath the clip's name header), and drag it to the right until the end of the clip reaches the beginning of measure 5 (shown as 5:1 on the timeline); it's a small adjustment.

6   Double-click the BeatFilter_E_125.aif clip to open it in the Waveform Editor (pitch edits need to be made in the Waveform Editor).

7   In the Waveform Editor, make sure you haven't made a selection, or press Ctrl+A (Windows) or Command+A (macOS) to select the entire waveform. Choose Effects > Time And Pitch > Stretch And Pitch (Process).

8   In the Stretch And Pitch dialog box, choose Default from the Presets menu.

9   Click the Advanced disclosure triangle. If necessary, deselect Vocoder Mode and select Solo Instrument or Voice, and deselect Preserve Speech Characteristics.

10 The BeatFilter_E_125.aif needs to transpose up two semitones so that its key is F# instead of E (E-F-F#). Click the Semitones field to select it, and type **2**. Click Apply.

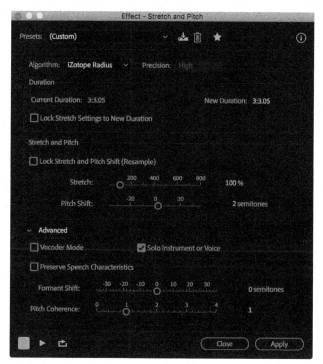

11 When the file is finished processing, click the Multitrack view button at the top left of the Audition interface to return to the Session.

12 Click Play. BeatFilter_E_125 is now in time and in pitch with the rest of the music.

Adding effects

The basics of the music are in place. You can now modify the music further: change clip levels, add processing, alter panning, and so on. In this section, you'll make the brass pad dreamier with some echo.

1 Click the FX button 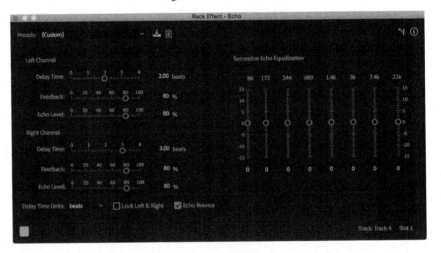 at the top left of the Editor panel, then drag the divider between Track 4 and Track 5 down (containing the Pad and Organ clips, respectively), until you can see Track 4's Effects Rack.

2 In Track 4's Effects Rack, click insert 1's right arrow and choose Delay And Echo > Echo. This turns on the Master fx button automatically.

3 In the Echo window, choose the Default preset from the Presets menu, and then choose beats from the Delay Time Units menu at the bottom left.

4 Set the Echo parameters as follows: Left Channel Delay Time to 2, Right Channel Delay Time to 3, and for both channels, Feedback and Echo Level to 80. Set all Successive Echo Equalization sliders to 0. Select Echo Bounce so the echo creates a wider stereo image. Close the Echo effect window.

5 Click Play to hear how the echo affects the overall sound.

6 The second clip in Track 4 seems a bit loud. To reduce its level so it sits more in the background, drag the clip's yellow volume line (if it's not visible, choose View > Show Clip Volume Envelopes) down to around −5.7 dB. Remember, the clip must be selected before dragging the envelope.

7 Play the session to compare the results. If the audio level is too high, adjust track volume controls to improve the mix.

8 When you have finished reviewing the session, choose File > Close All, and choose No To All if you are asked if you would like to save any files.

Review questions

1 What are the important characteristics of a sound library's construction kit?

2 Can you use files from sound libraries in commercials or video soundtracks?

3 Where can you find royalty-free content for use in your projects?

4 Can files be used if they have a different pitch or tempo than the multitrack session?

5 Are there any limitations to stretching time or changing pitch?

Review answers

1 The files are matched with respect to tempo and pitch.

2 The legal agreements for sound libraries vary; be sure to read them to avoid getting into possible copyright infringement issues.

3 Thousands of sound files are available by choosing Help > Download Sound Effects And More.

4 Yes, you can process pitch with the Waveform Editor's stretch and pitch processing function, and stretch a clip to a different tempo simply by dragging in the Multitrack Editor.

5 The greater the amount of stretching or pitch transposition, the less natural the sound.

16 RECORDING AND OUTPUT IN THE MULTITRACK EDITOR

Lesson overview

In this lesson, you'll learn how to do the following:

- Assign a track to your audio interface's input or your computer's default sound inputs so you can record into a Multitrack Editor track

- Monitor the interface input while you record

- Set up the metronome track for different patterns and sounds

- Record an overdub (additional part)

- Punch in over a mistake to correct it

- Record multiple takes and choose the best parts to create a composite track

- Export a completed session

 This lesson takes about 50 minutes to complete. Please log in to your account on peachpit.com to download the lesson files for this chapter, or go to the "Getting Started" section at the beginning of this book and follow the instructions under "Accessing the Lesson Files and Web Edition." Store the files on your computer in a convenient location.

Your Account page is also where you'll find any updates to the chapters or to the lesson files. Look on the Lesson & Update Files tab to access the most current content.

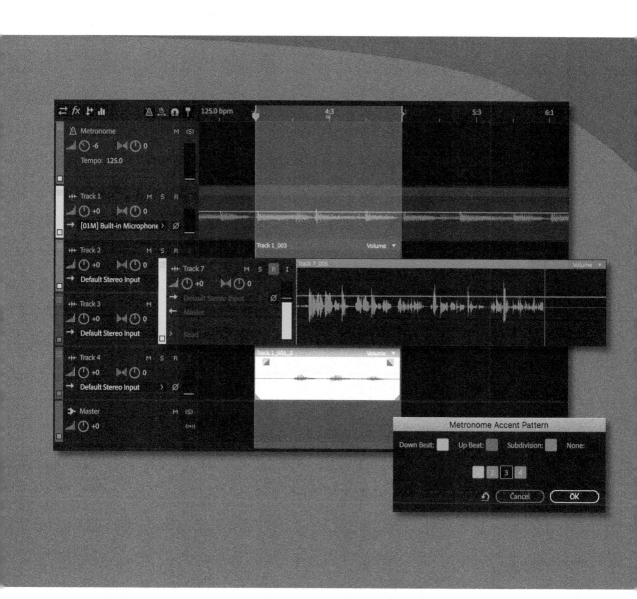

In addition to simply recording into a track in the Multitrack Editor, you can also punch in over mistakes and assemble multiple takes into an idealized, composite take.

Getting ready to record a track

Note: If you have not already downloaded the project files for this lesson to your computer from your Account page, make sure to do so now. See "Getting Started" at the beginning of the book.

You can record directly into the Multitrack Editor. For the purposes of this lesson, use any audio source that's compatible with your audio interface: a microphone, a USB microphone that plugs directly into your computer, a musical instrument (guitar or drum machine), any kind of audio player output, and so on. You'll also need a new multitrack session.

1 Choose the Classic Workspace, and reset the workspace by choosing Window > Workspace > Reset To Saved Layout.

2 Choose File > New > Multitrack Session, or press Ctrl+N (Windows) or Command+N (macOS). Name the new session **Recording**, and choose None from the Template menu. Browse to save the new session in the Lesson16 folder. Choose a sample rate of 44100 Hz and a bit depth of 16, and set Master to Stereo. Click OK.

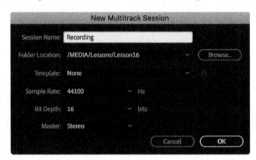

The default session includes 6 stereo tracks. When recording from a mono source, a stereo track will create dual-mono stereo (the same signal recorded on both channels), which is usually unhelpful.

Note: The Input field arrow points inward toward the Multitrack Editor; the Output field arrow points outward away from the Multitrack Editor.

3 If you're recording from a mono source (such as a microphone), choose Multitrack > Track > Add Mono Audio Track, and use the new track to record. For example, recording a voice would require a Mono track. Most drum machines have stereo outputs, on the other hand, so if you were recording a drum machine to lay down a rhythm part, you could use one of the existing Stereo tracks.

Note: If you add a Mono track, the input will nonetheless show Default Stereo Input. However, the default input will actually be the left channel, or lower-numbered input, of a stereo pair. For example, if your default stereo input is called 1+2, with a Mono track the default input will be 1.

4 At the top left of the Editor panel, above the track headers, choose Inputs/Outputs. Make sure the track height for Track 1 is enough to see the Input and Output options.

5 The input defaults to the Default Stereo Input, as described in Chapter 1, "Set Up Adobe Audition CC." Verify that your signal source is plugged into the correct default hardware input. If it is plugged into an input that is not the default input, you can change the default using the Input menu.

6 The output will default to the Master track output bus. If for any reason you want to bypass the Master track output and send the input directly to an audio interface hardware output, choose the appropriate Mono or Stereo output from the Output menu.

Note: Because the track's output is assigned to the Master track output bus, you should also see the signal level in the Master bus meter.

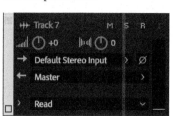

7 Click the track's Arm For Record (R) button and play your audio source. The track meter should indicate signal level.

As with most recording software, you'll need to adjust levels at the audio source or with your interface; there is no internal input level adjustment within Audition. Make sure that with the loudest anticipated signal the meter does not go into the red, and typically, that peaks don't exceed –6 dB in order to leave some headroom, just in case.

8 Click the Monitor Input button ![I]. The input signal will pass through Audition and to the default output. With slower computers, this may result in *latency*, which is an audible delay between what you're hearing compared to the input. For information on minimizing latency, refer to Chapter 1.

If you're using a live microphone, you will probably want to turn off live monitoring to avoid feedback.

9 Keep this session open in preparation for the next exercise.

Setting up the metronome

The metronome helps you record by providing a rhythmic reference during the recording process. The metronome signal is not recorded into any track but is routed directly to the Master track output bus so you can hear it.

When recording with a microphone, you'll always want to use headphones to avoid the sound of the metronome being included in the recording.

1   Click the Toggle Metronome button 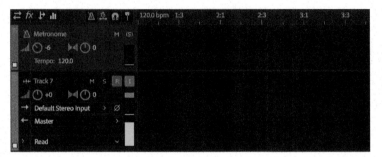 at the top left of the Editor panel. The metronome track appears above any audio tracks, but you can move it within a project, like any other track.

2   Click Play, and you'll hear the metronome.

3   Right-click the Toggle Metronome button, and choose Edit Pattern to define a rhythmic pattern. The Metronome Accent Pattern dialog box opens. You can modify which metronome sounds play on which beats.

The metronome plays four clicks. The default is a downbeat using one sound and three subdivision beats using a different sound: *TICK – tock – tock – tock.* However, clicking any beat square (labeled 1 through 4) cycles through four options for what that beat can play: Down Beat, Upbeat, Subdivision, or None.

4   Click once on beat 3 to select None, and then click OK.

5   Click Play, and you'll notice that the third beat is missing.

6   Right-click the Toggle Metronome button again, and choose Edit Pattern. This time click twice on beat 3 to select Up Beat (it will turn orange); click OK. Click Play, and you'll hear a different accent for the third beat.

7   Return the metronome to the standard setting. Right-click the Toggle Metronome button, choose Edit Pattern, and then click the Reset Accent Pattern button 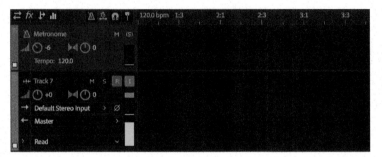 to the immediate left of the OK button. Click OK.

8 You can also change the metronome sound. Right-click the Toggle Metronome button and choose Change Sound Type > [*desired sound*]. Sticks is the most conventional, followed by Cymbals, Kit, and Beeps; other options are available for more unusual sounds. Click Play after choosing an option to preview it.

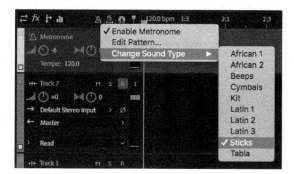

9 After choosing a sound, adjust the Metronome Tempo as desired. The metronome's Volume and Pan controls, and Mute and Solo buttons, work identically to other tracks.

10 Keep this session open in preparation for the next exercise.

File management

When you record audio into a track in an Audition session, it's stored as a new file in a subfolder next to the session file on your computer.

The newly created file will have the same settings as your session. For example, right now you're working on a session set to 44100 Hz, 16-bit. If you record into a mono track, a mono file will be created. If you record into a stereo track, a stereo file will be created.

The new file is named after the track, with a number extension that increments each time you record. So the first time you record a file on track Audio 7, the file will be called Track 7_001.wav.

Files you record into a multitrack session are also automatically added to the Files panel.

As for all media you work with in Audition, it's up to you to manage where it's stored and how it's backed up. Thankfully, Audition makes managing newly recorded audio easy to locate and manage.

By now, you will have encountered a warning that one or more media files are located outside of the Session folder. The *Session folder* is the folder that contains the multitrack session .sesx file.

If you choose the option to move the files into the session folder it will mean *all* files used in the session that are currently stored in a different location in your computer will be moved to the same folder as the session file. This might be a good idea, but it also might not—only you can know if the media files are where you want them.

If you choose to store your media so that it's in the same folder as the session files you work on, you will probably see this warning message as a reminder that you have been disorganized, which is quite useful!

If you choose to store your media in a separate location, you will probably want to check the Don't Show This Alert Again box, otherwise the warning will appear every time you save.

Recording a part in a track

Now that the levels have been set and the metronome is set up, you can record a part.

> **Tip:** If you can't select Arm For Record, it means no input is selected.

1   If necessary, return the playhead to the session start (recording begins at the playhead position) and make sure the track's Arm For Record button ⬛ is on.

2   Click the Transport Record button or press Shift+spacebar to begin recording. When you do this, several things happen:

- The playhead starts moving to the right, and the metronome plays.
- The Transport Record button glows red.
- The Arm For Record button remains dimmed until recording stops.
- A red-tinted clip shows the waveform being recorded (the color indicates that the clip is currently recording).

3 When you're finished recording, click the Transport Stop button or press the spacebar.

4 Keep this session open, ready for the next exercise.

Recording an additional part (overdub)

Recording an additional part is equally simple. This process is called *overdubbing* and is a mainstay of modern recording techniques. For example, a vocalist will often overdub an additional vocal part to create a thicker sound, or a drummer might overdub hand percussion parts (like a tambourine) over a standard acoustic drum part.

1 Create a new track, select an input, select Arm For Record and Monitor Input, and set levels.

2 Deselect Arm For Record on the previously recorded track.

3 Click the Transport Record button, and then click Stop when you're done.

4 Close the session; you'll be opening a new session for the next exercise.

► **Tip:** If you forget to turn off a previously recorded track's Arm For Record button and accidentally record on that track, a new clip records on top of any existing clip. When you're finished recording, simply click the accidentally recorded track to select it, and then press Delete.

Punching over a mistake

If you make a recording mistake, you may be able to edit it, for example, by finding someplace else in the song where you play the same part and then copying that part and pasting it over the mistake. But sometimes it's easier and more natural just to play the part again. You don't have to play the entire part, however; you can select only the section of the part with a mistake and record over that. *Punching in* initiates recording at the desired section, and *punching out* stops recording at the section's end.

When you record over a section of a clip in a multitrack session, the original section is not overwritten. The new recording is stored in addition to the original audio as a new, separate file. You can choose which recording you want to use (or keep both).

Although you'll be punching over a guitar part for the purposes of this lesson, use any audio source that's compatible with your audio interface: a microphone, a USB microphone that plugs directly into your computer, a musical instrument, a CD or portable music player output (iPod, smartphone, MP3 player), and so on. The point of this lesson is to demonstrate the process of punching more than to fix the example guitar part.

1 Navigate to the Lesson16 folder, and open the Multitrack Session named PunchingIn.sesx.

2 Play the session. Note the mistake between measures 4:1 and 5:1.

3   Make sure Snapping is selected, either by clicking the Toggle Snapping button 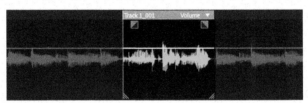 to the right of the Metronome button, or by pressing **S**. Select the Time Selection tool, and then drag from 4:1 to 5:1.

4   In the timeline, place the playhead before measure 4:1—at the beginning or at measure 2:1, for example.

5   Make sure the correct input is selected for Track 1, then click the Track 1 Arm For Record button. If you can do so without feedback, turn on Monitor Input so you can hear yourself play the part you're punching in. If you're using laptop speakers and a built-in microphone, enabling Monitor Input is likely to lead to a feedback loop; use headphones in this case.

6   Click the Transport Record button. Several events occur:

•   You can hear the previously recorded clip along with what you're playing into the interface input.

•   Recording (punch in) begins only when the playhead reaches the selection's beginning.

•   While recording within the selection, the previously recorded clip is muted.

•   When the playhead reaches the selection end, recording stops (punch out); you can again hear the previously recorded clip, and playback continues. The section that was punched in is tinted red until you click Stop.

7   Click Play. The punched part, being on top of the previously recorded clip, will play back and "cover over" the mistake.

Whichever clip is in front will be audible, so you can record multiple takes for comparison, and either move unwanted versions to one side (it's common to temporarily use an empty track at the end of the session), or right-click on the front clip and choose Send Clip to Back to hear the original version.

8   Choose File > Close All, and choose No To All when asked if you would like to save.

Composite recording

Some recording software allows for looping a selection while in Record mode so you can record take after take without stopping, and then choose the version you like best after you stop. Although Audition doesn't have that exact function, it provides a similar option. The process is called *composite recording* because you composite several takes into a single, perfected take.

This exercise explains how to create several alternate takes, and then choose the best one (or assemble parts of the best ones).

1   Navigate to the Lesson16 folder, and open the Multitrack Session named PunchingIn.sesx again.

2   As in the previous exercise, make sure Snap is selected, choose the Time Selection tool, and then drag between 4:1 and drag to 5:1.

3   In the timeline, place the playhead somewhere before measure 4:1 (such as measure 2:1).

4   Choose an appropriate input for Track 1, then select the Track 1 Arm For Record button and Monitor Input.

5   Right-click the Play button, and make sure to choose Return Playhead To Start Position On Stop is selected.

6   Click the Transport Record button, and record something during the selection. This will be your first take.

7   After the playhead passes the selection, click Stop or press the spacebar to stop. The playhead returns to where it started.

8   Click the Transport Record button again, and record something during the selection. This will be your second take.

9   Click Stop. The playhead returns to where it started.

10 Repeat steps 6 and 7 to create one more take (for a total of three takes).

11 Click Stop, and then disable the Arm For Record and Monitor Input buttons.

12 Drag the header of the clip you just recorded (take 3 in the selection area) straight down from its current position on top of the original clip to create a new track with only this take.

▶ **Tip:** When using the Time Selection tool, you can still move clips as long as you drag the clip by its header, rather than by the body of the clip.

13 Drag the header for the next clip (take 2) in the selection area down into another new track, and then drag the header for the next clip (take 1) in the selection area down into another track. Now each take is in its own track.

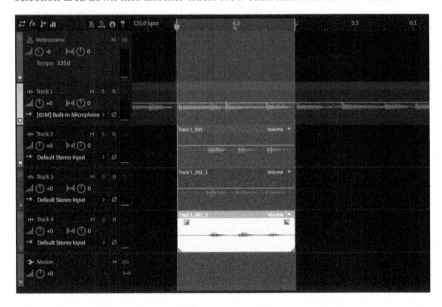

14 With the selection you made back in step 2 still active, click the original clip's header (the clip with the mistake in it) to select it.

15 Choose Clip > Split to separate the selected section from the rest of the clip. Now it's ready for deletion.

16 Click the header for the new clip section you just split to select it, and then press Backspace (Windows) or Delete (macOS), or right-click it and choose Mute.

17 Solo the original track, solo the track with the first take, and listen to how they sound together.

▶ **Tip:** If you can't solo more than one track at a time, Ctrl-click (Windows) or Command-click (macOS) a Solo button to select it in addition to other Solo buttons.

18 Toggle off the Solo button for the track with the first take, solo the track with the second take, and listen to how they sound together. Similarly, listen to the track with the third take.

19 If you like one take best, drag it into place in the original track, and then delete the tracks with the unused takes.

▶ **Tip:** To delete a track, right-click an empty space in the track to be deleted, and then choose Track > Delete Selected Track.

20 If you like different parts of different takes, trim to isolate the sections you like, and then drag them into place on the original track. Remember that if a clip is on top of another clip, the uppermost clip is what you'll hear. If you need to send a clip behind another clip, right-click it and choose Send Clip To Back.

21 Choose File > Close All, and choose No To All, when asked if you would like to save.

Exporting a stereo mix of the song

To export a stereo mix based on a multitrack session:

1   Choose File > Export > Multitrack Mixdown, and then choose either Time Selection (if you've defined what should be exported as a time selection), Entire Session (from the start of the first clip to the end of the last clip), or Selected Clips (exports a mix of only selected clips).

2   The Export Multitrack Mixdown dialog box appears. The Export options can be quite advanced but as long as you're happy to keep the settings that you chose when you created the multitrack session, you only need to choose a few: Enter a filename, the location where you want to save the file, and choose a format.

3   Click the Change button for Sample Type to change the sample rate and bit depth (resolution). The Convert Sample Type dialog box opens. In this context, Same As Source means the settings you chose when you created the multitrack session. After you've chosen your settings, click OK.

When you click OK, Audition exports the multitrack session as a stereo mix to your specified location. This process can take a while, depending on the session's length and complexity, but happens much faster than playing the file.

Exporting with Adobe Media Encoder

You can choose Adobe Media Encoder as an encoding application by choosing File > Export With Adobe Media Encoder. Although this is useful for exporting multitrack mixdowns, that need is already fulfilled well by the built-in export options in Audition. Exporting to Adobe Media Encoder shines when you are working on a video soundtrack, based on an Adobe Premiere Pro project. Because it's possible to view the Premiere Pro project video via Dynamic Link, you can post-produce your video in these broad stages:

1   Edit in Premiere Pro. Include audio level adjustments, transitions, and effects.

2   Open the Premiere Pro project in Audition, and continue working on the mix, benefiting from the adjustments already made in Premiere Pro.

Note: Audition can export multiple file types, including WAV, AAC, AIF, MP3, MP2, FLAC, OGG, Windows Media Audio, Windows Media Foundation WMA (Windows only), Ogg Vorbis, libsndfile, and APE (Monkey's Audio).

Tip: In the Mixdown Options section of the Export Multitrack Mixdown dialog box, click Change to open a dialog box in which you can choose to mix every track as its own file (a stem). This is a great way to back up a session or exchange a session with someone who uses a different recording program than Audition.

Note: Media Encoder presets are available as output options directly from Audition. If you would like more control on export, you can always send your multitrack session back to Premiere Pro (as described in Chapter 12, "Video Soundtracks"), and export from there.

3 Export the multitrack session to Adobe Media Encoder, combining the original video and the new audio mix in a finished file.

The Export With Adobe Media Encoder dialog box includes the option to choose audio channel output routing.

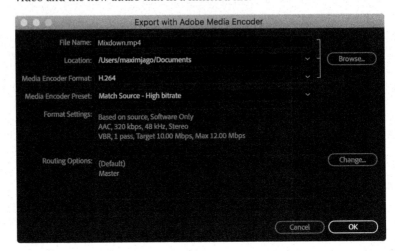

Export with Adobe Media Encoder

File Name:	Mixdown.mp4
Location:	/Users/maximjago/Documents
Media Encoder Format:	H.264
Media Encoder Preset:	Match Source - High bitrate
Format Settings:	Based on source, Software Only AAC, 320 kbps, 48 kHz, Stereo VBR, 1 pass, Target 10.00 Mbps, Max 12.00 Mbps
Routing Options:	(Default) Master

Browse... Change... Cancel OK

Review questions

1 What is the disadvantage of monitoring the input signal through Audition?

2 Is clicking the Transport Record button sufficient to initiate the recording process?

3 What is the purpose of the metronome?

4 What is punching in and punching out?

5 What is composite recording?

6 When would you most likely use Adobe Media Encoder to export a multitrack session?

Review answers

1 With slower computers, you may experience latency, meaning the signal you hear coming out of Audition is delayed slightly compared to the input.

2 No; you also need to arm at least one track for recording.

3 The metronome provides a constant rhythmic reference while you record.

4 Punching in initiates recording at a designated start time; recording stops at the designated punch-out time.

5 Composite recording involves recording multiple takes of the same part, and then assembling the best sections into a final, combined take.

6 Adobe Media Encoder is particularly useful for exporting combined video and soundtrack files.

INDEX